AF323307

FATAL GIFT

Jewish Intelligence and Western Civilization

BOOKS BY SEYMOUR W. ITZKOFF

Fatal Gift

Jewish Intelligence and Western Civilization

Seymour W. Itzkoff
Smith College

PAIDEIA PUBLISHERS

Ashfield, Massachusetts

Library of Congress, Cataloging-in-Publication Data

Itzkoff, Seymour W.
    Fatal gift : Jewish intelligence and western civilization / Seymour W. Itzkoff
        p. cm.--(Who are the Jews? ; 3)
    Includes bibliographical references (p.) and index.
    ISBN 0-913993-22-0 (hardcover ; alk. paper)
    1. Jews--Civilization. 2. Jews--Identity. 3. Jews--Intellectual life. 4.
Europe--Civilization--Jewish influences. 5. Intellect. 6. Sociobiology. I. Title.
II. Series.

DS112.I88 2006
909'.04924--dc22

                                                                        2005058686

Paideia Publishers
P.O. Box 343
Ashfield, MA 01330

Copyright © 2006 by Seymour W. Itzkoff
ISBN 0-913993-22-0

Printed in the United States of America

Dedicated to the Memory of:

. . . .

My Grandmother, three Aunts, two young First Cousins.

Murdered, "Babi Yar" fashion, Summer, 1942, in Russia/Ukraine, by Ukrainian volunteer auxiliaries, paid by the German SS

Table of Contents

Foreword

Fatal Gift is the third and final part of my series, "Who Are the Jews?" The purpose of this series has been to probe the scholarly literature and the internal Biblical writings in order to understand the unique journey that has united this people over the millennia, to probe their position in, and contributions to Western Civilization.

Most important to this writer has been the need to recall the varied historical, ethnic, and religious commitments that this people has made in their hegira into the contemporary world. In order to understand the future, one must recall the past.

In the first book in the series, *Soul of the Israelites,* a study was made of the origins of the tribal peoples as delineated in the Bible, thence as a nation and nations until the time of the destruction of the independent monarchies of the Jews, Israel and Judah, between c. 722 and c.582 BCE. A sub-theme of this book attempts to reveal their very disparate ethnic and historical origins, as well as the crucial role that a *real* Moses must have played in the shaping and self-definition of the Israelite rabble that he led out of Egypt. Later, the Priests, Judges and Prophets, the intellectuals of the time, tried to maintain and purify this rule of Law under their God, *Yahweh.*

It was the apostasy of this people, first epitomized in the breakup of the United Monarchy established under Saul, David, and Solomon, that became an underlying sub-text of eventual disintegration, a falling away from the faith. The Hebraic prophets chronicled it well, the national military and political defeat at the hands of northern Mesopotamian power, merely certified God's disappointment with *His* people.

A Nation of Philosophers takes up the study of the evolution of the faith and the people from the time of the return from Babylon of a small group of devotees to the Judean homeland. This, ironically, came at the hands of the liberal Persian monarch Cyrus, who released them to return home, if they would. It traces the evolution, even the revolutionary alterations in the religion of the Jews, roughly to the medieval era of Saadia Gaon, Rabbis Gershon, Rashi, and Maimonides, ending in the 12th century CE

What we call Rabbinic Judaism is a product of the interaction of a politically semi-independent priestly Judaism of the Second Temple, and the Greek Enlightenment. Judaism came onto the world stage in the Hellenistic and Roman eras. As a great and international rival to Rome, Judaism failed on the battle field, and was banished into a self enclosed politically dependent ethnic culture. Christianity, a daughter faith, standing aloof from the struggle, exploited the expansive possibilities for a universal mystery religion, building on the decadence of pagan Rome.

The Talmudic heritage of study, education, moral self-discipline eschewed universal proselytism. Instead, the Jews pursued their claims for God's "chosenness," to live a politically dependent existence within their own communities of belief. Once more they would be alone, a people apart in their devotion to eternal purity.

The past can clearly tell us the boundaries of where we have been, and what this faith and its ethnic carriers are today, as products of history and commitment. It cannot decisively spell out what the Jews should pursue as the next phase of their history.

The purpose of *Fatal Gift* is to spell out the circumstances which have over taken the Jews as they reentered the mainstream of modern Western Civilization, they now endowed with the most powerful intellectual heritage amongst their peers. The consequence for this latest contribution to Western Civilization, was the *Holocaust,* an enduring black cloud for the West, for the Jewish people, their millennial tragedy.

There is here important meaning for Jews and all others living today and tomorrow. As such, the arguments here laid out both in historical and contemporary analysis will have to be faced. The events of the 20th century, centered in the *Holocaust,* reflect the deep crisis our universal civilization today faces. It is of our own making. The experience of the Jews in the centuries leading up to this primeval event is key to any rational explication; if not by the general community, then above all, by the remaining Jews themselves.

1

Introduction

Perspective

The Jews gained their original identity as a community of religious belief at a time in human and Near Eastern history when belief in a higher system of powers, gods, guiders of the human destiny, protectors from the unseen dangers of unpredictability, was a core anchor of human existence. The solution of both the mysteries of human life in this dangerous universe, as well as the need for a system of regulation for the frailties of human behavior, was given to the Israelites by Moses, in the Sinai desert, out of the reach of Egypt, nor yet in the hoped-for land of milk and honey that beckoned from Canaan.

So began a long journey through history in which the Hebrew people, and Judaism itself became a significant guidance system for humanity, and a core element of what would be the Western Civilizational approach to nature and man.

But the Israelites/Hebrews in being able to surmount the various cultural challenges to their existence, a people of belief, and then of the Book, also became unified over time as an *ethne*, a group that set itself apart, to intermarry within the belief/value system. As such, they were able to cultivate what was sacred within their people, their relationship to God and each other as a community chosen, an exemplar for humanity itself.

Now, after so many millennia, the Jews are in crisis. Their numbers are dwindling, slaughtered in the *Holocaust*, and newly challenged as a belief system by the modern, scientific, secular world. Today, they are being forced to take stock. 'Who are we as a people, what is our future? How can we know our essence as an ethnic group? How can we come to terms with history?'

The State of Israel presents one solution. So much love, effort, wealth poured into this great experiment of Jewish political, military, religious independence. Yet not all Jews want to take the great venture of *aliya*, to establish themselves in the Holy Land. Nor do the Jews of Israel necessarily want the rest of the 13 million to immigrate. They need an outside source of assistance and relationships to protect them from the darkening menace both within their borders and outside, Arab demography.

Were not Israel the focus of Jewish mobilization around the world, what would become of this essential core of Western Civilization? What does the future holds for Judaism? *Fatal Gift*, the third book in a three-part series, which explores the journey of the Jewish people from the time of their hazy origins in the Near East, through the various events, the times and tribulations of religious and national self-conscious, here concludes with an examination of the origins and nature of the *Holocaust*. For, it is this event that has forced upon us the responsibility for understanding the 19th- and 20th-century evolution of modern Jewish identity in Europe, and thus at the beginning of the 21st century, the nature of the modern Jew.

To understand these "modern" events, we must of necessity see the Jews in the context of Western Civilization. For, it was modern representatives of this Western Civilization that initiated the social, political, and economic processes that resulted in the *Holocaust*. The *Holocaust* was a unique event. But it was preceded and succeeded by a series of deadly genocides that, in all, have defined Western Civilization in the 20th century.

Self-Awareness

Today's Jewish identity is comprised of two sides. One is a traditionalist approach, Judaic life and belief through the synagogue, with the Rabbi as leader. As pointed out in earlier books in this series, *Who Are the Jews?*, "synagogue" is a Greek term referring to a meeting house for Jews to study the holy writings, a place within which they can come together as a community. Today, it is less of a place of study. The *Yeshivah* also has ceded its role as a central institution of learning, to the public high school, which most assimilated Jews support. Then there is the modern university of secular knowledge, which practically all Jews attend.

Indeed, the synagogue looks mostly backward, a place of weekly worship and community allegiance, a place where the sacred moments of Jewish life are "celebrated," confirmations, weddings, funerals, a place where the ancient ethnicity rather than the modern core of philosophical and metaphysical understandings can be shared and debated, in contrast to the era before the 18th century CE, of the Talmud.

Thus it is that Israel looms large, even if its political incarnation in Jerusalem is not accepted by some of the orthodoxy. Israel is Jewish, modern, and secular. But it is in jeopardy. If Israel were to become a multi-cultural, multi-ethnic society, given its large internal Arab minority, the hundreds of millions of Arabs outside, at its doorstep, what then, Judaism?

If Judaism is to live, it needs to be attractive in and of itself as a belief system, as a way of life, a perspective from which Jews can look forward. Its ancient roots in human civilization are accepted, even revered. The present trend in cross-faith intermarriage, the distancing of much of its former constituencies from the community of Judaism threatens not merely the belief system, but also the ethnic community that has so richly grown about it. Judaism could come close to becoming a small peripheral sect of ancient believers, *e.g.* Samaritans, Zoroastrians, Bahai.

To live as a vital, modern system of belief and behavior, it must do more than what the 19th-century German Jews attempted—modernize the rituals, the services, the relationship between man and woman. It must look anew upon the world with the same awareness of the times that Paul opportunistically accomplished for his new vision, Christianity. This is not to say that the road that Paul traveled toward opening the doors wide for the Gentile masses was and is a correct pathway for the Jews. But Paul understood his times, and what was possible for a religious outlook to survive in an era of declining pagan belief, and then beyond, to prosper.

The Jews of Paul's day still entertained the vision of political independence. They recalled the ancient political and military beginnings of the United Monarchy, under Saul, David and Solomon. They remembered the more recent liberation from the Antiochene Macedonians by Judah Maccabee. Throughout the 1st-century of the Common Era and into the 2nd, they attempted once more to carve out this secular political breath of independence. They failed. But this did not mean the end of Judaism.

Our question still remains, would Judaism likewise fade were Israel to disappear as a distinct political/ethnic entity for the Jews?

The Jews do have something to tell to the world about their way of life and their religion as they carry it into their morality and life commitments. They have arisen out of persecution, the ghetto, the pogrom, but also from the study of Torah, the larger Hebrew Bible, the Talmud. Jewish life in Europe concluded with the unspeakable events of the *Shoah.* Israel is only a partial recompense. Here the Jews once more live under danger. Here the Jews have created a society from which the Western civilizational tradition can draw *nachis* and learn much. But can we endow so much of our Judaic identity on the long-term maintenance of an independent Jewish state?

This deeper historical and contemporary teaching that the Jews must learn about themselves, as well as offer to the West, now becomes the challenge. This is a theme for this book. It is a controversial teaching, one from which most contemporary Jews would run, much as they have run from the Sephardic and Ashkenazic heritage for the past several centuries. The survival of the Jews will not be assured until they recognize the controversial implications about what they have brought into the modern world. First, it is a rational, secular and scientific teaching. On a deeper level, these implications for Jewish survival lie at the core of the holiest teachings in their Books, about who they are as people, they who claim to be among God's *chosen.*

The trial undergone over the centuries by the Jews is most of all a concern of the West. For, the Jews are part of the West. What has happened historically to the Jews in the Christian West, in the Muslim East, and in our own time, constitutes a critical message for the survival of the West itself. The most vivid exemplification of this lies in the evolution of the State of Israel. The people of the West should see in the existence of the state of Israel, its close ties to modern Ashkenazic Judaism, and thus also to the European homeland.

Israel lives in the Mid-East surrounded by a world of humanity wholly different from the West. From this reality of difference itself, we should learn much about the uniqueness of Western Civilization, now undergoing inundation by a worldwide demographic explosion. Even the latent anti-Semites of the West ought to realize that Israel is the living proof that Western Civilization is in danger. Israel is at the frontier. Beyond exists a mostly alien world.

Ironically and tragically, the West allowed the Jews to be destroyed in the 20th century. The Jews were not the first nor will they be the last of able minorities, both ethnic and social, to become victims of genocide. Do we really think that we are beyond the horrors of this 20th century? Despite the smug contemporary advances in living standards in Western Europe, North America, and beyond, there still endures, the stain of the *Holocaust.* In addition there too is engraved on our collective consciousness, the worldwide 20th-century genocides, within Ottoman Turkey (the Armenians), the Soviet Union (Kulaks, Intelligentsia), Rwanda (the Tutsi), Cambodia (middle classes), Maoist China (vast silent populations), to name only a few. These still darken the benign image of Western Civilizational progress.

The *Holocaust,* plus the genocides of so many other gifted innocents, must be understood and resolved, first intellectually. Anti-Semitism still pervades our world. The ideological stigmatization that shunted the Jews into the Nazi gas chambers has not yet been confronted. And thus, as a consequence, others will suffer.

The West must thus be educated to the suppressed truths that allowed the *Holocaust* to occur, else the West itself may drown in a world inundated by the mindless spewing of hate. The hate is pervasive, and the Jews are but one recipient of terror. Ironically, the once dominating Christian dimension of Western Civilization should be alert, sensitive to reality. There is vulnerability in ignorance and ideology.

The Message

Western Civilization is a product of a unique quality and quantity of human intellect. This high conceptual intelligence was born in the north, perhaps a sport of human evolution. We see its first glimmering expression in the cave art and technology of the Eur-Asian Cro-Magnons, tens of thousands of years ago. What makes these untutored cultural emanations so special are the hints of abstract thought that are reflected in these cultural realizations. Esthetics and technology, yes. But also, conscious fabrications by minds searching for meaning; relationships in a world that must be probed for its structured causes and their consequences.

This mentality has expressed itself with sequential institutional developments in man's search to understand. In this book I trace this ancient Eur-Asian fortuitousness through the Sumerian discovery of literate civilizational life. Thence to the Greeks who uncovered philosophy, science, and the self-conscious cultivation of our esthetic hungers. The Jews were a part of this process of civilizational discovery, theirs being the probing of our deepest moral sensibilities, the need for humans to subordinate their own unconscious drives, to the Law, here given to humans by a higher authority.

It takes great intelligence to create a moral and literate civilization. Because of their special historical circumstances, the Jews often have had to live within Western Civilization in a self-protective cocoon, cultivating their unique defensive intellectual profile. It was a civilizational profile that treasured learning, scholarship, family life, intensively protective and united, to maintain its inner moral discipline.

Indeed, the Jews recognized heroic achievements, these quietly celebrated within the community, Talmudic scholars of deep dialectical mastery of the ancient laws. No great architectural or military monuments here. The Ashkenazim were hidden from the larger Christian world until the Emancipation of the 18th century. The Jews emerged to the external world clothed in a quaint and idiosyncratic culture. To the Enlightenment elite, this external cultural mantle was repulsive. As the Jews themselves looked out upon the glowing light of the modernizing world, they often returned the favor, on themselves..

They and the larger Gentile world did not understand the latent power that resided within this seemingly recidivistic *ethne.* The subsequent surge of Jewish intelligence within every institutional form that gentile intellect had created in this new scientific/secular, deeply creative post-Enlightenment world, was jarring. Suddenly these formerly odd looking and acting Jews had changed clothes, now becoming astute and dominating competitors. Here emerged the theme of the anti-Semites, even today. 'The Jews have too much power, they achieve too highly, they are cleverly aggressive.' But along with the anti-Semitism came Jewish self-hatred, in its own way equally vicious.

The core of significance in *Fatal Gift* emerges from an inquiry into the causes and meaning of the *Holocaust.* I document the cacophony of hate spewed against the Jew from the mid-19th to the mid-20th century. The 20th century was tragic, for the ideology of conspiratorial domination seeped into even the most seemingly idealistic socialist thinking. It was there in Marx's grim hatred for the achievements of himself and his own people. Given the conditions of social and economic dissolution in Germany and Austria, even throughout Europe, after World War I, it is understandable that the Nazis could be voted into power on the basis of their rabid Jew hatred. They were able to persuade the German people that the one percent of Jews in Germany had taken over this nation, prelude to their taking over the world.

The Nazis fully implied that the vilification of the Jews—the "lice" of the world, so Hitler's Hans Frank called them—was not merely to be political rhetoric. The Nazis really believed that it was high Jewish intelligence that could derail their march to power. Thus it was that Hitler's mad dream gradually became a policy reality. True, he allowed many German and Austrian Jews to escape. He then had not yet realized the power of the modern bureaucratic industrialized state. Nor did he expect such disinterest in the fate of the Jews outside of Germany. The inherent power of German industry and its army gave Hitler the opportunity to extend his hate and fear to all of Europe's captive Jews, except those in Britain.

No one will ever be able to understand the non-historical character of the *Shoah,* here invoked by all of the Nazi allies. It is an event beyond the grasp of the rational mind. But certainly the formal cause of this madness was that the Jews were not a slave people. They were seen to have higher intelligence than the average German or Austrian. You do not announce to the world that you are going to eliminate people of higher intelligence than your own. You must taint them, degrade them, first verbally, then socially. The perverted German propaganda machine was able to persuade educated intellectuals, even to this day, to agree with Hitler, that his bestial policies were a program of "eugenics."

Ironically, the world did not and has not seen through this fog of Nazi propaganda. It still does not understand the root impetus toward the *Holocaust,* and also the underlying impetus of those many other genocides that have made this 20th century the most evil in human history: the destruction of humankind's high intellectual potential.

Indeed, two world wars added to this millennial miasma by destroying the youthful potential of many millions of the finest young men that might have helped renew our civilization and short-circuit its ongoing suicidal descent.

Truth vs. Mythology

Our intellectual and social dilemma today arises from this problem of human intelligence differences. First, we do not understand the uniqueness of that cultural differentiator that we call "civilization". Our assumption is that all cultures equally satisfy the needs of humans. That may have been true when the great civilizations of history were only a geographical fragment on the face of this earth, many different ethnic groups living on our planet in diverse social and cultural patterns.

Today, Western Civilization has extended its tentacles around the world. What has arisen out of Europe and North America in the last two centuries has now enveloped our planet. This unfortunately, has not meant that the entire world has received and internalized the institutional and mental achievements of the West. Thus we experience today a serious condition of civilizational indigestibility, the demographic impact of Western medicine, not reciprocated throughout a poverty stricken globe, for example, with the population disciplines that the West has imposed upon itself.

The word *intelligence*, as an explanation for the inability of much of the world to join together in this civilizational embrace, is today under interdict. We cannot speak about such matters as cause for social differences. Every nation, and between the continents, must engage in euphemisms of demonology, much as the Jews suffered through in Europe, and even today between Israel and the Palestinians. Such differences are explained through a semantic of "oppression, discrimination, domination, conspiracy." Thus we set the stage for more unrestrained genocides of the innocent.

Again, we see this rhetoric shading into terrorism with regard to the Jews and the problems of anti-Semitism. The greatest exemplification of the continuing spleen of hatred is the burden Israel bears in the United Nations, and elsewhere, in the Islamic world, even in Europe, where the shadow of the *Holocaust* has hardly faded. The truth is that the Jews of Israel, without the incubus of the continuing and bloody struggle against terrorism, would live in peace and prosperity, a democratic light to all nations.

Sadly, its very existence as a humanitarian and secular civilizational outpost is a provocation to the anti-Semites. Why is not Israel like its neighbors, suffused with oil wealth, but yet weighed down in superstition, random assassinations, corruption, oligarchic autocracy, internal poverty? Why are the Jews successful?

Here in the United States this fear of truth and reality creates its own forms of anti-Semitism, now among the Jewish self-haters. For example, an anecdote told to me by its principal. A submitted manuscript on Jewish themes was rejected by the editor-in-chief of a publication house associated with a Middle Atlantic state university. This publishing entity also published scholarly journals, the editor-in-chief, himself a notable Jewish intellectual.

The rejection was based on the author's development of the well-studied subject that Jewish achievements in the modern world were prepared for by the intensive eugenic practices within the Jewish family, when it came to marriage, learning, the internal centripetal factors that kept Jewish life meaningful during their enforced pre-Enlightenment encapsulation. About the issue of Jewish intelligence development during this era, the editor stated, "no contemporary statistics, no truth", manuscript rejected.

Another example comes from a brilliant series of studies on anti-Semitism and Jewish intellectualism in the last two centuries, *Smart Jews*, by Sandor Gilman.[1] Gilman's point of view is that while the Jews have accomplished much, the conception of Jews as "smart" is a literary convention or construction. It is not real.

"Attributing 'intelligence' or 'cleverness' to the Jews provides a model to explain the relative quality of the observer's intelligence or cleverness. Such superiority comes to categorize the Jews' intellectual ability as deviant from the norm, as in a bell curve. The invention of the 'smart Jew' has little or nothing to do with the real accomplishment or virtue (or lack of accomplishment or absence of virtue) of individual Jews (however defined) in the modern world. No 'kernel of truth' in the reality of Jewish activities lies at the core of this 'philo-Semitic' myth of generalized Jewish intellectual superiority."[2]

Gilman, it is sad to say, is a representative example of a newer kind of self-hating Jew, a denier of the objective reality of Jewish intelligence, even when it stands before us universally in evidence in the scientific and historical record. To Gilman, Jewish intelligence is a construction, a mythology of assertion and interpretation. Perhaps, in a more sinister sense, Gilman implies that it may be an element in the thinking of certain Jews who would wish to denigrate Judaism (self-hating?) by putting the Jew over others, presumably white Christians, but also other racial and ethnic minorities. In this way the Jew supposedly invites hatred.

Symptomatic of a more realistic mini-trend is a discussion of high Jewish intelligence, of which this series of books, *Who Are the Jews?*, is a part. Such discussion has even reached the mass media. An article in *New York Magazine*, entitled "Are Jews Smarter?: What Genetic Science Tells Us" explores some of the recent and ongoing research in the genetic basis of intelligence that helps explain the argument.[3] I deal further with this issue in Chapter 10.

Can we ever resolve the dilemmas posed by history as well as our own fragile civilizational existence if we refute fact and truth in favor of momentarily salving mythologies? Here is the essential tragedy of the *Holocaust*. Had Western Civilization been able to proclaim the truth that Jewish accomplishment was not part of a sinister conspiracy to take over the world, here a people apart, tainted with peculiar cultural traditions, could we not have been able to stop the insanity of "National Socialism" and the other pseudo-egalitarian crusades against human accomplishment? Could we not have engaged in social policies that would have tangibly promoted the egalitarian ascent of all peoples, here perhaps taught in the light of the lessons learned fruitfully, if painfully, by the Jews?

After all, while wearing the mantle of "chosenness" in obligation as well as fulfillment, Jewish accomplishment, intelligence, does have secular roots in the factual life and social commitments of the Sephardim and Ashkenazim. These practices are not intrinsically foreign to the achievements of any people. The Jews, as a founding component of the Western Civilizational tradition, have something to teach humanity, having themselves learned so much from their ancient and contemporary pagan, Christian, and Islamic neighbors.

Here the strength of backbone to assert even unpopular truths might have prevented the tragedy of the twentieth century. Today, the Jews are obligated once more to raise their historic beacon of moral leadership, both for the benefit of their own future as well as that of the larger civilization that they are mandated to preserve.

Endnotes, Chapter 1

[1] Gilman, S. 1996. *Smart Jews: the construction of the image of Jewish superior intelligence,* Lincoln: Univ. of Nebraska Press.

[2] Gilman, S., *op. cit.* pp. 27-28.

[3] Senior, J. 2005. "Are Jews Smarter? What Genetic Science Tells Us," *New York Magazine*, October, 24.

2

Origins of Civilizational Intelligence

Animal Intelligence

First we must examine the relationship between intelligence and what we call "civilization," intelligence in the evolutionary sense, as applied to animals, the bearers of this adaptation. Intelligence is a behavioral term. From the earliest stages of life's beginnings, it connoted a characteristic of animal life, the ability to change behaviors within a generation. These behavioral changes are responses to what was occurring in the outside environment as it impacted on individual creatures. No longer fixed to the ground or casually free floating, animals were able to disengage from the species-wide stereotypical behavior that was embedded in their genes. Here animal behavior first took on personal individuality. Certainly, the leeway given to engage in intelligent responses was also rooted in their genetics.

This kind of "individualism" was gradually built into animals as a product of Darwinian adaptations and the selective process that gained for it a place in evolutionary history. The range of responses was dependent on the received stimuli from the external environment communicated by the evolving sense organs of animals as organized by their neurological structure and then the forward-placed brain. Ever more movement for personal survival was thus allowed for in an ever-changing external environment. This is the key to understanding animal life.

Animals are motile. Nature has nodded positively, through natural selection, to their adaptive turn toward movement, reactivity to changes of place as well as existing conditions. For this they needed the brain, ever more shaped into an adaptive tool, a guidance system allowing for changed behaviors. Intelligence is a natural response to an external bio-physical world in flux.

Many simpler forms of life have also changed, evolved over time. Here the genetic mutations are usually smaller in their biological impact, imperceptibly changing both the internal functions as well as external configurations. All of life is in some kind of genetic flux, such that over the generations, even the most embedded one-celled animals or plants can survive the inevitable changes in the external environments. Here we see populations of creatures, genetically varying from one to the other, even while maintaining their species-like consanguinity. Some forms will make it, others will pass into history.

Animals will mutate often so as to allow for a greater measure of variability in their species or genus-wide taxonomies. Here the variability is "blessed" by natural selection conditioned by the dynamics of change on the outside.

This tradition of genetic instability exists amidst inter-fertility even when there are large somatic (external) differences. This feature may have originated as an instability in the chemical structure of inheritance. As sexual reproduction replaced earlier forms, inevitable "errors" occurred as part of the exchange of genetic materials between the sexes. Naturally such exchanges by themselves added to the adaptive equation, because for the most part sexual reproduction mixed up the genetic character of each subsequent generation and thus could have pre-adapted the line of creatures for changes in the external environment.

If not all, some members of the new generation of "mix and match" variations on the species theme might be able to respond positively to external environmental changes. In this way lines of sexually reproducing creatures developed a wide range of phenotypical forms, some thus passing on their morphological/structural and behavioral characteristics to a new time-line sequence in evolutionary history.

If animal creatures did not change as rapidly as the external environment, or if the external environment changed in the extreme, most of these creatures would perish. A selective limit on mere random, uncontrolled mutation would occur if the changes in the chemistry of animal reproduction were too chaotic, and they missed the adaptive balance with the existing environment. But that there is a record of continuity in the animal world amidst extensive and repeated extinctions of animal lines, the intuition is that some of these variable members of a species or genus had the right stuff to survive, thence to pass on these successfully adaptive characteristics to the next generation.

That some creatures had it right for the long run is attested to by many of our one-celled animals, also worms and many other ancient relics who are doing quite well. But others took on the road of experimentation and adventure. Instead of finding a comfortable niche within which to feed and reproduce through the eons, they took the road leading to ever greater rhythms of genetic mutation, and thus were endowed with a larger brain to allow them to successfully change behaviors within one reproductive generation.

Here, the line leading to humans, chordates, those creatures originating perhaps a billion years ago, a rudimentary spinal chord with which to resist casual external forces in the seas. With a spinal chord and a brain at the head, thus giving directionality, both toward the prey, and away from danger, the body plan was established. The brain became an important genetic element in this long evolving adaptive strategy. As time went on, these adventurers moved ever more deliberately onto the pathways of evolutionary change, behavior gradually taking over as the critical adaptive and selective element, displacing successful adaptations featuring gross physical elements. And the Earth did its selective winnowing in continually changing its face. Movement required high energy levels, and thus predation gradually became a key element in the brain/adaptation/selection equation.

Intelligent behavior had to be both a positively adaptive response to the inanimate bio-physical world as well as in competition with the rapidly multiplying and diversifying, animal lines. Natural selection shaped the mutational rhythms of these creatures, speeding up the rate or slowing it down. Clearly, the animal brain was an adaptive element in evolutionary history. A bigger brain often meant more successful adaptation, thus survival into the next generation. This large brain made possible the organization of greater reserve ratios of both mass and energy to resist the next challenges, inanimate and animate.

Evolutionary Pathways of Intelligence

Animals are opportunists. As the millennia unfolded on earth, many different animal lines were shaped by many different environmental opportunities. Some of these opportunities tended toward the big positive "hit." Such animals began to specialize in both organs and behavior to take advantage of their successful adaptive niche. This usually resulted in creating a large domain of close relational forms. One line of animals (dinosaurs) luxuriated for a long while. Then came external change, what was once security now became despair. We see these extinctions from the fossil record, often accompanied by ecological clues, weather, geological/continental changes, new, more modernly adapted challengers to the particular niche of survival.

We humans are of the line that never quite made it big, until recently. In each dynamic moment of evolutionary opportunism inevitably exist lines of animals that while not quite kings of the mountain, do not fall off the edge, either. Around the great dinosaurs there already were sea reptiles, flying and

perching reptiles. We are now even giving more notice to the existence of ancient placentals, 300-150 million years ago, contemporaries of the evolving
mammals, *e.g.,* fish, sharks, and skates, amphibians, then reptiles such as modern snakes. These creatures carved out a niche in the darker more hidden edges
of the dinosaurian world, remained diminutive and relatively brainy in defense.

Eventually they developed more aggressive skills, emerged from the woods
with larger brains, and pressed the dinosaurs into oblivion. Placental mammals
were the descendants of ancient animals having inherited the chordate survival
skills over one billion years in the making. Today this line of animals is found in
every evolutionary niche, in the seas and lakes, in the air, and here on land. For
the most part these highly intelligent outsiders were defensive creatures in the
eons of their evolutionary gestation. The larger chordate brain connotes defen-
siveness, both for protection and to evade recognition and predation.

When, as with large mammals as well as great fish and reptiles, good opportunity beckoned, the line jumped forward, immersed itself in nature's good
tidings. Success implies opportunity for growth in size and numbers beyond the
limits of survival. Those without the specializations necessary for the big time
will remain at the periphery, hoping to survive long enough so that as inevitable
environmental/ecological change shakes the powerful from their niches, they,
the outsiders, can move into the vacuum. To survive, they will need all their wits
about them to avoid being devoured or frozen out of food sources. Note, this
teleological language is only descriptive. Nature has made the rules that govern
the destiny of the entire planet, not necessarily the living inhabitants. They and
we are unaware actors and actresses.

Our ancestors: creatures of great sensory acuity linked to brains that organize perceptual information into a language of movement, change in behavior.
Evolutionary definition of success: the creation and protection of the young, the
next generation. A panoply of such behavioral mechanisms for successful survival have been tested over the eons. Here, the brain has ever been the key to the
discovery of new evolutionary horizons.

Our own ancestral line of defensive, evasive, even nocturnal mammals, the
primates, were the least successful of the avalanche of mammals as they rushed
forth after the dinosaurian debacle some 80-60 million years ago. We humans
are the end product of over a hundred million years of placental, often nocturnal,
miniaturized mammals. These roaming, searching creatures inherited the
mainline land surfaces, an ecological niche that ushered in true *Homo* some five
million years ago, perhaps even earlier.

Human Intelligence Evolves

To understand humanity today one must be aware that at the earliest stages
of *Homo*'s surge into dominance, he was accompanied by many other closely

related hominid cousins, *Australopithecus* now being one variable exemplar among many others. They emerged into evolutionary dominance from an African environment of savannah, mixed forest and plains. Their higher intelligence, brain power, and environmental energy made them good learners within the generations. A growing brain had been set into dynamic interaction with a new adaptive opening—walking, running, land roaming.

A few of the large apes retreated into the African (chimpanzees, gorillas) and then Asiatic (orangutans) jungles; the Old World monkeys and baboons had earlier opted out of competition The rich variety of existing African land roaming apes was obliterated by some 10 million years ago. Only proto-*Homo* and its many hominid branches moved into paleontological reality, c.5 million years BP (Before Present). *Homo* eventually won the ensuing struggle, its many branches spreading into a wide variety of species and races.

The first diversification originated in Africa, thence spreading around the world from about two million years ago. In all probability when these small social groupings met, fought, or socialized, they found themselves to be an interbreeding life form, over-spanning surface phenotypic differences. Heightened interfertility is a characteristic of all wide-roaming animals. They may change in surface appearance when separated by as much as a million years or so, but when they meet again, it is likely that they will create fertile hybrids.

The fossil record gives evidence to the fact that at all times after these humans first appeared in abundance from c.5-4 million years ago, the trend was toward larger brains and a correlated articulated material cultural repertoire, *i.e.*, stone tools. A larger brain was now being extruded, millennium after millennium, but not as an outgrowth of a struggle with other mammal rivals, predator hyenas, lions, leopards. There is no evidence for either human defensive or offensive physical adaptations—claws, teeth, speed of foot—that would hint at close competition with such rivals.

The only explanation for our evolutionary dominance is a slowly evolving environmental competency, and perhaps social, aggressive coordination. More intellectually retrogressive hominids were pushed into peripheral ecologies, thus reducing their reproductive efficiency, leading eventually to the extinction of the respective species or race.

The Neanderthals are perhaps the most recent exemplification of this process. Having a large, but primitively organized skull and brain, they produced tools that were primitive as compared with their rapidly advancing rivals, Cro-Magnon of Europe and West Asia, c.45 KBP. By 27,000 BP the Neanderthals had disappeared, probably leaving behind hybrid progeny. Their tool culture, the only evidence we have for their abilities to think, behave, defend themselves, was primitive compared to the rich and variegated stone culture of the Cro-Magnons. These latter people, our direct Eur-Asian ancestors, had modern and capacious skull structures, by implication, highly-honed hunter/gathering, and probably aggressively expansive dynamics. As more of the Cro-Magnon children lived to puberty, this culture thrived, then diversified in the rich hunting grounds of Europe and West Asia.

Our Civilizational Ancestors

What kind of brain did Cro-Magnon, *Homo sapiens sapiens*, have? Certainly, the testimony of our human history is that we are no longer defensive creatures huddling at the edge of survival. The answer is given in evolution. Likely the earliest mammals, c.150 million years ago, were tiny mice-like creatures quietly and busily hustling for survival under the feet of massive carnivorous dinosaurs. But as their intelligence and energies allowed them ever increasing defensive maneuverability, and they succeeded in holding on to a broad ecological niche, they grew in size and brain, *i.e.*, successful behavior. One hundred million years later, they were lunching on dinosaur eggs and hatchlings, now highly successful, aggressive creatures.

The behavioral possibilities for aggression, predation, carnivorousness are rooted in the ancient chordate/vertebrate body plan, which allowed for a forward situated brain closely informed by sensory organs, roaming over a wide area, taking advantage of a variety of opportunistic delicacies. Even defensive creatures, from fish to mammals, will often dine on meat proteins, insects, worms, and other small animals.

As hominids grew from their 5-3 million years ago height of two to four feet to modern humans of five to over six feet, with a concomitant brain and nervous system expansion, the opportunity to move to the top of the food chain exploded human aggressiveness. Interestingly, fossil remains thus far reveal no evidence that Cro-Magnon engaged in cannibalism, nor the genocide of the Neanderthals. (There have been discoveries of mass killings of transitional humans in the Sudan, c.30,000 BP).

The growth and restructuring of *Homo's* brain from its well-grooved utility as a primitive hunter/gatherer instrument to its now raging power, psychological complexity in creating the panoply of cultural expression in civilization, were epochal. How do we explain this growth and transformation? For, with it came a delicate bone structure, crowned by an eggshell-thin skull. One word in the literature is *orthoselection*. This term connotes the directionality of evolutionary change, in this case an expanding brain unaccompanied by any other specializations except that for spoken discourse, possibly unique to *Homo sapiens sapiens*, or Cro-Magnon.

For millions of years, larger brains in primates had proved positively selective. The feedback of such phenotypic success to our genetic structure established a precedent for further mutations along the same adaptive pathway. Thus it is not unlikely that as these mutations for an ever-larger brain continued to reappear and be successfully transferred from generation to generation, they would tend to reappear with increasing frequency.

Something happened to this brain of *Homo* some time between c. 300-150 KBP. And this likely took place in the north amidst the ebb and flow of the glaciers and the warm/cold cycle. The largest pre-*Homo sapiens sapiens* skull and brain belonged to the northern Neanderthals. This brain/body model was an expanded form of the basic *Homo erectus* type of human that had lived upon the earth for well over a million years. The Neanderthals were cold adapted in their nose and breathing structure, the thickness of their bones, short stocky build, and probably their hirsute skin covering.

The Cro-Magnons were unlike the Neanderthals, being tall, thin-boned, with no cold-adaptive features, but not either of a tropical heritage, as they were white of skin like their Eur-Asian descendants. As with their Neanderthal neighbors, many had light-colored hair and, often, blue eyes. One guess is that they originated in the trans-Caucasus region, much like their Indo-European descendants. But the mystery of their origin does not lie in geography. Rather it lies in the radical restructuring of the entire body and brain structure of Cro-Magnon (*Hss*). This alteration goes beyond the revolution hinted at by *orthoselection*, evolution in a straight line of an ever larger brain and the skull within which it was contained.

This newer revolution of reconstruction is variously described by the words, *neotony, paedomorphosis, infantilization,* which terms describe processes leading to the slowing of individual ontogenetic development, so that sexual maturity occurs while the individual is still largely "infantile" in body structure, often behavior. Thus we note the retention of the characteristics of the immature form of the animal as it reaches sexual maturity. Here, humans grow tall into sexual maturity (here delayed relative to other primates and earlier humans) with thin bones, the sutures of the skull not fully enclosed (which allows for continued brain expansion into maturity), an infantile face, late-surfacing of permanent teeth, perpetually endowed until great old age with the playfulness and sexual energy of the young of other forms of man or ape.

Such radical reconstruction that occurs in evolutionary history usually takes place in animals undergoing selective siege. Under such conditions of survivalist stress, given variable genetics scattered throughout the interbreeding group, certain fertile individuals who are youthful in structure, perhaps exhibiting camouflaging spots or stripes or even experimental behaviors, are positively selected. Nature, given this positive adaptiveness, allows for their successfully reproduction under these perilous conditions. These successful characteristics, following the laws of natural selection, will be passed into the next generations. Often the external environmental siege will be lifted. The line of inheritors of this new "rate gene" restructuring here obtains a new lease on survival, then proliferation.

This was likely the case for the pre-cursors of *Hss*, already brainier types, caught in the deep winter of one of the oncoming glaciations of the Pleistocene period. A few neotenous/paedomorphic cousins in the group, now endowed with higher nervous energy potential, cognitive organizational capacity, could have seen new possibilities for life amid stress. They aggressively took their extra share of leadership and planning, thereby gaining more wives, more nutrients, more progeny living into sexual maturity. Eventually, a larger family, then band, soon an incipient tribe, was followed by a split from their original and more lethargic brethren, now starting a new line of cousins.

The evidence seems to be that the Cro-Magnons rapidly moved both west and south, c.45,000 years ago, multiplying rapidly, then invading the Neanderthal zone of occupation. The lure was to exploit the great hunting opportunities of Western Europe, now fabricating a creative technological tool-kit of hunting weapons. They had the intelligence and the foresight to develop the social organization needed for such hunting (and even fishing) success. Thence they settled into a world of cave shelters high above rich valley ecologies of animal life, spontaneously creating what can only be called, a proto-civilization.

Biological Conditions of Civilization

The term "proto-civilization" is controversial. Though the Cro-Magnons were not literate in the later Sumerian sense, and they were not urbanites, living in a complex institutional setting, they were already engaged in abstract intellectual inquiry. Alexander Marshack was the first to interpret the odd geometric lines and dots on slate and ivory plaques that appear to be attempts to register symbolically the regularities and rhythms of the world around them; the phases of the moon, the female menarche, the drift of the sun, south and north over the seasons, the movement of the stars and planets, the migration of animals, birds, fish. Their survival depended on relating the causes and consequences of such phenomena. Think of the hunter and his vertical and then horizontal slashes on the wooden butt of his rifle, here denoting animals killed.

The Cro-Magnon brain had overshot the formerly tight relationship of instinct and survival that we see in other primates. It had grown far beyond its gross competitive needs, here against nature, but not against fellow humans. Such hypertrophy had happened before, in the gigantic herbivorous dinosaurs, the ivory tusks of the mammoths and mastodons, the great antlers of the Irish Elk, the canines of the saber-toothed tiger. Here, too, this human brain could ultimately become prelude to biological disaster. But, for then and now, it was a great tool for *understanding*, mapping out a domain of causes and their effects, organizing one's and the communities' memory, in myth, story, or speech. The world was rich in potential information. A conceptual understanding of the workings of the outside world allowed the community to plan for the worst, and the possible best, far beyond the compass of eye and ear.

The tools that humans make to build, to fabricate, or to hunt are incomparable to the limited efficiencies revealed in animal instinct. With humans, the extraordinary growth of the cortex has intersected the traditional mammalian repertoire of behaviors. Along with the substitution of experience and learning within one reproductive generation, for the mechanical sureties of instinct, has evolved the almost complete elimination of behavioral regulation by the autonomic system.

Even the tiniest human infant has surrendered the instinctual freezing reaction of young animals when under threat. Human infants can reveal their whereabouts in crying, danger or not. This small fact tells us that the defense of human life by the social system has been so successful in protecting the young, and over many millennia, that the lack of instinctive control of behavior has not caused the human community to suffer a fateful Darwinian deficit.

This shift in the structure and function of behavioral systems in the neonate must go back to the dawn of human evolutionary history. Consciously fabricated tools can be confirmed from about one million years ago. By then, voluntary linguistic communication among these early *Homo* erectines was possible.

The softer qualities of cultural behavior, dance, songs, decoration are archaeologically ephemeral. We cannot say for sure what kind of brain power was necessary to create a unique tribal culture. Likewise, we do not know when cultures themselves evolved as integrated symbolic entities.

We know that Neanderthal humans probably had a distinctive sociality. Their tools, the so called Mousterian, were functional, perhaps having distinctive cultural traditions over the extensive geography of this race. Their product was highly repetitive, without much esthetic quality, as compared to the beautiful tools of Cro-Magnon. The art of Cro-Magnon was of the highest skill levels, and deeply moving in its depiction of the surrounding fauna. The clothing decorations were as advanced as in many cultures found in our historical period. In addition, the care for their home-sites, their burial patterns, methods of garbage disposal, strongly suggest the mentation of the modern civilized mind.

The human brain and the symbolic mind is a product of natural evolution on planet Earth. Yet, unlike the stereotypical socio-biological model that is argued for, there is little in our supposed survival and procreative interests, part and parcel of this biological heritage, to which we cannot say *no*. Culture, voluntary choice, human freedom, all come into play in the operation of the so-called iso-cortex' (new-cortex) war against the determinism of the more ancient instinctually driven brain/behavioral system.

From this confluence of two brain heritages—the older primate structure, and its adaptive plan, perhaps 70-90 million years in the making, and the newer cortical expansion, certainly no older than 500 KBP—arise the possibilities for civilizational behavior. Older human communities had cultural institutions and patterns, but the Cro-Magnon brain became the core model of modernity, the pivotal event in human evolutionary history. And it is from these human effusions into public observability that constitute the mystery that we call culture, and culture's paradigm, civilization.

The Search to Understand

When we look around at the present state of humanity and the world cultures that surround us, then look back in human history at the condition of civilized people throughout the world from the time of the discovery of literacy, we cannot objectively speak of progress. We have just endured a century of unspeakable genocides, perpetrated by some of the most advanced nations upon this earth. We today see an outpouring flood of humans, without seeming limits, and the consequential desecration of our biological and physical nature. The condition of these masses, by any standard of history, can only be described with the words, tragedy, squalor, degradation.

Reason should tell us that we still have not grasped an understanding of the human brain, its proclivity to create high civilization, as well as social debasement. It should not surprise us that our fathoming of the cultural nature of the human brain remains ephemeral. This hypertrophic mammalian iso-cortex; does it not now seem to be without Darwinian adaptive or selective restraint?

We need to find the key to understanding the significance of the creation of this new brain and with it the nature of modern *Hss*. One answer lies in the power and complexity of the brain created by biological nature, a process beyond, seemingly immune to the conscious governance of humans. True, it is in part a neurological inheritance from our mammalian and primate past—*in nutria*. But nowhere is it clear how it can be understood in terms of the possibilities for the internal cultural self-governance of people. We have learned of and use its power over physical and biological nature, but nowhere in consonance with any inner understanding of what it *is*.

Ironically, the growing brain worked for *Hss*, even without self-conscious understanding. The orthoselectively expanding brain was practically efficacious. It allowed for more foresight of causes and their effects, more integration of perceptual information into a map of experience, the ability to put this experience into organized form. But there were other powers latent, in the high emotionality and possible ferocity that energized humans into dominance, now over other relic humans, and animal life. The functioning of the *Hss* cortex and the cognitive linguistic organization that accompanied its growth, was not instinct-governed. This growth unleashed a seemingly free set of behaviors that first had to be inchoately experienced as meaningful for survival. Then as it dawned on humans that some actions worked, others not, a more cognitive awareness of its success came into the public domain, the origins of learning.

We find fossil skulls in Israel, dating back to about 90 KBP, Qafzeh and Skhul. These are clearly hybrid humans, with large inflated skull capacities, Neanderthal brows and heavy bones, and also with a Mousterian (Neanderthal) tool-kit. It is probable that the Cro-Magnons were about, interbreeding, some perhaps joining well-settled Neanderthal groups. At any rate, the Cro-Magnon culture at that time level seems not yet to have been established. More recently, c.35 KBP, in Bohemia, we find humans with similar skulls indicative of this more ancient heritage, Predmost and Mladec, now surrounded by Aurignacian (Cro-Magnon) tools.

Between these two time periods, 60,000 years, the Cro-Magnons gained the capacity to create surplus beyond basic subsistence. Success was translated into demographic expansion, more children survived into reproductive maturity. Thus we begin to see their cultural remains from 45 KPB in a surge west into the rich hunting valleys of Central and Western Europe.

The Social Structure of High Intelligence.

Considering that it is extremely doubtful that proto-Cro-Magnon, c.100 KBP, in their wanderings for food, shelter, security did not come upon other human forms, evolved erectines, also Neanderthals. It is also doubtful that hybridization did not take place, hybrid children and women taken into the band. It is likely that variable intelligence always existed, a heritage from the ancient Cro-Magnon past as well as these added newcomers. At all times in a life of rigorous challenges to the survival of the band or tribe, there had to be selection for those who could breed and then be accepted into the life struggle of the group. It is not unlikely that lower intelligent humans, as they were recognized in communally experienced behavior of both male and female, would have been excluded, if not ejected from the group,. Thus a tight genetic similarity infused all of these small populations, often cousins marrying cousins, as in later medieval and early modern traditions around the world.

Here we speak only of the internal selective process that maintained the intellectual levels of the people. This intelligence was now honed in an environment of constant struggle. Certainly, there had to exist enough "time off" so that the hunters could indulge their inner and spontaneous artistic urges, now expressed in the mysterious darkness of the cliff-side caves. The inner cohesiveness of the group as with all struggling subsistence agricultural communities depended upon no one person or family falling down on the job, a job that universally required alertness, persistence, and cooperative intelligence.

Elsewhere, individual or small group wanderers to the south and east found other human lines, probably already hybrids in their evolutionary and ethnic heritage. Did we evolve as one human species or several? We are speaking here of a timeline of at least one hundred thousand years during which humans, constant wanderers, met other humans to exchange genes and their ancient racial heritages, always to be forming the new. What happened then is happening now.

Birth of the Civilized Mind

Anthropologists speak of the universals of human cultural expression. The list contains such items as technology, religious ritual, plastic arts such as painting, sculpture, practical crafts such as decorated pottery and house wares, music and dance traditions and styles, governmental traditions of leadership and political participation, warrior elites. Often these universals have been interpreted so as to connote a universal cultural relativism. Thus the satisfaction of living within a cultural tradition that embodies these universals seems to place all human cultures and their constituent people on an even plane. This would lead to the conclusion that no antithesis exists between the generic term, culture, and the seemingly more exclusive word, civilization.

And yet to the secular observer from afar, one can see the differences in the qualitative realizations of the cultural tradition of the Cro-Magnon peoples of Eur-Asia, some thirty five thousand years ago, and some of the so-called primitive or subsistence cultures found during the 16th to the 19th century, the age of discovery. Yet it was precisely the state of cultural difference between the world of the so-called civilized West and these feral worlds that was clearly apparent to all concerned, discoverers and the discovered.

We here argue that the difference inherent in the ancient Cro-Magnon proto-civilization, whose people moved steadily south into the river valleys in the post-glacial historical era, c.12 KBP, embodied a difference in cognition and intelligence. The Cro-Magnon brain was unique. Its spontaneous expressions indicate an overpowering symbolic realization in the manipulation of these cultural universals. Here lies the primal revolution in the evolutionary traditions of *Homo*.

What is different in the behavior of the Cro-Magnon and their descendants is the inner content that flows from these minds. This brain pours out self-conscious interests of the mind—religion, language, sport, dance, political organization, decoration, perfume, style. Why these universals? Are there more to come as culture and civilization advances? What new universals as yet unrecognized might we expect, nuances of meaning immanent in human brain structure and thought?

The flow of symbolic images of meaning joined with our lower brain's affect and emotionalism become the grist for creating these cultural interests and involvements. *Intentionality* connotes the diverse universal interests of a human brain that has surged beyond the practicalities of socio-biological necessity, procreation and gross physical survival. Even human sexuality explodes far beyond the needs of biology. At its acme, it can become love. And we see this not merely in the voluptuous Venuses that the Cro-Magnons fabricated, but in the occasional outlines of a "modern" female face, nose upturned, hair carefully arranged. We can recognize such women walking down a Parisian boulevard.

The word objectification hints at this greater symbolic capacity to engage in abstraction, to envision a map of meaning within which each of these psychological intentionalities of mind (the religious, esthetic, ritualistic, technological) is subject to high cognitive ordering, organization. What is exhibited in Cro-Magnon culture at the very beginning of *Hss'* journey into civilized life is the immediate and spontaneous richness, the diversity of intellectual expression. This intellectuality is demonstrated in the character of the art, the technology, the economy of plenty, the community life, the search for theoretical meaning, to find order and cause in the world into which they had naïvely and spontaneously entered. It was a world that the brain was fitted to investigate. Then it became subject to the inner mental needs of Cro-Magnon and their descendants.

Most important, the proto-civilization of these Eur-Asian populations was spontaneously created. No one told them that it is "good" to penetrate the darkness of the cave up on the hill, to fabricate the lamps out of oval-shaped stones, vegetable wick embedded in animal fat, the clays and vegetable juices thence pounded into paint. Then, under the flickering lamps, to draw and color in three dimensions using the undulating face of the stone wall to create a sense of depth and dynamism in their artistic enactments of animal life. The same applies to the ivory, bone, and stone jewelry, the decorative embellishment to clothing or body. The mind spontaneously created the desire, this need for symbolic envisionment. Then came the critical assessment of their work, students and critics of their own minds, and the analysis of the stimulating world of things and life outside.

Bibliography, Chapter 2

Aitken, M. J, *et al.*, eds. 1993. *The Origin of Modern Humans...*Princeton, N.J.: Princeton.
Arsuega, J. L. 2004. *The Neanderthal's Necklace,* N.Y.: Thunder's Mouth.
Bar-Yosef, O., and Cavalli-Sforza, L. L., eds. 1996. *The Origin of Modern Man,* Forli: ABACO Edizione.
Blum, H. 1951. *Time's Arrow and Evolution,* Princeton, N.J.: Princeton.
Bone, Q., Marshal, N. B. Blaxter, J. H. S. 1995. *Biology of Fishes,* London: Blackie.
Brues, A. 1977. *People and Races,* N.Y.: Macmillan.
Calvin, W. 2002. *A Brain for All Seasons,* Chicago: Univ. of Chicago.

Cassirer, E. 1955 (1923-1929). *The Philosophy of Symbolic Forms*, 3 vols., trans. R. Manheim, New Haven, CT: Yale Univ. Press.

Cavalli Sforza, *et al.* 1993. *History and Geography of Human Genes*, Princeton, N.J.: Princeton Univ. Press.

Christian, D. 2004. *Maps of Time*, Berkeley, CA.: Univ. of California Press.

Colbert, E. H., and Morales, M. 1991. *Evolution of the Vertebrates*, 4th ed., N.Y.: Wiley-Liss.

Coon, C. 1962. *Origin of Races*, N.Y.: Knopf.

Dawkins, R. 1995. *River Out of Eden*, N.Y.: Basic Books.

De Duve, C. 1995. *Vital Dust*, N.Y.: Basic Books.

Deakon, T .W. 1997. *The Symbolic Species*, N.Y.: Norton.

Gould, S. J., ed., 1993. *Life*, N.Y.: Norton.

Itzkoff, S. W. 2000. *The Inevitable Domination by Man; An Evolutionary Detective Story*, Ashfield, Mass: Paideia.

Jerison, H. 1973. *Evolution of Brain and Intelligence*, N.Y.: Academic Press.

Klein, R. G. 1989. *The Human Career*, Chicago: Univ. of Chicago Press.

Langer, S. K. 1957 *Philosophy in a New Key* Cambridge, Mass.: Harvard Univ. Press.

Marshack, A. 1972. *The Roots of Civilization*, N.Y.: MacGraw-Hill.

Mayr, E. 1997. *This is Biology*, Cambridge, Mass.: Harvard Univ. Press.

McNeill, W. H., and McNeill, J. D. 2003. *The Human Web*, N.Y.: Norton.

Morris, S. C. 2003. *Life's Solution*, Cambridge, U.K.: Cambridge Univ. Press.

Pilbeam, D. 1972. *The Ascent of Man*, N.Y.: Macmillan.

Schopf, J. W., ed. 1992. *Major Events in the History of Life*, Boston: Jones and Bartlett.

Schwartz, J. 1993. *What the Bones Tell Us*, N.Y.: Henry Holt.

Simpson, G. G. 1944. *Tempo and Mode in Evolution*, N.Y.: Columbia Univ. Press.

Stanford, C. B. 2003. *Upright: The Evolutionary Key to Becoming Human*, Boston: Houghton Mifflin.

Swisher, C. C., *et al.* 2001. *Java Man*, Chicago: Univ. of Chicago Press.

Tattersal, I. 1995. *The Last Neanderthal*, N.Y.: Macmillan.

Trinkaus, E., and Shipman, P. 1993. *The Neanderthals*, N.Y.: Knopf.

Trinkaus, E. 1983. *The Shanidar Neanderthals*, N.Y.: Academic Press.

Wilson, E. O. 1996. *In Search of Nature*, Washington, D.C.: Island Press.

Yablokov, A. V. 1974. *Variability of Mammals*, New Delhi: Amerind.

3

Sumer: First Literate Civilization

Considerations

The Sumerians, amid the vast marshlands of southern Mesopotamia, at the confluence the Tigris and Euphrates river system, c.4000 BCE, created the first literate, urban civilization. The Greeks c.3000+ years later, after c.600 BCE, in an environment of stony desiccation, created the first self-conscious philosophical civilization, the first explicitly articulated democratic urban way of life.

As such, both these peoples exemplify the next phase in the evolution of our inner mentality, the cultural possibilities of life in an environment of rich and diverse surplus. We must remember that the Cro-Magnon Upper Paleolithic, Eur-Asian proto-civilization was restrained by the disciplines invoked in Ice-Age rigor. The timeline duration of this Upper Paleolithic Stone Age culture involved upward of thirty-five thousand years. During this time, the Cro-Magnons migrated into Central and Western Europe, their setting for the highest refinements of this civilizational existence. They quickly created the forms and institutions that still awe us, lived in disciplined plenitude within their hunting and gathering existence.

By c.12 KBP, the glaciers were retreating, the forests advancing. Rather than the earlier trickle of wanderers south, it must have become a stream. There were soon changes in the physiognomy of the people in the burial parcels in Mesopotamia, and the Near East in general. The newcomers seem more aligned with the implied migrants from the north. This pattern continued during the early Holocene, our own post-glacial interstadial. Migration patterns were always from the north to the south.

Our inquiry: 1. What were the natural, historical, and social conditions that allowed these peoples to build unique civilizational models of human life? 2. How did they evaluate their own achievements, even deficiencies? 3. To what extent were their creative civilizational achievements a natural outflow of human intelligence onto new ecological, historical circumstances? 4. In each of these civilizational entities, was there an inner self-conscious awareness of what was being created? 5. Finally, what were the conditions that caused them to fall away from their achievements, to allow this luminescence of creativity to dim? An outflow of inevitable historical changes? Or perhaps, an unavoidable accident of an historical moment?

Origins

The original Sumerian homeland may have been near the Caspian Sea, from a city-state they called Aratta, with whose people they later had trade and political relationships throughout their rule in the south.[1] Clearly, this is a relatively late post-Ice Age date for the first northern civilizational occupation of such an important economic source of sustenance, this, the area of the rich river valleys. Their predecessors have been called "Proto-Euphrateans," "Ubaidians," or, later in time, "Subarians." Many of the root Sumerian words for cities, rivers, vocational occupations, reveal a non-Sumerian character, now attributed to these earlier productive and acculturated people who were absorbed into the Sumerian city-states.[2] Also, there exist on some of the earliest Sumerian written inscriptions, writing, itself a truly Sumerian innovation, loan words, here the names of a number of adopted deities of seemingly Semitic origin.[3]

Where did they come from, with their very different spoken language, perhaps related to the Uralic/Altaic family, Hungarian Magyars, Turkic peoples, Kazakhs? The awareness of their separate heritage perhaps was accentuated by the fact that they were dark-headed people in contrast to the light-haired Semites and early dominating North African Hamites. This may hint of a people in contact in their northern homelands with peoples of mixed Mongoloid heritage. The Sumerians could have been a people who swerved south instead of wending their way east, as did so many of the advancing northerners—first, Amero-Indians, later, people of Pazaryk (Siberia), and the Tamir, Celts, Tokharians, the charioteers of the Shang Dynasty in Sian.

The Sumerians literally called themselves the "black-headed" people in contradistinction to other ethnicities around them and at a distance. "After An, Enki, and Ninhirsag / Had fashioned the black-headed people, / Vegetation luxuriated from the earth, / Animals, four-legged (creatures) of the plain were /

brought artfully into existence."[4] {Genesis in the Hebrew Bible?} In the epics of the Sumerians, Emmerker, lord of Erech goes on a journey to Aratta to make it a vassal state. He joins with seven heroes, especially the hero Lugalbanda; they arrive at Mt. Hurum.[5] Samuel Noah Kramer argues that Mt. Hurum was the original home of the Hurrian people (probably Indo-Europeans) who figure so largely in the Hebrew Bible, "in the neighborhood of Lake Van," now in eastern Turkey.[6]

The Tigris/Euphrates valley had begun to arise from its glacial inland sea after c.6500 BCE. The gradual desiccation of the southern world saw the soil rise to emerge from the Persian Gulf, from today's Nasariyah, northwest. It was then still a great freshwater marsh with a rich variety of wild animals, birds, shellfish, vertebrate fish and other water-attracted creatures.

.The cultural artifacts that we find from this period are a composite of the new and the ancient Upper Paleolithic Cro-Magnon proto-civilization, still part of their living mental heritage: "stone sickles, blades, scrapers, stone ornaments, pendants, beads sown on clothing (belts), alabaster vessels, pottery of different sizes and shapes, figurines of females and animals. Grave goods, semi-precious stones, carnelian and turquoise—the latter probably from Iran, also copper pendants."[7]

It is in this context that we meet up with the Sumerians. There seems to have been a cultural change, c.4500 BCE, evidenced in the type of pottery ware that was being used in southern Mesopotamia and in the trade of the region from that time period. From c.4000 BCE, we find true urban settings with temple sites that indicate a more intensely settled cultural scene. Eridu, Uruk, Ur, Lagas, important Sumerian cities in their heyday, from c.3000 BCE, are sites that reveal the existence of more ancient temples upon which these towns were built, going back to the dim horizons, evidence of a people branding the terrain with their cultural symbols.

They transformed what was a wide ranging and developing cultural trend (agriculture, water management, domestication) among all the Cro-Magnon peoples who had descended into the south. Now the stabilization of secure communities along these water courses allowed for a gradual development into a full-fledged literate civilization, a civilization critically self-conscious of its accomplishments as compared with the then-contemporary level of life among its neighbors.

By 4000 BCE, it is clear that these people were well settled in the rich marshy environment of the southern Tigris/Euphrates valley. Perhaps they looked at its potential with new eyes, as foreigners often do. In contrast to the harsh barrenness of the northern steppes, this land teemed with resources that invited disciplined exploitation. A potential Garden of Eden, the Sumerians saw opportunity.

Based in the city of Uruk, a thousand-year evolution can be traced, the transformation of cultural life into a full civilization. A companion city, perhaps even older and holier, Eridu, became victim to one of the turns of the wayward river Euphrates. It was finally abandoned, its achievements buried in the sands as the river moved to another course. A shrine in Eridu, dated to 4500 BCE, home city of Enki/Ea, later "stranded deep in a sandy and rocky desert," was finally transferred to the nearest city, Ur, to stay within the complex of the god, Nanna, patron god of Ur. "No one lived there {Eridu} after the early dynastic period, c.2600 BCE."[8] This god, Enki, as we will later discuss, became the thematic Sumerian god of myth, as with Apollo of the later Greeks, his activities emulating the youthful spirit of this innovating people.

Uruk: Civilization's City
Technology:

"Most of the significant developments that were involved in that transformation seem to have taken place in the Uruk period which follows the Ubaid. {5000-4000 BCE}, monumental architecture, public art, specialization and standardization of industrial production, the invention of writing and greatly expanded trading horizons....The continuity with the Ubaid period is epitomized in the famous sequence of temples at Eridu, enlarged time and again through the centuries, the latest surviving remnants of the temple's platform are in fact from the Uruk period....Excavation from the Anu ziggurat at Uruk itself have shown that the Uruk period temple on its platform was also built over the site of an Ubaid period temple....It is fair to conclude that the major cities of the Uruk period are in part at least an indigenous development."[9]

"Technologically, it was a time of rapid and important changes. In metallurgy we see the use of sophisticated casting processes for the first time. In pottery we see the use of the fast wheel; perhaps most significantly of all we see the introduction of the first pictographic writing on clay tablets. This was accompanied by the introduction of the cylinder seal. The Uruk period was arguably the most innovative and important in the history of Mesopotamia and its influence was felt as far as the Mediterranean and the Anatolian plateau."[10]

"...extensive irrigation systems, and of techniques of alloying and casting not previously found on the plain itself....Some may have been brought in by immigrants from the Iranian plateau, for instance, but they all appear within the span of a few hundred years and transform life. No comparable innovations can be attributed to the succeeding Early Dynastic, Agade or Ur III periods {3000-2000 BCE}; they seem to have built on the new techniques and refined them, but fundamentally the technological tool-kit remained unaltered. So too did the range of raw materials available to the craftsmen."[11]

Uruk period craftsmen and craftswomen embarked upon a course of systematic experiments, some of which succeeded while others failed. Attempts at building in concrete in the Uruk VI period, temple foundations partially made of concrete/cement, 3500-3400 BCE, were abandoned in favor of clay, the more traditional material. Of a number of experiments with alloys, the smiths of the period invented the viable formula of tin bronze at the close of the period, 3200-3000 BCE, but in one site only. On the other hand, the invention of the fast wheel for pottery making, c.3800 BCE, explains the plain undecorated mass production pottery of the period.

So, too, the discovery of iron, which enriched human culture for millennia, propelled the influence of this culture. Advances in metallurgy, mostly of imported materials, trade with Aratta in the mountains of northern Iran, or again with Anatolia, are exemplified in smelting copper into wire, sheets, the lost wax casting techniques; single and bivalve moulds. Lead, for the making of bowls, used as a single or compound/alloy, was mostly for repair. As in later Greek and Roman civilizations these advances in metallurgical and other technology were primarily directed to the temple for cultic paraphernalia. Stonework advanced mostly for seals—administration—or works of art.

In Iran, in the city of Susa, bitumen and woolen textiles were exported in exchange for Uruk metal tools. Uruk-type beveled bowls are to be found in Pakistan (Makran Province). Raw materials for chipped stones from Iran, obsidian and metals from Anatolia, chert from Canaan are to be found in Uruk sites, alabaster vessels from the Taurus Mountains, pottery from Anatolia.

Uruk-type terracotta cones, used in the decoration of the great temples, painted in different colors, show up in the Nile Delta of Egypt, presumably transported by ship, or overland on sledges or wheeled vehicles. Domestication of the donkey as a beast of burden took place during this time. The names Dilmun, Meluhha, Magan appear in the later written record signifying distant but long-standing trading partners, Indus River valley, Persian Gulf oases, Ethiopia in East Africa, and again, more surreptitiously, with the Nile River valley.

Uruk farmers continued the experiments of their predecessor domesticators. They attempted to domesticate antelope and/or gazelles. We have discovered illustrated signs that depict the head of such an animal with an ear of corn at its mouth, implying its feeding with grain.[12]

Concept of Life

"With the creation of the Uruk corporate entity, {c.4000 BCE} this essentially prehistoric development—the community as the most important social component, came to its climax....The Uruk corporate entity, short of introducing any major subsistence innovations, did the trick by realistic analysis, rational administration, common consensus and intellectual attraction. It simply committed no mistakes and there was hardly any escape from the tyranny of its all pervading success.

"The Uruk culture managers assessed the economic potential of all their component communities, determined the type of enterprise most suitable to every single one of them and arranged for the distribution of results, maintaining a steady flow of goods throughout the entire community and buffering the impact of unexpected events. Tasks requiring specialized knowledge were carried out by the centres and the products released into the redistribution network. Some of them involved seeking alternative solutions by testing several hypotheses, the erroneous ones of which were subsequently abandoned" {metalwork}.[13]

"The founding fathers of the Uruk culture must have 'run their homes precisely on schedule.' The ideal of the Uruk culture leadership must have been a society in which no one actually starved, as the best individuals racked their brains to procure for everyone what he or she needed and to release the potential of the natural resources in accordance with a preconceived vision of the external world in which non-economic aspects were not absent."[14]

The sociopolitical terminology of leadership is interesting. *Ensi* was the term for head of state during the Early Dynastic period, c.2900-2600 BCE. This term meant, in the early Uruk period, c.4000-3500 BCE, "tenant farmer of the god," later, c.3500-3000 BCE, it connoted, "the lord who established the foundation of the temple." *Lugal* also meant "great man." First, in the Uruk period, 4000-3000 BCE, it denoted a leader of the community. Then in the Dynastic period (city states in competition with each other), after 3000 BCE, *lugal* became the king who lived in the "lu-gal" or great house, the palace.[15]

Uruk, 4000-3000 BCE: "In all spheres of society the principle of universality and equality comes to the fore and struggles with the particular and concrete manifestations of the visible world in order to make way for human advance. In the spiritual sphere, the torrents, twists, and turns of the mythopoeic thinking in symbols embedded in reality are surmounted, if not straightened out, by application of universal principles and rules. The world perceived as a unity in diversity is accordingly organized into a social whole. The natural variability of communities, in most cases linked principally by the factor of co-residence and accompanied by industrial sites and service holdings {is} interspersed by groupings that see themselves as manifestations of divine will, communities divided among elites and commoners is constantly leveled. The material standard of living is equalized by means of redistribution; external threats are eliminated by garrisons posted to ward off any attack.

"Everyone is close to everyone else, people meet in assemblies to discuss and decide matters of common interest with at least some of the resolution put down in writing. All receive the same treatment both in life and in death. The world is an organized place where the economy thrives because all the discoveries and inventions of previous ages are now put into practice and systematically exploited. Unity of purpose drives the best brains of the epoch to experiments both economic, some of which fail and social and spiritual, some of which succeed. The flow of goods throughout the community is directed and scheduled....The world is weighed, measured, disposed of in organized form, from cake baking to manipulations of time and space."[16]

Literacy

"From the fourth millennium {3999 BCE} on, what we can call an urban high civilization flourished. It was complex and original, and it was the first in world history. Numerous elements were gathered in this civilization, {from 3999 BCE}: social and political organization; the creation of institutions of obligations, and of laws; the production of all goods of use and exchange, procured over-abundantly by a planned effort, and their circulation in the interior of the country as well as abroad; the appearance of superior and monumental art forms, the basis of the scientific spirit {divination and neocromancy, the functions and status of the gods} characterized first of all by a constant urge to rank, to classify, and to clarify the universe.

"And finally, around the year 3000 BCE, came the last great innovation, doubtless the most decisive discovery of an importance that can barely be measured: the establishment of a system of writing. It was at first {4000-3500 BCE} a simple mnemonic device, but in a few centuries it enabled the recording of all that is expressed by the spoken language, and in the way it is expressed by it. This ability of the script allowed people to objectivize knowledge, to organize it in an entirely different way, and to propagate it. Hence knowledge became rapidly more extensive and more profound."[17]

We have tokens from Mesopotamia, Iran, Jericho that date from shortly after 4000 BCE. These are made of clay and are in the shape of spheres, cones, bicones, tetrahedrons, sometimes with incised marks, indications of personal or corporate exchange. People are negotiating and recognizing these marked agreements over time and space. From the mid-fourth millennium, c.3500 BCE, in Uruk and elsewhere in Sumeria, these tokens contain pictographic symbols, human heads, trees, animals.

Soon, hollow clay balls were devised, *bullae*, again found widely throughout Mesopotamia, north Syria and Iran (Elam/Susa). These had incised symbols on the outside to coincide with the clay-enclosed tokens. Such often thumb-sized cylinder seals would be rolled over clay to identify their owner, soon to be followed by pictographic symbols, often denoting the meaning content on small clay tablets. Soon, conventions about meaning had to be established among these pictographs, and more abstract symbols added to clarify rebus and homophonic elements unclear from the pictographs. The requirements of this urban, economic, political revolution necessitated the establishment of clear, accepted legal public agreements, economic, business exchange, long-distance trade between cities, governmental and temple laws.[18]

"The fact that the Uruk tablets, c.3000 BCE, were located in the enclosure of the great temple of that city, and that the pieces clearly constitute accounts of the movements of goods, listing numbers first in detail and then totaled, make us think that this script was established mainly in order to memorize the numerous and complicated economic operations centered in that temple. The temple was the exclusive or principal owner or redistributor of the products of the labor of the land....In other words, Mesopotamian writing did apparently grow from the needs and necessities of the economy and the administration, and therefore any kind of religious, or purely intellectual preoccupation seems to have been excluded from its origins."[19]

"The script, created deliberately by Uruk's sages, put at their disposal both an ordered series for things of the visible and invisible worlds which they could manipulate to their hearts' content and an efficient device for the tracing of movements of material goods throughout the complex circuits of the Uruk corporate entity. Thus they {scribes-*soferim*} rose to the status of masters of the visible world, guardians and managers of its fertility and creators of a cosmic order. Nevertheless, they bowed low before their gods who represented the highest values of Uruk culture/society, reserving for themselves {the gods-temples} all the most precious goods and justifying the mobilization of a considerable amount of manpower for all-community projects.

"The gods had to determine and to decide first of all the *destinies* of all things, in order to produce and govern the world and the people from day to day. Their orders had to be *written down* in order to give them substantiality, publicity, and force. Utilizing as pictograms and ideograms the *things* to come, which they created as needed, they impressed in them the 'individual words' of their decrees....Whoever understood the code used by the gods, {cuneiform writing}...could decipher the signs and read in them the irrevocable will of their authors.... Priests, scribes, and kings could thus associate themselves with a higher order of powers and the future events. The search for meaning in the external world of mostly unique events, beneficial or dangerous, as well as the powers of humans organized to secure their lives, took on a mythological, religious cast. This required of every city its higher commitment to the will of the gods and the temples, as symbols of both dependency as well as the resurgent intelligence of the community under its gods."[20]

Transition:

Per Charvat claims that the Uruk period was unique in its treatment of life and death. "The citizens who came to the shrines where they sometimes left their personal articles as tokens of faith even tolerated an absolute break in the treatment of their dead who departed to the nether world in a manner radically different from those of the preceding periods. No veneration of the dead was now possible with the new policy of mass graves or the incineration of the dead. Thus we find few graves, the disappearance of cemeteries, as compared with earlier periods."[21]

This claim raises an interesting conundrum. For, in the succeeding Dynastic Period, we find much evidence of cemeteries close to towns, often within living compounds, at the least, of the extended family. There are, of course, the royal burial tombs in Ur, discovered by the British researcher C. Leonard Woolley. They were discovered, along with a great urban cemetery of c.2600 BCE, hinting of a radical reversion in cultural practice as represented in the transition between the Uruk and Dynastic periods, from c.3000 BCE.

A supposition about this transition can be made from the Epic of Gilgamesh, a great Homeric-antecedent tale of adventure and misadventure that is now believed to have been written c.2700 BCE, but refers to events, such as the great flood, presumed to have taken place c.3000-2900 BCE. This flood had such an impact on the psyche and history of Mesopotamia and the Near East that it reappears in a more moral/religious setting nearly 2000 years later in *Genesis* of the Hebrew Bible, now featuring Noah and his sons.

It is not at all unlikely that this catastrophic event, and the necessity to rebuild the Sumerian cities, gave rise to a wholly new cultural outlook and destiny for this people.

Sumer's Achievement
Timeline of dominance:

Fifteen hundred years, 4500-3000 BCE, approximates the Sumerian adaptation to life amidst the swamps and fields of the southern river system. A vast accommodation had to be made by a people wandering from the mountains and plains of the north. Thence, the maturing cities of Sumer became increasingly self-conscious of their history and covetous of their achievements. Eventually they became engaged in disputes and conflicts with their neighbors as we enter what is called the "Dynastic Period." Certainly, irrigation rights and other economic contestations figure highly. But also pride of place should not be discounted, as urban centers such as Ur, Lagas, Nippur, Uruk, Kish, Larsa, Isin, Umma, begin to figure in the documents. Writing, computing, surveying, all are perfected within the cuneiform system during a five-hundred-year-plus period of Sumer's international dominance, c.3000-2400 BCE, a dominance that made its civilizational impact well beyond its geographical boundaries.

Whereas in Sumer the development of writing and monumental architecture can be traced back to the fifth millennium BCE, in Egypt it appears suddenly after 3000 BCE, to be taken up as a passion by the ready Egyptians, *i.e.,* "why didn't we think of that?" The Sumerian merchants and technicians had clearly visited the Nile kingdoms.

The influence of Sumer over the ancient world lay as much in its conception of civilization as it did in its material achievements. Sumer reached a peak in Ur, as exemplified in the above-mentioned discovery by C. L. Woolley, 1920s, of the royal tombs of that city. Here artifacts amid the sacrificial suicides of a king's entourage, c.2600 BCE, first revealed the extraordinary achieved level of craft and esthetic skills of this people.

Over time the Sumerian cities became a magnet for the gradually infiltrating Semites of the valley and surrounds. They increased in proportion and influence. There were no "outside" Sumerians to repopulate the area. The Sumerians were *sui generis* in Mesopotamia, as compared with the Semites, thus with no other known related kin. About 2340 BCE, Sargon, from *Agade,* an Akkadian Semite conquered the cities of Sumer to create an empire that extended to the Mediterranean. Culturally and intellectually, he was a Sumerian, even if of a different ethnicity. After one hundred fifty years, his empire was felled by Gutian (perhaps Indo-European-Tokharian) tribesmen from the north. They seemingly acclimated themselves to this urban culture and ruled for almost one hundred years, thence to be ousted by a new Sumerian dynasty, from Ur (III).

This reinvigorated Sumerian dynasty achieved a peak of systematization, a Sumerian forte, in every area of life, political, educational, economic and cultural. Sumer was now united by a dynastic force of great brilliance; its language and heritage flourished amid this ever-multiplying Semitic demography. It was a relatively brief century-long *nova.* Its disintegration, c.2100 BCE, after another one hundred years plus, was accompanied by a wholly new force of diverse peoples from outside, the Elamites, once a satellite people to the east, the Amorites a semi-nomadic Semitic people to the west and north. It was from this latter and seemingly barbarous infiltration that a new cultural center based in the new city of Babylon (Hammurabi) arose from the Sumerian base.

The Belief System

Twenty-five-hundred years separate the Sumerian and the Hellenic renaissance, 3000-500 BCE. Both were civilizations of the city state. Each city had attached to it its own tutelary god, which represented the local ethos and protective hand. While the Greeks were in the process of creating a written literature, now including philosophy, science and drama, which the Sumerians had not yet developed, both had absorbed ancient mythological systems and literary epics (*Iliad, Gilgamesh*). These latter explained to their ordinary citizens the meaning of their existence as vulnerable beings upon this earth.

During the Akkadian Semitic dynasty of Sargon (from 2340 BCE), there was catalogued a series of forty-two hymns, including the Hymn of Enheduana, quoted above, by the daughter of Sargon, high priestess to the Sumerians at Lagas. These were recorded as referring to the Dynastic Period, c.2600 BCE, and represented thirty-five cities, each one with its indigenous temple and gods. They extended from Ur, Eridu, Lagas in the south, to Kazallu, Marad in the northwest, to Sippur in the north, Esnunna and Der in the northeast hill region. Although the non-Sumerian peoples who came to rule over Mesopotamia throughout its independent history (before the Indo-European Persians and then the Greeks) added their own special gods to the pantheon, the original Sumerian deities remained a critically important element in this conjoint cultural heritage.[22]

The myth of Enki (called Ea by the Semites) represented to the Sumerians a poetic exemplification of the inner values and understandings of their own achievements. Enki, one of the great gods (originating god of the city of Eridu, later transferred to Ur), offspring of Nammu, universal primordial mother, is lazy. He invents humans to do the work of the gods.

"The triumph of Enki was not only to have invented mankind, an enormous technical success, but also in finding a function for all the human types, even the imperfect but usable ones…(sterile women, the court officer, the blind, a-sexual humans for the court, etc)…Thus Enki is at the same time civilizer, inventor, keeper of all cultural values, but also the most intelligent, the most clear sighted, the prototypical technician, the only one capable of overcoming all hurdles, and of adapting everything for his purposes, of molding matter for every possible use."[23]

"What Enki/Ea does, what he has to do, is never defined in terms of power, of government, or of political authority, but only in terms of organization, of control, of the promotion of life and, to that goal, of intelligence and technical and practical success—and all this, always, in the supreme interests of the divine society {the stable order of things}.

"In the end he was portrayed as being at the head of an enormous and extremely complicated mechanism, which he guarded and animated. Beginning with his infallible directives and passing through his 'foremen,' the minor deities, which he charged with a section of this gigantic machine, this mechanism reached all the way down to the 'workmen,' the people who made it actually function. These people were first of all the 'technicians.' Enki/Ea is the *only* god who, according to the entire tradition, is the patron of all of them and of all technologies, as if he had established all of them: from agriculture and husbandry to writing and exorcism."[24]

"Enki/Ea used the *apkallu*, the scholars, sages, craftsmen to introduce culture in the history of his country, the great technical advances, the successive elements of high civilization that had made, first Lower Mesopotamia in general, then Babylon the cultural center of the world....At the side of authority, of power, of efficient command, of commanding appearance, there was indeed need for a clear and profound vision, of intelligence, of wisdom, to give a positive sense to these orders—what we call 'the technical function of power,' eminently incarnated by Enki/Ea."[25]

"The entire civilization of the country, their entire life and their way of living was first of all based, since the beginning of time, on communal work, the extensive production and transformation of usable goods. In such a system, in the end, everything is directed by a spiritual activity that researches, invents, promotes, and perfects procedures, not so much to *see* better, but to *do* better.

"All knowledge, all intelligence, was thus polarized by production and action, and was materialized equally well in the 'practical judgment' of the artisans, and what we would call 'craft' as in the sagacity of the tactician and his ability to adapt, and as in the 'good sense' and the astuteness of what was known in the old days as an 'upright man'—both on the collective level and in individual achievement...this type of wisdom was incarnated...in a younger god, Enki/Ea as if to stress his capacities not only in knowledge but also in action, in speed and in versatility, which cannot be detached from the 'technical function' or from the 'functions of government' that formed the double aspect of power."[26]

Myths, poetry, a bardic tradition that is imputed in such ancient stories as Enki/Ea, reflect only one aspect of a culture that, by the late Uruk, had found a place in its ideals for leisure, play, song and dance. Illustrations on a carving from an Early Dynastic Period, c.2900 BCE, depict banquet scenes with lyres, flutes, cymbals as musical entertainment. There are also stone plaques that show wrestling matches, plus other entertainments, dice, complex gaming boards and their pieces—before the mid-third millennium in Ur, c.2700 BCE.[27]

"Some material culture items do bear out a non-negligible function of dance (a pin in the form of two nude female dancers....The fact that in the 'Curse of Agade' {Sargonic period, from c2340 BCE}, Inanna {goddess} assigns dancing as a historically distinguishing feature for young women. This could indicate the existence of age grades or age groups as early as the Uruk period..." (4000-3000 BCE).[28]

Even love merits the conscious efforts of humans to go beyond mere procreation. Here, we can better understand the sacred sexual/fertility sacraments celebrated on the day of the spring New Year by a high priest or priestess. As with the Greek god Dionysus, whose major role in the mysteries was centered at his temple in Eleusis just northwest of Athens, here was proclaimed a conjunction of sex, wine, and the sacral. Such invocations were not merely salacious events, "Sadie Hawkins Day." Rather, they were the ritually inscribed and disciplinary representations of a powerful human drive.

Twenty-five-hundred years separate Sumer and Athens. So, too, twenty-five-hundred years separate Athens from contemporary 21ˢᵗ-century Rome. In our own era, Vatican Rome's celebrations are royal and mysterious, invoking the sacredness of the non-explicit sexuality of the mass, supposedly held in check by priestly celibacy. How much further have we advanced in the human understanding, the symbolic and ritual acting out of this unique human biosocial force?

"A famous episode found in the first two tablets of the *Epic of Gilgamesh*, c.2700 BCE....In it is explained how Enkidu, the wild man of the steppe, hairy and barbarous, only intimate with animals and living a life like them, *becomes a man* in the full sense of the word:...a civilized man, a city man who eats bread, drinks beer, and grooms and dresses himself. This transformation is the work of a courtesan from Uruk who came to look for him in the steppe and who introduced him to love; hence not simple intercourse with a female, but love with a real human. Thus, human and refined love, *i.e., free love.*

"Once he had discovered it and had acquired a taste for it, Enkidu could only follow his teacher *to the city*, where she taught him to eat, drink, and dress, and where she completed his transformation. Thus free love is presented as being the point of access to a life that is truly cultural and human. It is difficult to better indicate its worth and its importance."[29]

Marriage contracts guarantee economic, social position, and value. Children from marriages established by elders inherit the economic and social base of settled urban life. Such marriages are *pro forma*, and, thus, not usually based on love or emotion. Man is also privileged to take concubines, slaves for work and sex, if his economic base allows for it. Love, if it could be searched for, however, is the real key to civilized life.

Beyond Barbarism

Fundamental to the obsessive efforts of the Sumerian to free themselves from the chanciness of the old order, a wandering subsistence existence always threatened by nature and man, was their awareness that the good life for humans is a constructed life, built from the possibilities of individual intelligence and conjoint human social efforts. The struggle was against disorganization, disorder, and the primitive, accidental flow of events. Here, discovered consciously, expressed in both life actions and the myths and temples that gave intelligibility to their efforts, they would attempt to extricate themselves from the unknown, from chance.

The democratic form of cooperative efforts came naturally, as much a part of this new social and economic system as the ancient Cro-Magnon band or tribal unity that undergirded the hunter-gatherer economy on the northern plains many thousands of years earlier. Key to understanding the creativity of the early Uruk period Sumerian achievements, a rich heritage that was mined in subsequent centuries and millennia, was the sense of the possible, the need to push back the mysteries of nature out of which they expected to realize the life vision they hardly understood, but knew they had to find.

The end of the Dynastic Period (2600-2340 BCE) is characterized by dominating elites that tried to use the temple as a repository of secular power. The palace and its *lugal* or *ensi* ("big man") developed independently of the more community-centered tradition invested in the ancient temples. Thus ensued a struggle between individual achievement and the ancient Uruk community classless traditions. Yet, "this age, terminated by the Akkadian (Semitic) conquests of the forties and thirties of the twenty-fourth pre-Christian century {2340 BCE}, saw the emergence of the principle of statehood, the embryonic forms of political democracy, but also the foundations of modern thought, including mathematics, metrology and the first ethical categories, when such notions as freedom or justice but also guilt and sin found their way into human literary culture. One of the most creative periods of Mesopotamian history, this epoch (the Dynastic—signifying kings and competitive Sumerian states, 2900-2340 BCE) enriched human civilization with achievements that affect the lives of humankind up to this very day."[30]

The Sumerian heritage of the free citizen and the secular culture was epitomized in the fact that rarely did Kings try to transform their secular power achievements into theological ordinations, as gods. Narum-Sin of the Semitic Sargonic era, 2290 BCE; Shulgi, c.2060 BCE, a Sumerian of the Ur III, reestablishment; Ishbi-Erra of Isin, c.1950 BCE, possibly an Amorite, are the few that attempted thus to anoint themselves. Considering that Mesopotamia had its share of autocrats and warrior kings over a period of almost 2,500 years before Cyrus, the Persian, he of religious tolerance, conquered Babylon/Chaldea in 539 BCE, this civic restraint was remarkable. These kings, if not gods, however, felt the need to proclaim that they were "called" by the gods to rule.[31]

What strikes as the gift of Sumer, here extended throughout each succeeding dynastic empire, was the commitment to preserving, copying, and cataloging the heritage accumulated over the millennia. Thus the sanctified role of the scribe, the scholar, the scientist/medical doctor never waned, in Nineveh (Assyria) as well as Babylon. The last king of Babylonia/Chaldea, Nabonidas, under whose rule the Israelites lamented in Nippur, sent his eldest daughter to be high priestess in one of the restored Sumerian temples in the south (550 BCE).

The Mesopotamians always feared that descent and disintegration could come from the wilderness both within and without the nation.

In the time of the rule of Su Sin, Sumerian king during the Ur III re-establishment (c.2030), after the Agade dynasties of Sargon and the Gutian hill people, the Amorite nomads of the western desert then beginning to overrun the walls along the Euphrates are thus described: "A tent dweller...wind and rain,...who digs up truffles from the hills, but does not know how to kneel, {plant crops}who eats raw meat; who has no house during the days of his life, and is not buried on the day of his death....Since that time the Amorites, a ravaging people, with the instincts of a beast...the sheepfolds like wolves, a people which does not know grain...."[32] A few generations later (c.1900 BCE), the widely disseminated myth of the marriage of Martu made its rounds in the ancient cities. Martu was the god of the Amorites (city of Mari, along the northwestern Euphrates River region). Martu arrived among the southern city dwellers. He engaged in a series of wrestling matches with the king's heroes. Martu won. The king offered him gold and silver as a reward for his achievements. No, he wanted the king's daughter in marriage. Her friends warn her away, "He is a tent dweller, eats raw food, has no house...." She goes ahead and marries Martu.[33]

These Amorites, whose West Semitic dialect (also Hebrew) could not be understood by the Tigris/Euphrates East Semites, became the Babylonians of Hammurabi, he who introduced new concordats of laws, created a rich and glorious city, to continue and amplify on this powerful civilizational tradition.

Most scholars see the living Uruk tradition modifying and limiting the excesses in class and inter-city warfare until c.2600 BCE of Sumerian dynastic experience.[34] By the time of the Amorite takeover of the ancient civilization, c.1900, BCE, Sumerian was no longer spoken, even in the ancient cities of the Uruk period, Ur, Lagas, Uruk, Kish, Nippur. It was, however, the language of the scribes, taught in the academies, and was the secondary official language of the cuneiform tablets.

"....Sumerian remained, until the very end, the scholarly and liturgical language, as Latin was to us in the Middle Ages. That is undoubtedly the best proof of the intellectual preponderance of the Sumerians in the Sumero-Akkadian cultural complex."[35]

In giving a postscript to the achievements of the Sumerians, we should understand the inner character of Sumerian advance as constituted of literacy, urbanization, and bureaucracy. This civilizational pattern was subsequently disseminated to the rest of Mesopotamia and the ancient world.[36]

Endnotes, Chapter 3

[1] Kramer, S. N. 1963. *The Sumerians*, Chicago: Univ. of Chicago Press, pp. 42-43.

[2] Kramer, *op. cit.*, pp. 40-41.

[3] Kramer, *op. cit.*, pp. 42-43.

[4] Kramer, *op. cit.*, p. 286.

[5] Kramer, *op. cit.*, p. 275.

[6] Kramer, *op. cit.*, pp. 291-299.

[7] Charvat, P. 2002. *Mesopotamia before History*, N.Y.: Routledge, pp. 22-27.

[8] Postgate, J. N. 1992, *Early Mesopotamia*, London: Routledge, p. 299.

[9] Postgate, *op. cit.*, p. 24.

[10] Postgate, *op. cit.*, p. 170.

[11] Crawford, H. 1991. *Sumer and the Sumerians,* Cambridge England: Cambridge Univ. Press, pp. 118-119.

[12] Charvat, *op. cit.*, pp. 120-131.

[13] Charvat, *op. cit.*, pp. 158-159.

[14] Charvat, *op. cit.*, p. 131.

[15] Mallowan, M. E. L. 1965. *Early Mesopotamia and Iran*, N.Y.: McGraw-Hill, p. 88.

[16] Charvat, *op. cit.*, pp. 158-159.

[17] Bottero, J. 1992. *Mesopotamia*, Chicago: Univ. of Chicago Press, pp. 47-48.

[18] Saggs, H. W. F. 2000. *Babylonians* Berkeley. Univ. of California Press, pp. 46-51.

[19] Bottero, *op. cit.*, p. 70.

[20] Bottero, *op. cit.*, p. 101.

[21] Charvat, *op. cit.*, pp. 150-152, 237.

[22] Postgate, *op. cit.*, p. 26.

[23] Bottero, *op. cit.*, p. 240; also see Postgate, *op. cit.*, p. 299.

[24] Bottero, *op. cit.*, p. 246.

[25] Bottero, *op. cit.*, pp. 248-249.

[26] Bottero, *op. cit.*, p. 250.

[27] Crawford, H. 1991. *Sumer and the Sumerians*, Cambridge, England: Cambridge Univ. Press, pp. 118-119; Saggs, *op. cit.*, Illus. 38, p. 64.

[28] Charvat, *op. cit.*, pp. 158-159.

[29] Bottero, *op. cit.*, p. 193.

[30] Charvat, *op. cit.*, p. 239.

[31] Saggs, *op. cit.*, p. 136.

[32] Postgate, *op. cit.*, p. 84.

[33] Saggs, *op. cit.*, pp. 92-93.

[34] Bottero, *op. cit.*, p. 238.

[35] Bottero, *op. cit.*, pp. 47-48.

[36] Postgate, *op. cit.*, p. 302

4

Hellenism: The Modern Civilization

Origins

The Greeks were Indo-European migrants from the north. As with the general Indo-European movement, out of a probable Trans-Caucasus region of origin (possibly similar to the original Cro-Magnon—*Homo sapiens sapiens*—origins), these migrations radiated east, west, and south after c.2000 BCE. The Persians, Hindi, Tocharian (Sinjiang Province in China) migrants went east. The Kassite conquerors of the Mesopotamian valley, c.1700 BCE, and possibly others before them, were Indo-European, as were the Hurrians (Mitanni) and the Hittites. They went south. The above may be true for the Hyksos who invaded Egypt from the north, c.1700 BCE, ruling Egypt from its Delta (Joseph and Moses in the Old Testament). These latter had absorbed the Semitic culture and language they found in place as they wandered south. This adoption of the language and culture of heavily populated societies usually encountered by roaming adventurers was the norm for many of these wanderers, especially those who entered the well-ensconced societies in the Mesopotamian river valleys.

In the East (Persia) and West (Europe), the lands were relatively unoccupied, the indigenous peoples early absorbed. The peninsula that became the homeland of the Hellenes did not have the economic potential of the other lands for which the Indo-Europeans reached. Their economic and demographic development was slow. To the south in Crete, a Mediterranean people, the Minoans (certainly ancient wanderers from the original Cro-Magnon outflow, c.12,000

BP) had developed a rich and unique culture from Knossos, their religious and political/economic center. This culture had flourished, especially in the Egyptian trade, from about 2500 BCE.

The influence of the Minoans, and indeed all the trading centers of the Eastern Mediterranean, undoubtedly had an impact on the Greek migrants. By 1500 BCE, the Mycenaean culture, so called after the fortress town in the Peloponnese, had become a factor in the trade and politics of the Mediterranean. It is possible that immigration or an actual invasion was a factor in the transition of Crete from Minoan to Mycenaean governance, with a natural and consequent weakening of the sophisticated Minoan cultural tradition. The Linear B writing that dates to c.1300 BCE has been translated as a Greek dialect. It is another brick in our awareness of the quickness of these inland wanderers (as with the Sumerians), to learn the *techne* of seafaring in the Mediterannean Sea.

The Dorians, a northerly Hellenic branch, migrated south, c.1000 BCE, and seemed to have militarily caused a break in the existing feudal structure of Mycenaean culture, amid much subsequent chaos and scattering.

The Egyptians suffered from external military stresses at the hands of such outside peoples, c. 1200 BCE. Some of these were clearly Mycenaean Greeks, Philistines/Sea Peoples. The so-called Cherethites (Crete/Greeks) figure in the Davidic tales of the Old Testament as mercenaries and migrants to the area, c.1000 BCE. And, of course, the Homeric description of the struggle for Troy in the *Iliad* (this against non-Greek Indo-European Anatolians) by invading Mycenaean "heroes," c.1200-1100 BCE, probably metaphorically represents the general migration of Mycenaean Greeks east into Anatolia, which the Greeks called Ionia. The Homeric poets, writing c.800-750 BCE, were islander Ionians of the north Aegean Sea. The *Odyssey*, by contrast, seems to be a symbolic representation of the subsequent migration of the Greeks west into Sicily, Southern Italy and beyond, into North Africa, especially Libya.

The Greeks rapidly took to ship building, navigation, and trading. Thus by the time of the Dorian invasions there was some non-agricultural wealth, and with it population increase. In sum it is thought that the migrations first east to Ionia then west to Sicily and Italy were stimulated by the social chaos of political instability, *e.g.*, from the Dorians, the lure of richer lands on all sides of the original archipelago, the press of population. All of this led to a considered policy of establishing colonies from the mother cities. The Dorians had brought iron weapons as part of their arsenal, and the Greeks were not averse to the method of war as part of their political/economic sense of destiny. They became notorious mercenaries for all the great empires of this period, 1500-200 BCE.

Understanding the Greeks

There is great similarity between the Greeks and the Sumerians of the Uruk period, before 2900 BCE. The latter were discoverers, passionately engaged in rolling back the tychistic, the unknown dangers of chance and fate. Their gods were city gods, as with the later Greeks. Temples were repositories of holiness/aspiration, monuments to the unknown powers in the universe and the weakness of humankind, physical testimony to their urge to understand human fate and vulnerability. Was the Acropolis in Athens anything less of such a symbol as their ziggurats, the greatest at Ur? The Sumerians wanted to achieve competence, to know and then to do, always under the guidance of the gods such as Enki.

In the end the Sumerians achieved their practical ends, but at the ultimate cost of the open door of secular progress into the future, and, of course, their freedom. Wealth seduced power. Kings, priests appropriated the gods. Greatness of empire became the historical theme of the Tigris/Euphrates valleys.

Later under the Macedonians and then the Romans, this historic sequence would be repeated for the Hellenes. As with the Sumerians (4000-3000 BCE), a long period of gestation and learning, c.1300-300 BCE, would allow the Greeks to exploit opportunity, have their historic moment in creating a new platform upon which civilization could be built. Do not think that the Greeks were any less self-consciousness about their own destiny than we.

The civic gods of the Greeks were an ancient inheritance, a primeval shaping in the light of the experience and power emanating from the east. The gods, however, did little to enhance the wealth and power of the home cities of Hellas. The poets Homer and Hesiod sanctified their existence in the life of man, but also ridiculed their behavior as mere reflections of human strength and weakness. It was this bardic poetry, written down in an alphabetic language accessible to all, here inherited from the Aramean East, that cast a glow of human individuality over the Greek people. The poetry was a reflection of an inner passion to know *how*, reflected first in the riotous enthusiasms of Achilles, then in the clever journeys of inquiry by Odysseus.

By the period 800-700 BCE, argues Eduard Zeller, the intellectual dialogue of the Hellenes was represented by these inspiring poets. Here, too, and influential, were the ancient theologians, as Aristotle called them: Orpheus from Thrace in the northeast, who earned a place alongside Apollo at Delphi. Musaeus, and Epimenides of Crete the latter purified Athens after an end of 7th century defilement. Pherecydes of Syros fabricated a sun dial for the center of his town. He wrote a famous quasi-mythological tale of the origin of the universe.[1]

Then, shortly after in time, these mythic figures were supplemented by the modern wise men of Greece: Solon, Phocylides, Theognis, Bias of Priene, Pittacus of Mytilene, Thales of Miletus, not to mention the poets Sappho and Archilocus of Lesbos, among others, dating from 700-600 BCE. Except for Solon of Athens, the powerful influence of the Ionian Greeks on the islands of the Aegean and the wealthy mainland towns—Miletos, the first center of a school of naturalist philosophers, also Ephesus and Colophon—spread the cultural ideals of this people.

Soon, to the West, a number of Greek settlements took form, Agraka and Syracuse in Sicily, Croton, Elea, Tarenton, and Neapolis on the Italian mainland. From here, too, we see individuals of universal importance to the Greeks, philosopher Pythagoras, who migrated from Samos in the Aegean to Croton where he founded his semi-religious/philosophical order. Also in the West flourished the philosophers, Parmenides and Xenophanes.

Here we pass into the 6th century BCE (599-500), an explosive century of creative inquiry. In the artistic arena, in architecture (Doric, Ionic, and Corinthian) and the design and painting of pottery, a unique vision of experience seems to tumble forth onto the civilized world.

Unquestionably, the Greeks were profiting from the intellectual and craft traditions of the east, those on the Phoenician coast of the Mediterranean, where many of their own and other Indo-European migrants had absorbed the indigenous Semitic culture. Also, the rich scholarly tradition, along with the religious theophany and myths in the syncretic Sumerian, Semitic, Indo-European Tigris/Euphrates civilizations, were powerful stimulants.

But there was something unique about this Hellenic peoples' approach to natural and human experience that elicited a special curiosity of mind. Only the always tumultuous political scene colored their life. Uppermost a secular curiosity shone through, always the free release of their creative imagination expressing both the stimulation and opportunities of life. Religion was a weighty element. As a civic heritage and ceremonial evocation, it set no limits for their ranging minds.

An Evolving Civilization

The dynamics of this evolving consciousness of life was lived according to a plan, implicit to a great extent, but unique and self-defined, nevertheless. It accepted the inevitability of conflict, war. The western colonies of the Greeks seemed to have flourished, economically and culturally. They traded to the north of Italy with the Etruscan towns. (The Etruscans were Anatolians, Indo-Europeans but not Greek, migrants.) The local Italic tribes were not yet developed enough to offer competition in economics or war. The Carthaginians along the North African coast, near present-day Tunis, colonists from the Phoenician east, were strong competitors, sometimes in war with the Sicilian Greeks.

In the east along the Ionic coast of Asia, the wealthy Greek cities, in commerce with Lydia, Phrygia, and Mesopotamia to the east, were soon to be pressured by invading Persians from the northeast Iranian plateau. The Persians first conquered Lydia (King Croesus), c.546 BCE, then went on to occupy most of the coastal Greek cities, absorbing their comfortable wealth. Cyrus, the Persian leader then turned his hot knife cavalry and archers through the soft butter of the declining neo-Babylonian/Chaldeans, they who had earlier arrivied from the adjoining Arabian peninsula (today Kuwait). The Chaldean ruler, Nabonidus, a sophisticated man, was far off, in northern Arabia, engrossed in the study of comparative religions. He scampered home, giving no defense. Cyrus found him lurking in the great Temple of Babylon, Nabonidus' priests having opened its doors to the Persian ruler.

Cyrus had no bother with religious, cultural, or philosophical involvements. He was interested in the wealth of the Mesopotamians and Greeks, not with their ideals. Thus, he quickly, 539 BCE, allowed whatever part of the captive Jewish population that wished to, to return to Judah (now the enlarged Persian province of Yehud).The Greek Ionian islanders (except for close-lying Samos) mostly remained independent.

Even before the Persian conquest of Ionia, events in the wealthy Lydian cities, such as Sardis, under their King Croesus, would revolutionize the political/economy of the world. The invention of coinage, c.650-625 BCE, as the new method of economic exchange gradually pushed the old hereditary land owning economy to the edge of oblivion. The mortgage came into being. The international impact of coinage and the end of barter as the predominant means for the exchange of value was a socio/political earthquake in impact.

On the mainland of the mother country, these dynamics were eagerly grasped by the Greeks, now stimulated by a new industrial trading and manufacturing mentality. Cities such as Corinth, Megara, Aegina, then Athens, soon realized that an economy based on scraping the stony earth for the planting of grains would yield little in the way of economic recompense. Thus began among the Greeks a mutual competition for the creation of value and the political/military power that would come with liquid wealth.

We witness large-scale planting of olive trees, vineyards, the manufacture and decoration of the pottery receptacles for the oil and wine, now to compete for the international market, a trade that involved the exchange of silver and gold coins. This mentality of mercantilism spread over the entire Mediterranean. Here impacted the economic thrust of modernity, now creating the social conditions both for political emancipation from the autocracy of familial based monarchy, as well as the liberation from feudal/oligarchical control of economic and political life. It did not come easily. This was a time, 600-500 BCE, of fratricidal revolutions and wars.

Sparta, in the Peloponnesus, a potentially great player in this ongoing social revolution, would not play. Its own early, 7th-century, cultural revolution was stimulated by indigenous poets and artists, but was gradually transmuted into a military state idealized by the old Homeric vision of an heroic, if egalitarian feudalism. Sparta gradually began to subject and hold under iron military control a large population of neighboring, now subservient Greeks. This policy was successful to the extent that the Spartans could muster enough well-disciplined and numerous young fighters from the fecund and boisterous Spartan female population.

It was in Athens that all these new historical elements came to a creative head. A series of leaders, from Dracon and Solon to Clisthenes, just before and during the sixth century BCE, restructured the legal basis of the society, to set it onto a new national course of industrial manufacture and international trade, away from the quiet hierarchies of agricultural feudalism. Athens opened up its *agora* to craftsman, its port, Piraeus, to the residency of talented foreigners, merchants, and sailors.

Most Greek towns were extremely ethnocentric, bound into a local patriotism through their city gods, their sense of familial genealogy. To an Athenian leader such as Clisthenes, c.525 BCE, such atavistic loyalties would endanger the stability of a large and growing democratically guided city devoted to future possibilities rather than traditional verities and loyalties. And he put into law measures to break up these hereditary political and economic cliques.

The west, Magna Graecia continued productively wealthy and relatively peaceful during this sixth century BCE. Events in the east, however, served eventually to precipitate the great war for the freedom of Hellas. The states along the eastern edge of the Aegean were involved in successive revolts against their new Persian overlords, always with the surreptitious, and then overt, aid by a homeland now expansive in wealth and power.

Thus "provoked," the Persians embarked on a series of invasions that would undermine their own hegemonic dominance, eventually to open themselves to the conquest of the Persian homeland. The result of the fall of Indo-European Persia would be the infusion and domination of an international Hellenistic culture, now to spread over the entire civilized world.

The Persian Wars represented a complex series of events, more than the simple invasion by Persia of Hellas, and then their defeat by the allied Greek cities. These two campaigns took place approximately ten years apart, 490-479 BCE. The Persian leadership, successively Darius and his son and successor Xerxes, was clever and persuasive enough to invade the Greek mainland, give battle with the major city/states, Athens and Sparta, with the accompaniment of many Greek allies, and many mercenaries.

However, the Persians were not capable of subduing armies and navies/marines that had been largely raised voluntarily from a democratic populace, individually armed with the most modern weaponry and armor. These Greeks could employ the most adventurous tactics and strategies that might be mustered by a free people. Contrast this with susceptible self-protective mercenaries, along with whip lashed and relatively unarmed often non-Persian conscripts. The democratic Greek phalanx and trireme were to be proved invincible over this culminating eastern empire.

Herodotus: "The sovereign virtue of Democracy is demonstrated not only in a single particular but in a general way by the experience of the Athenians. Under despotic government the Athenians did not evince a military superiority over any of their neighbors, while they had no sooner got rid of their despots than they won by a long lead. This demonstrates that, so long as they were held down they deliberately malingered out of a feeling that they were working for a master, whereas, after their liberation, each individual citizen felt the impulse to achieve victory for his own advantage."[2]

The self-conscious morale boosting achievements of a people who would sacrifice everything, the Athenians abandoning their city and Acropolis to the Persian torch, thence to fight and win, proved culturally explosive in consequence. Let us not think that this victory, which took place twice in an eleven-year campaign, was assured. After the final land battle of Plataea, in which the Spartan general Pausanius united a mixed force of Athenians, Spartans, and their allies to victory, a great celebration was held in place on the battlefield. Part of the Persian army was held captive along with its vast supply train, both male and female slaves.

Herodotus: "It is said that Xerxes on his retreat from Greece {479 BCE} left his tent with Mardonius {the Persian commander killed in the battle}. When Pausanius saw it, with its embroidered hangings and gorgeous decorations in silver and gold, he summoned Mardonius' bakers and cooks and told them to prepare a meal of the same sort as they were accustomed to prepare for their former master. The order was obeyed; and when Pausanius saw gold and silver couches all beautifully draped, and gold and silver tables, and everything prepared for the feast with great magnificence, he could hardly believe his eyes for the good things set before him, and, just for a joke, ordered his own servants to get ready an ordinary Spartan dinner. The difference between the two meals was indeed remarkable, and when both were ready, Pausanius laughed and sent for the Greek commanding officers. When they arrived, he invited them to take a look at the two tables, saying, 'Gentlemen, I asked you here in order to show you the folly of the Persians, who, living in this style, came to Greece to rob us of our poverty.'"[3]

One need not recapitulate the rise of Athens to civilizational predominance in Hellas, in its early phases welcoming creative individuals in every area of human symbolic cultural expression, later producing in its own citizenry some of the greatest creative minds in history, and in all the various political, esthetic, philosophical, scientific dimensions of life, and here participated in by a majority of its population. Indeed, political controversy surrounds the wealth that Athens rightly or wrongly expropriated from the Delian League's mutual defense funds, seeing how it was that the Athenian fleet had earlier destroyed the enemy and now ruled supreme in the waters touched by all the Greek states. The result of this tax on Greece's wealth was the erection of a new Acropolis, this time of marble and granite, replacing the wooden temples burned by the Persians.

The great era of liberation and civilizational advance lasted fifty years, c.480-430 BCE. At the end, the creative political energizer of this civilizational thrust, Pericles, was dead. Sparta, still powerful, had feared this modernist trend and the loss of its titular leadership in a Hellas that still remembering the valiant achievements of Homeric-like fighters. Sparta was the model for this heritage. Athens was proud, sophisticated, and arrogant. As the war began, 431 BCE, disease within the walls of a now-congested *polis* destroyed almost a third of the populace of Attica and laid the nation low. For civilization, this fratricidal war was a disaster. It ran on for almost thirty years, until 404 BCE.

The patriotic fruit of this democracy, Socrates, refused to flee his civic responsibilities, even given his challenge to traditionalist religious and philosophical prejudice. Mass hysteria, a democracy at the brink, brought him to drink the hemlock in 399 BCE. Fellow revolutionaries in thought, Euripides and Aristophanes, had fled. Philip of Macedon finally closed the door on Athens' democratic independence at Cheronaea in 338 BCE. However, Plato's Academy and Aristotle's Lyceum would make the Athens of the 4th century and forever, philosophy's home.

Freedom of Mind

What allowed or stimulated these people to unchain themselves from tradition, the religious modality of thought, aligned as it always was with the autocracy of hierarchical rule? Clearly, the religious, ritualistic domain was not shut out in Athens or Greece. The holy festivals, both religious and artistic, took place at ancient and meaningful markings of the Hellenic tradition, Dodona in the north, Olympus, in the Peloponnesus, Delphi, north of Athens along the western migratory route going south. The rituals, the sacred priestesses, the observance of holiness continued.

Here, religion was divorced from an establishment clergy usually under the thumb of the political/military rulers. The Greeks were a free people, living in relatively small towns, separated from each other by water and land, yet com-

municating and sharing in their conjoint heritage. Culturally integrated in literature by their revered poet, Homer, they freely probed the inner workings of the
intellectual and creative potential of *Homo sapiens sapiens*.

Indeed, they were not saints. They were constantly at war with each other,
as with the Sumerian cities in the post-Uruk period. Within their own cities, the
struggle continued, in the case of the Greeks, social class conflicts. Yet, still ob-
scure to our understanding, conditions for the release of an extremely high level
of creative expression were in play. As with the Sumerians, these Hellenic discoveries were of the nature of a catapult for the Western Civilizational tradition.

It should be remembered that the era of the Homeric writings, c.800-750
BCE, came at least a century after the first setting down of parts of the Hebrew
Pentateuch, the "J" and "E" traditions (*Jahweh*-Judah and *Elohim*-Israel). The
semi-mythological and heroic figures of Abraham, Isaac, and Jacob, along with
the powerful judicial/law-giver Moses, seem to hint, as with the Homeric heroes,
of a period in the maturation of the West of a more universal turning point in the
historic self-consciousness of the human species.

Where the Jews struggled amid political chaos, continuous conflict with
their neighbors, both Judah and Israel being way-stations on the pathways of the
great powers in their successive wars of domination, the Hellenes in their forma-
tive period were alone, free to wander throughout the Mediterranean without
great opposition or counter-migratory incursions. The Jews found succor in their
deep search for moral and spiritual understanding, amid constant conflict and
tragedy; the Greeks were seduced by the natural, the secular.

There were no heavy burdens of conquest and enslavement for the Hellenes. The well of Greek intelligence flowed into the diverse capacities of the
revolutionary *Hss* brain. Hinted at in the creativity and affluence of the Ice Age
Cro-Magnons, and then the literacy and urbanization that the Sumerians had
mastered, the Greeks made this human potentiality available to our own eyes,
2500 years later.

One cannot say that this explosive creativity, this incessant and unencumbered search for knowledge, both in theory—as curiosity to know—as well as
for practical results, was theirs alone, a unique ethnic genius. We recognize the
same kind of explosive curiosity, a balance between the abstract and the practical, first in the northern Italian Renaissance, then in northern Europe proper,
c.15th-19th century. By the mid-twentieth century, it is fair to say that *theoria* has
stepped back in favor of *techne*, application.

In perspective, the Greeks took the civilizational career of humankind far
forward and faster than had any people before, the Cro-Magnons and Sumerians
excepted. They did this by giving us the broadest perspective yet of the intellectual possibilities within human nature. If they did not equal the Old Testament
Hebrews in depth of understanding of the metaphysical and moral conditions of

humanity in a dangerous and lonely universe, it is because they had not yet felt the full bite of individual, tribal, and national anguish. To the end, they were Apollonians, even with the introduction of eastern Dionysian elements into their mental pantheon. This latter devotion of mind, they participated in with ecstasy, almost joy.

We can say in summary that the civilization of the Greeks, perhaps to the era of the beginnings of the Roman Imperium, surged forward in discovery, of all the cultural symbolic capacities of humans, their ability to objectivize experience in law and form. At the same time, they infused their cultural products with the mammalian juices of emotion and beauty.

The Advance of Hellenic Civilization

The tendency today is to downplay the Greeks' achievement in our understanding of science, but also in philosophy, in engineering and the material emoluments of urban life. We can concede that even if the air in Athens, 5th-century BCE, did not smell singularly worse than Rome, 1st century CE, the Greeks did not strive to make the technological improvements in urban life that the Romans did. The Greeks, however, had absorbed several thousand years of technological progress achieved both by the Mesopotamians, from the days of Sumer, and the Egyptians in their heyday, after 2700 BCE, and applied this knowledge for their own civic enhancement. In their best days, they engaged in commerce sufficient to create the wherewithal for their subsistence physical well being. At all points in their material life-style, in architecture and the plastic arts, the vases, amphorae, which they decorated the better to sell their wines and olive oil, the Greek mentality was so directed as to achieve a balance of the "necessary."

The important question is, that, taking into consideration the achievements of any civilizational entity, what is the total dynamic profile of this civilization? Where did they pour their efforts when it comes to moving the institutions of cultural life forward? Here, it is clear that that the Greeks disregarded few areas of life in their striving for creativity, potency. The high intelligence and mental orientation of the Greeks allowed them to look anew always, at the intellectual essence of life, even the seemingly emotional dimensions of the arts.

Take for example, the Parthenon in Athens, built on a high escarpment in the center of the city. One does not need to compare this architectural and engineering effort with the massive symbolism of the Egyptian pyramids, c.2600 BCE. Yet the Parthenon on its completion, c.438 BCE was the largest sacred and civic shrine in the world, a building into which people could walk, celebrate the holy festivities of the city, all the time surrounded by a rich variety of painted sculptures, friezes, and esthetic decorations. This building required for its construction the long-distance transport of massive marble blocks, which were then lifted onto the Acropolis, there to be trimmed and set.

Its engineering was good enough for it to survive into the early modern world almost unscathed, considering earthquakes and other disasters, human and natural, that impugned its integrity. It was served an almost-fatal blow when it used as an arsenal during the 15th-century wars between the Ottomans and the Venetians. The stored gunpowder was hit by a shell, which blew up and threw down large portions of the building. Not only was the engineering of the Parthenon masterful, but the esthetics integrating the architecture has become a model used even today in our modern teachings (art, architecture, engineering) and the prototype symbolism of official national architecture throughout the world.

In evaluating any civilization, including our own fading embodiment of Western Civilization, c.2006, we have to ask how far did the Hellenes progress in pushing forward the boundaries of knowledge and the formal sensibilities of the human mind?

In our own moment, we have made great strides in technology, feeding off the theoretical breakthroughs in physics and biology of the early 20th century. At the same time, the general quality of life, the mental aspirations of the average citizen in the world of the 20th century cannot be compared to the life of the mind and the heart of the Greeks throughout the Mediterranean world of the 6th through the 4th century, 500-300 BCE. That world was then abuzz in intellectual inquiry, in the artistic exemplification of their inner intelligence, and in every area of human perception and conception that *Hss* has yet explored.

Yes, certain symbolic forms of human perception and cognition have gained for us more power over nature. Middle-class humans live with conveniences in our physical life, including the medical, that the Greeks could not have hoped for. Yet for those citizens of Athens, taking away the almost genocidal costs of their wars, men and women were born to live out their three score and ten years in great cultural richness.

We must constantly train our attention on the interaction of human mental biology with both the events of nature surrounding culture as well as the complex tensions within the mind of *Hss*. This high intelligent mind seeks the freedom and the cultural initiative to explore the universal invariants of thought, philosophy, science, even politics and the forms of high culture. It does not contemptuously rebuff the deep and nearer-to-home dimensions of our thought, those that apply to the uniqueness of creativity, in ethnic depth and intimacy, the language of poetry, the intercourse of the marketplace, the heat of music and love, all parts of our ancient mammalian emotionality.

The Greeks discovered the right combinations of political and religious freedoms that allowed them to explore the world. Deeply intellectual, with soaring cortex, they plumbed inner and outer experience to search for the laws of nature, as well as the moral and political laws that applied to humans. They thus expanded the boundaries of our knowledge of reality. This inner curiosity of mind did not stop when they were no longer politically independent, when they were subject first to Macedonian and then Roman hegemony. Greek education became the model for all ethnic groups, and into the modern era.

It is difficult to compare across history the esthetic and unique cultural contributions of different peoples. It is not like engineering, where the criteria are universal across space and time. However, it is not unfair to argue that in drama, architecture, sculpture, music and poetry, their work will never be out-spanned, though perhaps paralleled by an Italian Renaissance, or the European eruption in the arts and literature up until the mid-20th century. Truly, we pretend to know more now than did the Greeks, especially in philosophy, the sciences and technology. However, the wars and genocides of the 20th to 21st centuries argue that we are not yet up to the Hellenic achievements in politics and social awareness, life lived at the crest of creative innovation. The barbarity of our times should tell us that we need more Sumerian social practicality, more Greek wisdom and individual *arete'* to live the civilized life.

In Xenophanes, Protagoras, Socrates, Thucydides, Plato, and Aristotle, the Greeks came to a deep and objective understanding of the perennial human condition. The poets of their maturity, Pindar, Aeschylus, Sophocles, Euripides, Aristophanes, likewise echoed this search within poetry and the drama, for the inherent meaning of civilization.

Genius and Loss

Greek creative insight did not end with the absorption of the Greek homelands into the Macedonian Empire, thence becoming the linguistic core of a multi-ethnic civilization, the Hellenistic. Greek scientists, artists, dramatists, philosophers continued to be at the forefront of innovative thinking into the Roman period, and finally into the latter era's final petrification into Christendom. Greek philosophy undergirded the transformation of Christianity from one of many eastern mystery religions into a powerful philosophical lure for the more intellectually inclined leadership of the Empire. Indeed, as we shall note in the next chapter, Judaism itself was transformed by its contact with and tense accommodation with Greek Hellenistic patterns of life. It served importantly as a civilizational model for the philosophical buttressing of the more ancient eastern Judaic traditions.

One thus cannot ignore the reality that even after the decline of the powerful city states, Athens, Thebes, Syracuse, Agraka, Miletus, Corinth, and Sparta, the boundless genius of the Greeks thence spread throughout the ancient world. Sociopolitical conditions had changed, but the talent, the intellectuality, the curiosity was still embedded in the genoplasm of this race.

How did these people remain, often despite themselves, committed to secular reason? How were they able so often to place into leadership persons who respected the intelligence of the *hoi polloi*? We must remember that even the reactionary social and cultural system of Sparta had embedded in its core principle, the democratic ethos, the search for the best leaders in the populace, and the determination to avoid dividing Sparta by social class. In so doing they did create a citizenry, male and female that would fight to the last for the *polis*.

Why did the world lose the Greek sense of openness, the lure of high intellectuality, and above all, the demand for freedom, the recognition of individuality? Indeed, within the Hellenic world, this was always a demand met with conflict and ambivalence, the desire by some in the polity to return to less adventurous modalities of thought, *viz.* the tragic execution of Socrates by the Athenian democracy.

The answer comes in the role played by Plato, Aristotle and their Cynic, Epicurean, Stoic, and Skeptic followers, all representing schools of thought that sought for an explanation as to the why of the defeat of the vision of the good life, lived independently. The 20th-century classicist Gilbert Murray once summed up this defeat, as the Greek "failure of nerve." There is general agreement that the inability of the Greek cities to join in an alliance that could turn back the newly awakened semi-barbarous peoples to the north and west, as well as the ongoing ambitions of the deadened civilizations of the east and south, and feed them the ideal of democratic independence, was a key in the defeat.

The Peloponnesian Wars destroyed much of the young genius in all the cities of Greece. When it came to facing up to a modernizing and expansive Macedon, the dream for the unification of Greece was held high by the Athenian Isocrates. His rival, Demosthenes, held out little hope for the unification of the Greek world under Macedon. Not a young man, he went out as a hoplite (infantryman) in the consequent defeat of the allied Greek armies at Cheronaea in central Greece (338 BCE), finally fleeing to Athens before the Macedonian spear.

The universality of power, plus the universality of the Hellenistic language, its institutions and mind, now comprised the theme. Alexander used well and creatively the military knowledge and cultural cohesion of his Hellenic forebears. Eventually Rome, too, would learn from the Greeks. But they would offer a wholly new practical legal orientation to the concept of the universal state, and the universal culture. Broadly accepting of diverse cultural and religious elements within this extended empire, even going beyond the cohesive syncretism of the role of the Latin and Greek languages, Rome demanded only political and military obedience. She offered up a universal Greco/Roman education to all, but did not demand it.

There was, however, a core element of this universal unification and Roman stereotyping of culture and power that could not be accepted by one constituency of this vast Hellenistic/Roman Imperium. Here, the Jews began to figure on the world scene, in genius, influence, revolt, and dispersion.

Bibliography, Chapter 4

Anderson, W. D. 1966. *Ethos and Education in Greek Music,* Cambridge, MA.: Harvard Univ.
Barr, S. 1961. *The Will of Zeus,* Philadelphia: Lippincott.
Bataille, G. 1962. *Death and Sensuality,* N.Y.: Walker.
Boardman, J. et al., eds. 1991. *The Oxford History of Greece and the Hellenistic World,* N.Y.: Oxford Univ. Press.
Bowra, C. M. 1957. *The Greek Experience,* Cleveland, Ohio: World.
Bowra, C. M. 1971. *Periclean Athens,* N.Y.: Dial.
Burnet, J. 1914. *Greek Philosophy: Thales to Plato,* London.
Dudley, D. R. 1960. *The Civilization of Rome,* N.Y.: New American Library.
Farrington, B. 1953. *Greek Science,* London: Penguin.
Gagarin, M.et al., eds. 1995. *Early Greek Political Thought from Homer to the Sophists,* Cambridge, Eng.: Cambridge Univ. Press.
Glotz, G. 1929. *The Greek City and its Institutions,* London: Paul, Trench, Trubner.
Herodotus.1954 (c.440 BCE). *The Histories,* tr. A. de Selincourt, London: Penguin.
Jaeger, W. 1934 (1923). *Aristotle,* London: Oxford Univ. Press.
Jaeger, W. 1943. *Paideia: The Ideals of Greek Culture,* 3 vols., N.Y.: Oxford Univ. Press.
Jaeger, W. 1947. *The Theology of the Early Greek Philosophers,* London: Oxford Univ. Press.
Jones, W. T.1952. *A History of Western Philosophy,* N.Y.: Harcourt Brace.
Murray, G. 1925. *Five Stages of Greek Religion,* London: Oxford Univ. Press.
Naum, M. C., ed. 1947. *Selections from Early Greek Philosophy,* N.Y.: Appleton-Century-Crofts.
Osborne, R. 1998. *Archaic and Classical Greek Art,* N.Y.: Oxford Univ. Press.
Randall, J. H. 1960. *Aristotle,* N.Y.: Columbia Univ. Press.
Sassi, M.. M. 2001. *The Science of Man in Ancient Greece,* Chicago: Univ. of Chicago Press.
Shorey, P. 1933. *What Plato Said,* Chicago.
Shorey, P. 1933. *What Plato Said,* Chicago: Univ. of Chicago Press.
Taylor, A. E. 1927. *Plato, the Man and his Work,* N.Y.
Taylor, A. E. 1953 (1933). *Socrates,* N.Y.: Doubleday/Anchor.
Thucydides, 1954 (c.410 BCE). *The Peloponnesian War,* tr. R. Warner. Baltimore: Penguin.
Toynbee, A. 1959. *Hellenism,* London: Oxford Univ. Press.
Wolpert, L., ed. 2002. *Science and Mathematics in Ancient Greek Culture,* N.Y.: Oxford Univ. Press.
Zeller, E .1962, 13th ed. (1883). *Outline of the History of Greek Philosophy,* N.Y.: Meridian.
Zeller, E. 1880. *Stoics, Epicureans, Sceptics,* London.
Zimmern, A. E. 1931. *The Greek Commonwealth,* Oxford, Eng: Oxford Univ. Press

---

Endnotes, Chapter 4

[1] Zeller, E. 13th edition, 1962 (1883) *Outline of the History of Greek Philosophy,* N.Y.: Meridian, pp. 17-37.
[2] Herodotus of Halicarnassus (c.440 BCE). *The Histories,* A de Selincourt, tr., London: Penguin, 1954. Bk. 5, Ch. 78. (Acclaimed in Athens, Ionian Greek of half-Carian (Anatolian) descent).
[3] Herodotus. *The Histories,* Book 9: 83, A. de Selincourt, tr., London: Penguin, 1954, p. 609.

5

The Shaping of Jewish Identity

Prologue

Here is a long and still evolving story. Earlier, in looking toward dim horizons, we noted the Sumerian's gradual disappearance into an enveloping sea of Semites. These Semite tribes had earlier been magnetically pulled into the rich Tigris/Euphrates civilization created by the late-arriving Sumerians. The Semites continued this civilizational tradition at an extremely high level of intellect and innovation. But eventually, Mesopotamian civilization bogged down, mostly due to the duress of imperial warfare, the centralization of religion and kingship, which led eventually to the draining away of the blood intellect of the people, as with the Greeks, by dint of perpetual war. Behind the millennial facade of creativity, we always note the desiccating weight of priest and temple.

Religion did not erode the juices of innovation and free thought for the Greeks in the same way as it did for the Mesopotamian civilization. The Greeks: perpetual, never-ending wars, mostly fratricidal, the spurious heroism of man against man, the ongoing quest for revenge and vendetta. Ultimately, no Dracon or Solon could excise such fixations from this ethnic *élan*, even on a national and international level.

Mesopotamia thus suffered its slow decline. Beyond the Persians, Macedonians, Romans, and Parthians, new peoples, made their way in by force or involuntary immigration. Under Islamic rule, new institutions such as quasi-industrial concubinage, slavery, polygamy eventually caused the slow descent of these peoples into a more primitive level of cultural life. The ancient Sumerian/Semitic religion that once harkened to philosophy, science, and poetry declined into the pedantry of revenge and *jihad*.

In Greece, migrations of new groups had also changed the basic Hellenic ethnic glue. Christianity reoriented the people into a wholly different, centripetal outlook. Here, too, as in Mesopotamia, but without the massive waves of African slaves, the economy slumbered and the people could barely recall the ideals of their past.

The Jews, part of the ancient Semitic/Indo-European assemblage of Near Eastern peoples, have preserved long memories. They, too, have been touched by history, and grievously. The following question does retain its bite. Why still the Jews and not the Sumerians? Where in that expanse of the two rivers can we today find the Sumerian creativity, discipline, practicality, inventiveness? It is with poignancy that we can ask a similar question about the spirit of the Hellenic Greeks. Why such a fading? We still need their optimism, skepticism, depth of mind, vision of rationality.

But the Jews remain the only highly creative inheritors of this ancient tradition. Why?

Origination

The Sumerians appeared on the world stage, c.5000-4000 BCE. The Greeks made their impact, starting about 1500 BCE. With the Jews this veil of originating clues is so linked to and dependent upon a series of holy writings, though ever revised through time, that the debate as to origins seems eternal. The brief recounting here laid out should be considered tentative, awaiting further news. (See this series, "Who Are the Jews?": Vol. I. *Soul of the Israelites*; Vol. II. *A Nation of Philosophers*.)

The first source is the Pentateuch itself. We identify two primary writings, the so-called "J" source, the Yahwist setting down that occurred late in King Solomon's reign or that of his son, Rehoboam (Judah), late-10th to early-9th century, 950-875 BCE; the "E" or Elohist source that was written in the northern kingdom, Israel, between the 9th and 8th centuries, 890-800 BCE. Both were based on explicitly noted earlier writings as well as the oral tradition. They were revised and sewn together to make a continuous narrative in later centuries, first with the addition of a "P" or Priestly source, this perhaps in Judah, c.700-650 BCE, or even later during and after the so-called Babylonian Captivity, 586-539 BCE, and beyond. The speculation continues.

The writing in the Pentateuch is both historical and theological in nature. It arose from the newly formed self-consciousness of the Hebrews as they became a nation, as they left behind the benign memories of their scattered tribal interminglings and wanderings. The push toward national unity was clearly a reaction to the ever-heavier press of migrants from the Mycenaean world of the Greeks, after c.1200 BCE.

We know that the Egyptians engaged in an ongoing struggle with the so-called "sea-peoples" in this timeframe. And as noted in Chapter IV, the Philistines and Cherethites figure largely in the history of Hebrew tribes. The settlement of the Philistines along what is known today as the Gaza coast pressed the hill peoples into defensive alliances that culminated in a nation. The Philistines were never defeated until the coming of the Assyrians, c.722 BCE.

Three elements comprise the probable origins of this one nation, and then its division after three generations, c.100 years. The divided monarchy comprised the ten northern tribes in Israel and the two tribes of Judah, with its capital in the old Indo-European city of the Jebusites, Jerusalem. The role of the incoming Indo-Europeans in shaping the destiny of this part of the Middle East was ubiquitous, *e.g.,* Abraham, Isaac, and Jacob. The tribes, even the Egyptian leadership, must be viewed as an amalgam of migrating and indigenous elements, Hamitic, Semitic, Indo-European.

The first component of this Hebrew nation-to-be were the refugees or expellees from Egypt. Led by Moses, imbued with Moses' all-encompassing ethical monotheism, this vision became the intellectual/moral core in the evolution of this people. They were probably Semite migrants and then workers/slaves in the *corvée* of the, Delta rulers of Egypt, Rameses II, Merneptah, and Rameses III (1250-1150 BCE--Asiatic in origin). Moses' monotheism bears strong resemblance to the monotheistic trends in the realm of the revolutionary Pharaoh Akhenaton.

Akhenaton created a new capital city, Tel Amarna, c.1360-1330 BCE, along the Nile River, to celebrate his religion of Aton, the one sun god. After his death the priestly establishment regained control of the Egyptian temples and their power and reinstated polytheism, which included worship of their animal gods. Moses may have been a descendant/follower of the religion of Aton, coming to live under a new dynasty, Rameses II, c.1275 BCE. The timeline between the death of Akhenaton and Rameses II is barely two generations.

The second group is symbolized by Jethro the Midianite, father-in-law of Moses. Jethro appears over and over again in the Old Testament. His presence is witness to the fact that the worship of one god, Yahweh, was not unique to the Israelites. Other non-Hebrew individuals, Othniel, Caleb, Rehab, Jael, Heber, Shamgar, indeed Ruth and King David himself, reflect a strong southern (the Sinai, Arabia, the Negev, Jordan) tribal element that early on, in the days of Moses, as well as late in Biblical history, such as the time of Jeremiah, 590 BCE, were part of the Judean Yahwhist tribal circle.

The northerners comprised the third element that contributed to the unification of Israel. These were the writers of the Pentateuch in Shiloh, Bethel, "E"

Elohim or El, followers of the traditional theist pantheon of the West Semites. The tradition reveals itself in Genesis with the story of the rape of Tamar, Jacob's daughter, and her brothers' revenge on the Shechemites. {Genesis 34} Indeed, the tribes of Dan ("Danaoi," possibly of Greek origins), Assur, Gad, all reflect names associated with non-Yahwist traditions. They were certainly an integral part of the tribal system, anywhere from twelve to fifteen, that appear in various parts of the Old Testament.

The breaking off of these northern tribes, the "E" traditions in the Pentateuch, all point to the fact that these former Apiru (Hebrew) raiders against the Indo-European Canaanite towns mentioned in the Amarna Letters to the Egyptian Pharaohs, Amenhotep III, and IV—Akhenaton, (c.1350 BCE) and hinted at in many of the tales in Joshua and Judges (*e.g.,* Gideon in Judges, 8) had a separate historical memory.

The two monotheistic entities, believers in Yahweh/Elohim had many subsequent generations of cooperation as well as occasional conflicts. Israel, of the north, was by far the wealthier. But Jerusalem, Judah's capital was the city of David. As yet there was no strong ethnic bond to keep them together, excepting the exhortations of priests and prophets to maintain the discipline of Moses and the Commandments of God. This was an overly demanding task for these simple agrarians, to which the Old Testament testifies in detail.

Moses and his intellectual scholarly descendants struggled with the *am ha aretz*, the tillers of the soil, the tendency of the ordinary folk in field and town to fall back into easier more primitive religious patterns, festal orgies, fertility worship of female goddesses, figurines of *Asherah,* and, of course, sacrifices of first-born daughters (Jephthah-Judges 11:34) and sons in the fires of the valley of Hinnom, just south of Jerusalem.

This was yet an impure syncretic religiosity, not far beyond King Solomon's own sacrilege of worship, encouraging his many foreign wives to worship their many gods. Except for those few scholar/priests who devoted themselves to the preservation of the historic traditions that had created this political, religious, moral entity, the Israelite community itself differed little, ethically and socially, from its surrounding neighbors, with their pagan rituals and anthropomorphic gods, their constant readiness to enthusiastically embrace the opportunity to engage in ever new wars.

Chronological Overview

1) Noah, the flood and Noah's sons—Great Sumerian Flood, c.2900 BCE.

2) Abraham, Isaac, Jacob—Southern migration, Semites and Indo-Europeans, c.2000 BCE.

3) Joseph in Egypt—Hyksos in Hamitic Egypt, (Semites and Indo-Europeans, c.1700 BCE.

4) Moses and Exodus—Mixed Semitic population leaves Egypt, c.1250-1150 BCE. Moses, the royal Egyptian follower of the monotheism of Akhenaton (1330 BCE).

5) Sea Peoples and Philistines, Greek migration to Phoenecia/Egypt, 1250-1150 BCE.

6) Tribal Interregnum—1200-1030 BCE—Amalgamation of tribes, worship of one God.

7) Coronation of Saul, of Gibeah in Benjamin, united against Philistines, c.1030 BCE.

8) Two Monarchies, Judah, under Rehoboam, Israel, under Jeroboam, 925 BCE.

9) Israel, conquered by Assyria, population dispersed/replaced, 722 BCE.

10) Judah, conquered by neo-Babylonians, Temple burned, elite deported, 597-586-582 BCE.

11) Cyrus, Indo-European/Persian, conquers Babylon, returns Jews to Jerusalem, 539 BCE, beginning of reconstruction of the Temple

12) Ezra/Nehemiah preaches to Yehud peasantry, interprets Holy Writings, c.450 BCE.

13) Alexander, Macedonian/Hellenic culture, conquers east, 330 BCE.

14) Maccabean revolt, 166 BCE; Judaic control to 37 BCE; Rome (Herod) from 37 BCE.

15) Revolt of Jews, destruction by Rome of 2nd Temple, 67-70 CE; international Jewish revolt, Cyrene, Cyprus, Alexandria, Adiabene, Ctesiphon—115-117 CE; Bar Kokhba revolt, 132-135 CE, Defeat, Jerusalem destroyed—Ultimate Dispersion.

Evolution of the Faith

Ancient sages tend to think in allegorical terms. Thus the first periods of Israelite history, (Chronology--1-5), are more symbolic of events that needed to be stitched together meaningfully, than the chronologically disciplined timeframes ordered by the modern historian. That certain events did happen, the flood, the migrations into Canaan, the coming of the sea peoples to the Mid-East, we know to be historical. For example, we have statuettes found in Canaan, along the Mediterranean coast that depict men in the traditional "sea people" headdresses. These figurines date to c.1800 BCE. These could have been Minoan (Cretan), explorers/traders, else early Mycenaean mainlanders.

Certainly, Moses as an historical figure is not undercut by the fact that we have no archaeological evidence for his personal existence. We have no archaeological evidence for much that fits together as historic fact from this civilizational timeframe. The power of Moses' teachings, his Egyptian name, the closeness in time, 60-80 years, of the Nile River monotheism of the court of Akhenaton to the events of Exodus all seem to parallel the drama of the Israelite escape/expulsion from Egypt.

Further, the existence of a tradition of one major fiery/warrior God, *YHWH*, held to by the desert peoples of south and the adjoining wilderness, makes the possibility that a powerful, well-educated human figure such as Moses could be the leader of such an exodus, a likely reality. He was revolutionary in shaping the deeply-held life experiences—especially the *intelligentsia*—of these nomadic subsistence agricultural Shasu (Sinai)-Habiru (Canaan) peoples.

The next stage, (Chronology--6-8), in the evolution of the sense of self of these people arose from the reality of fighting and defending their homeland against the encroachments of a truly foreign enemy, the uncircumcised and swine-eating Philistines. The Israelites adopted circumcision largely from aristocratic Egyptian as well wilderness tribal practice. For wanderers, goats, sheep, oxen were possible livelihoods for herding. They could not cultivate the farming of pigs, as did the urban, sea trading, and sedentary Greek Philistines.

Formalizing in writing these traditions of selfhood and nationality became an essential role for a literate, educated, priestly cadre. This period marked by the surrender of tribal freedoms for national consciousness and defense, c.1000 BCE, comes long after the dissemination of alphabetic literacy to this part of the Middle East, c.1500 BCE. It is noteworthy to reflect on the closeness in time of the events of both the Homeric and Mosaic tales, c.1200 BCE. The writing down of this largely bardic tradition was also paralleled, c.950-850 BCE, for the early versions of the Pentateuch, and c.850-750 CE for the authors of the Iliad and Odyssey. The far more ancient Sumerians had their own mythic text, the Gilgamesh narrative, written in the era of c.2900-2600 BCE.

With regard to the events in the two rival kingdoms, we observe a discontinuity between this educated leadership, the prophets, the aristocratic ruling classes, and the peasantry on the farms and in the villages. The military and economic leaders removed religion and morality from the opportunism and advantageousness of the moment.

The descent of the Israelite kingdom's leadership into Baal worship was prompted by the fact that, as the northerly political unit, it was deeply involved in the economics and politics of their more powerful northern coastal neighbors, and they intermarried following these less rigorous religious patterns as well. The ordinary people felt a greater emotional connection to the celebration of festal days spent on heights in the countryside than to the disciplines imposed by a distant Temple high on Mt. Zion in Jerusalem.

Judah in the south was surrounded by wilderness, and the foreignness of Egypt, a desert away beyond the Sinai. Much poorer, Judah tended toward defense. The priesthood could therefore exert a stronger moralizing influence, to exhort the people to stay the course of religious conformity to the Commandments and the Covenant with the Lord.

Yet this was a powerful tool wielded by this educator class in Judah, and to a lesser extent in Israel. To the intellectually emancipated groups, the enlightened, the insights of Moses, the Judges (Samuel), the Prophets, who came forth from all parts of the ancient tribal confederation, the *Laws* of YHWH/*El*, *Covenant*, and *Commandment* were powerful intellectual as well as moral magnets.

These principles derived from an all-powerful Deity on high, goaded all Hebrews to aspire to a higher intellectual understanding of the universe, one suffused with moral tensions and ambiguities. In Holy Writ was a message for humans, complex, full of restrictions, yet clear as to the struggle to which all humankind was engaged in order to gain meaning and understanding. The Laws illuminated a reality with which we weak humans must forever grapple. The purification of one's soul for eternal salvation connoted a hard-fought battle in a world of ever-present danger.

Eventually, both Israel and Judah were crushed by greater powers in the eternal political ebb and flow of national advantage, (Chronology--9,10,11) The prophets saw the razing of the Temple, 586 BCE, as an exemplification of the moral defects of both Israel and Judah, their disobedience to the tenets of the Book. Assyria, typically, dispersed the existing population of syncretic practicing Israelites. The ten tribes disappeared, probably adopting the religion of "place" of their new homelands. The newcomers to Israel quickly asked for local Hebrew priests to teach them the ostensible religion of Israel/Samaria.

The Chaldean/Babylonians, they from the southern deserts of Mesopotamia, already contesting the old Assyrian Empire with the incoming Indo-European Medes and Persians, had a more benevolent policy for the "duplicitous" Judeans. They allowed the people of the land to stay and harvest their crops, took only several thousand of the elite to the Nippur region along the Euphrates for purposes of repopulation, and to have the Judeans as a community, reap some wealth for themselves and their overseers.

Forty-seven years later, the Indo-European Persian Cyrus conquered Babylon and allowed all those Jews who wanted to return to Jerusalem, now as part of the Persian province of Yehud, to return. They could rebuild their Temple. A few, carrying the ransomed remains of the gold and silver artifacts of the old incinerated holy shrine, did return, 539 BCE. Over the decades, more and more returned to Jerusalem, and its surrounds as a community began to form. Many others stayed behind, maintaining their religious connection with Jerusalem, but enjoying the seemingly endless renewable wealth that was centered in the great Mesopotamian river valleys.

Jerusalem and the Yehud were under the easy governance of the Persians from 539 to c.330 BCE, over two hundred years, twice the length of the United Monarchy. Israel had been an independent state for a similar length of time, c.925-722 BCE, Judah, an additional one hundred and twenty-five years of independence, until 597 BCE, the first Chaldean conquest.

As the life of the Jews of Yehud under Persian hegemony took form, it was clear that a new dimension to the faith was being shaped. Under the geographically extended Persian hegemony, many diverse peoples and religions coexisted. Even within the small provinces of the Yehud and Samaria there could be little hope for the political maintenance of any religious orthodoxy.

Later, (Chronology—12) under the prophets Ezra and Nehemiah, not only was the Second Temple completed, but a new perspective on the faith was adduced. The Persians were only uncomfortable with political unrest. They would tend to support the orthodox authority of those they selected to run the province. Ezra and Nehemiah came from diverse parts of the empire, c.450 BCE, the former from Babylon, the latter from the Persian court itself, in Susa. The Babylonian exilic completion of large parts of the Holy Writings, and their compilation, made it ever more important to communicate the message to the masses, many of whom were forced migrants to Yehud and Samaria (Judah and Israel) by the Assyrians. Others had fallen away from strict observances during the approximately fifty years of Chaldean occupation.

It is significant to note that Ezra and Nehemiah demanded that the Jews not marry outside the faith. They urged the abandonment of non-tribal Israelite wives. Close reading reveals that these lectures were accompanied by oral readings, with explanation of the Holy Writings. It had by now been over four hundred years since the setting down of the original drafts of the Torah. And at best the understanding and commitment to the Law was probably as weak inside the independent Israelite states as it had been during Moses' long hegira into Canaan.

Alongside the now growing semi-official power of the priesthood of the new Temple came an effort to disseminate the meaning and obligations of the teachings of the LORD, now in written form. The flourishing of the *soferim* (scribes) derived from this need. Out of this movement of scribes into the communities would later come the *Pharisees*, offering legal counseling services to a largely illiterate population, but also help in understanding the Holy Writings.

Unlike the instabilities of the earlier Jewish monarchical tradition, the pacific nature of Persian rule made it possible to disseminate an official state-sponsored religious tradition throughout the Yehud, again centered in Jerusalem. The Persians cared more for political quiet than any particular sectarian religious orthodoxy. The rejection of representatives of Samaria, the divided monarchy's old capital of Israel, now largely occupied by the immigrants from Assyria, to participate in the rebuilding of the Jerusalem Temple, was a signal event. This putting off of a dominant Samarian political figure such as Sanballat, considering the growing wealth of this region, soon led to the separatist Jewish movement (claiming to be more orthodox), the *Samaritans*.

By 409 BCE, the Jewish colony at Elephantine, on the upper course of the Nile, which was created as an Assyrian era military outpost, would appeal to both the religious authorities in Samaria (Shechem), as well as Jerusalem for help and guidance in rebuilding their local temple after Egyptian priests had had it destroyed. The now Persian occupiers of Egypt would allow for its rebuilding.

It is in this era, also, that the traditional canonical division of the Old Testament began to take shape: 1. *Torah* (Law-*Pentateuch*); 2. *Nevim* (Prophets); 3. *Kethuvim* (Writings), equaling TaNaK. Ezra and Nehemiah constitute the final prophets. The other writings were well debated until early in the 1st CE, when the Rabbis made their final distillation, adding, deleting, and redacting the ancient texts. The Samaritans, seeing the prophetic tradition so closely allied with Jerusalem and Judah, rejected the *nevim* and the *kethuvim* as not having special holy status. They adhered to a strict interpretation of the Torah, not too distant in belief from that of the later Sadducees, the Priesthood party of the Jerusalem Temple.

Revolution of the Faith—Hellenism

The Hellenes were out and about prowling the seas far back in time, raiding Crete, Egypt, and, of course, Troy. Cyrus had his eyes on the Ionian Greek city states even before attacking nearer-at-hand Babylon. After swinging down to capture Sardis, 546 BCE (King Croesus), and then the Greek towns, he then, in 539 BCE, breezed into defenseless Babylon. The growing Greek wealth was the lure, not stagnant Mesopotamia. It is hardly likely that the western coasts of

Mediterranean Asia had not been many times touched by Greek traders and influence. In fact, one probable view is that Ezra and Nehemiah were sent to Jerusalem c.450 BCE, to help secure the routes to Egypt because of the epochal failure of the Persians and their international allies and subjects in the campaign against the Greek heartland, 490-479 BCE.

It has also been suggested that the concern of Ezra and Nehemiah to interpret the holy writings and thus help communicate their meaning to the ignorant peasants and craftspeople was stimulated in part by the growing literature that was emanating from Greece. Here was developing a powerful and literate civilization, largely democratic in political governance. Their industrial manufacture, the artistically decorated pottery, the computers of the era, at the least, testified to a growing influence of Hellenism. The strongest wave was yet to come, c.330 BCE, with Alexander.

The hint that we get from the Egyptian Jewish colony at Elephantine, c.409 BCE, reveals the growing extent of the Diaspora, yet its commitment to *Israel.* The Jewish colonies in Babylon had spread into Persia, thence with the Persians, back again into Anatolia as well as Egypt. The Prophet Jeremiah and a few followers had fled to Egypt in 582 BCE, following an attempted coup against the Chaldean-established Jewish regency in Jerusalem. The Jews thence spread into a number of Egyptians cities. Jeremiah was able to correspond with the Babylonian exiles of 597-586 BCE.

Alexander arrived, c.330 BCE, (Chronology—13). The rapid establishment of a new Hellenic city along the Mediterranean, named after Alexander, became a magnet for opportunity. A politically powerless Jerusalem was less of a centripetal glue than in the era of the First Temple. There was a quiet stream of Jewish migration from the home country and elsewhere into more economically opportune climes. As borders evaporated, the Jews took their Holy Books with them.

About 280 BCE, a scant two generations after the founding of Alexandria, the call came from the growing Jewish community of that city: the young no longer knew Hebrew or the Aramaic lingua franca of the Near East. Greek was the "modern" language. Probably from Jerusalem, assistance was forthcoming to translate the Torah into Greek, the *Septuagint.* The version that comes closest to what was used as the Hebrew source was the Samaritan Pentateuch; the orthodox Rabbinical, Masoretic version, c.200 CE, is a later distillation.

Clearly, a large prosperous community had quickly grown up in the region of Alexandria. These migrants felt their closeness to the faith through the holy writings, because soon after the *nevim* and more modern writings of Jewish seers and thinkers, *kethuvim,* in all the languages of the region began to appear in successive versions of this *Septuagint* (the supposedly seventy translators of the Torah into Greek). The *Septuagint* in its final form, which differs in content as well as style from the Masoretic text, was the basis of Christian translations into Latin and other languages.

The vision of Ezra and Nehemiah for a literate Judaism was now being accomplished in the surge of a modern literary culture that the free-thinking Greeks were stimulating throughout the Hellenistic world of their conquests. There was now another pole in the centrality of Judaism. Not merely Jerusalem, its Temple and priests, with the tithes, sacrifices, concordance with the ruling powers of the day. Now the Jews, as Elias Bickerman has noted, became "the people of the book."

As early as the days of Herodotus, c.450 BCE, Greeks had wandered the world not merely in trade and/or conquest but to learn in a secularly unshackled manner what the non-Hellenic world was about. How could it be understood in terms of its interaction with the Hellenes; what larger meaning could this strangeness connote? The conquests of Alexander opened the doors to travelers to more easily learn about these peoples who had been joined in Hellenistic hegemony.

Encountering the Jews, with their strong, moralistic monotheism, the commandments given by God to Moses, the Greek scholars were impressed. The Hellenic philosophers had long persuaded the educated Greeks to view their own polytheism metaphorically. The 6th-century philosopher Parmenides first enunciated this perspective of the unity of nature, later, the encompassing perspective of Plato penetrated the outlook of the educated Greeks, offering a sense of openness and inquiry as regard the deeper mysteries of nature, society, and man.

Here was a people, the Jews, that held to a view that all questions concerning the challenges of human existence could be sourced and answered in and from the writings and sayings of one supreme deity, a God, abstract, not to be pictured or reduced to a concrete image. Wherever the Jews were found, Greeks such as Hecaeteus, Megasthenes, Theophrastus of Lesbos, Clearches of Soli, all 4th-century thinkers, many, students of Aristotle's Lyceum, termed the Jews "a nation of philosophers." Here is exemplified the rebounding impact that the Jews in turn had made upon this new Hellenistic international culture.

The *Proseuche*, (place of prayer), *Synagogue*, (bring together) both Greek terms, also called *Bet 'am*-(house of a people), along with a new group of *soferim*, scribes, writers, interpreters, the Pharisees (Parash—stand apart) now began to espouse the "Oral Law," that which is implied in the Holy Writings, yet explicitly given by God to Moses. This new movement of local interpreters of these Holy Writings, moved in a world external to, both physically and in religious practice, to the Temple priesthood. The Pharisees began to make their way in thought and practice into the language and social ferment of Jewish Hellenism.

It is agreed that this new outlook, and the new institutions noted above, arose within the Diaspora, probably from Alexandria, now a dynamic center of Jewish life, as earlier, Babylon had functioned. This new trend within Judaism spread rapidly throughout the Jewish world, which now flowed outward everywhere that the Macedonian conquest extended, and then beyond.

The reflexive orthodoxy both of the Samaritans and then the Sadducean Temple alliance was rapidly being overtaken by an international Judaic experiment, both in institutional structure, plus a now active written culture. Other groups such as the Essenes, the Qumran secessionists, soon added to the mix of experimental Judaism, all rooted in the wisdom of the Torah but now under the auspices of Hellenistic Greek secular openness of thought. The Pharisees even introduced elements of the syncretic orientalism sweeping the Hellenistic world-into the mix of the Written and Oral Law. They explicitly argued for the coming of a Messiah {Isaiah 7:11} and the immortality of the individual human soul, ideas that the Christians later added to their program. However, events in the political arena would decide the ultimate direction of this revolutionary Judaic historical change.

End of the Dream of Nationhood

The Hellenistic intellectualism of the Ptolemies, Macedonian inheritors of the Egyptian domains of Alexander that long controlled Judea, was benign. To the great museum in Alexandria flocked the cream of the Hellenistic science, art, and philosophy. For awhile, Alexandria was an oasis of tranquility and intellectualism. The Jews prospered here. But as the Ptolemies were softening with prosperity, their Macedonian rivals the Seleucids, based in north Syrian Antioch attacked and took Jerusalem from them, about 200 BCE. By this period, increasing wealth was flowing into the Temple, contributed locally as well as from the Jewish Diaspora. The ambitions of this Macedonian family first led them west into Europe, becoming the dominant Hellenistic entity there until they met the growing Roman military presence, fresh from its extinctions of the Carthaginians.

The Maccabean revolt, (Chronology--14), and the subsequent Maccabean/Hasmonean dynasty (Rome concurred) that ruled Judea took its fundamentalist energies from the overreaching of Seleucid ambitions. Soon, Rome officially intervened, placing the converted Idumean(Edomite)/Jew, Herod, on the throne as vassal. Thence after, Rome ruled. The religious intellectual factor in the revolt seems to have been secondary to the attempted Sadducean selling and the Seleucid looting of the Temple by Antiochus IV, c.173-167 BCE.

Withal their priestly orthodoxy, the Jewish elites in Jerusalem were entranced with Greek culture, the *ephebia, gymnasia*/education, theatres, hippodromes, baths, nudity, above all the military efficiency that Alexander brought to the region This respect for the Greeks is already hinted at several hundred years earlier in the Biblical writings, *Chronicles*, c.375 BCE, during the Persian period. The Sadducean aristocracy was not at all ashamed of the possibility of placing a Greek temple or fortress on Zion, opening up the Temple to a variety of syncretic worship, seemingly as long as the wealth poured in and the ritual traditions of the Pentateuch, the festivals continued apace.

Ironically, the descendants of Mattathias and Judah Maccabee were named Jason, John, Alexander, Salome/Alexandra, all served to institute a full-fledged Hellenization of Judea. This trend was continued under Herod, with the retention of certain traditions such as circumcision, Temple worship, exclusion of human images on coins. Included also was required conversion to Judaism to allow for provincial investiture.

In general, the ordinary Jew on the land or in the towns now held true to the older Biblical injunctions concerning moral life. In the writings of Jewish Hellenes, there were stinging criticisms of the more "primitive" anthropomorphic religious institutions of the Greeks, and of the Orientals as well. These bitter critiques centered on their looser morality, here including homosexuality. An amazing phenomenon began to occur, amplified upon the commencing of Roman rule. Mass conversion to Judaism was occurring, both of an official nature, as well as from a broader circle of consanguinity of ostensible Jews aligned with the Hellenistic community.

Gregory Sterling gives these approximate population figures: Jerusalem, c.100 BCE—35,000. One hundred fifty years later, c.50 CE—70,000-80,000 (after Herod, and now including converts); Alexandria, 50 CE, total population—600,000, Greek/Egyptian free citizens—300,000, Jewish citizens—180,000, slaves and aliens—120,000. In the kingdom of Adiabene (Assyria/Kurdistan), on the upper Euphrates, the royal family led in its conversion to Judaism early in the 1st century CE. Soon, the growth of Jewish demography and its subsequent surge into positions of power led to inter-religions/ethnic strife, especially in Alexandria, the second city of the Empire.

The ascension as Emperor of Caligula, who in his madness proclaimed himself god, and demanded emperor worship, reacted sharply against the Jews, especially in Judea, but also in Alexandria. When he gave opportunity to anti-Jewish sentiment, c.38 CE, riots broke out in that latter city. Several delegations, one led by the noted anti-Semite Apion (of Josephus fame), the other led by Philo, the philosophical member of an extremely powerful Jewish clan. The attempt was both to calm the waters of inter-ethnic conflict, and to insulate the Jews from Caligula's mad demands. Fortunately, he was soon assassinated and his successor, Claudius, attempted to dampen the fires.

In all parts of the Roman Empire, (Chronology—15), Judaism became the attractive alternative to a dying pagan religious tradition; some estimates give up to seven million Jews, thus more than ten percent of the population of the Empire. The old pagan religious tradition was in decay. Born of community identification and local place, it had now been pulled out of shape and context into an intercontinental expansion by virtue of Macedonian and then Roman military and political organizational power. To the conquered it was foreign and oppressive.

To the locals in Rome, it was a matter of going through the civic rituals of tradition, amidst a philosophical and political enlightenment that robbed it of its old meanings. Thus, in the Jewish populations, the growing sentiment of uniqueness and apartness began boiling up into revolt, given the Roman needs for ever heavier taxes, political and military control. No longer attracted to Hellenism, the Jews felt themselves ever more sharply burdened. These impositions were felt especially heavily in the non-Hellenic/Roman domains of the Empire.

For the Jews of Judea, the ancient homeland, the alienation from this foreign and hateful occupation led to a break. In 68-70 CE, they revolted. They were bloodily defeated, and the Second Temple was razed. The Pharisees, unlike the Samaritans, crushed along with the Sadducees, stayed aloof from the conflict, maintaining an educational center in Yavneh, an old Philistine town near the coast. They were largely out of power, located in the towns and villages among the *am ha aretz*. From there, the final development of the Oral Law was framed, to accommodate modernity with the moral/theological vision of the Torah and the Prophets. Christianity was simultaneously moving away from its Judaic, even pharisaic origins.

The famed Rabbi Hillel, during the reign of Herod, 37 BCE-4 CE, had arrived from Parthian Babylonia to take his pharisaic place in the intellectual debates. Hillel's grandson, Gamaliel was a teacher of Paul, the disciple of Jesus. The New Testament cites Gamaliel's vindication of Paul's heresy in a Jerusalem Sanhedrin {Acts 5:35-39}, this, before the wars.

After the war, Judea still flourished in population and education, as turmoil in the other Jewish communities boiled beneath the surface of Roman rule. The accession of Trajan, 98 CE, who had dreams of a greater Empire than that bequeathed by Augustus (d. 14 CE), and his followers, began a great and expensive military campaign. Trajan was not anti-Jewish. In fact he was accused by Alexandrian gentiles of having a Senate full of Jews. However, his final campaigns, in the East against Parthia, 115-117 CE, and the chaos that ensued with war on all sides, set off an international revolt of Jewish populations throughout the western Empire.

.   Alexandria again exploded. In Lybia, the great city of Cyrene saw Jewish kings taking the helm of that province, marching east to liberate Alexandria and then Judea. Cyprus was engulfed in revolt. Trajan conquered the Jewish kingdom of Adiabene, from there the capital of Jewish controlled Parthia, Ctesiphon.

He thence marched to the Persian gulf, and quickly lost this capital, as well as his life, in one stroke. His successor, Hadrian, unhesitatingly drew Roman lines backward in space, in accord with Augustus' admonition for "safe boundaries." The chaos that followed in Parthia saw a Jewish Kingdom in Ctesiphon (the ancient Babylonian exile heartland), and for almost fifteen years.

The revolutionary Judean, Simon Bar Kokhba, supported by the renowned Tannaim, Rabbi Akiba, led a final revolution for liberation against Rome between 132-135 CE. Destroyed by Hadrian's legions, Judea was emptied, as Jerusalem itself was sacked and destroyed, a new Roman town erected on its ruins. All of these Jewish attempts at revolt and political/military dominance outside and within the ancient homeland, failed. Jewish Hellenism was the ultimate victim of the thrust for political/military independence from the gentiles. Alexandrian Jewry melted back into the hazy backwaters of history. After Philo (died c.54 CE), no intellectually "enlightened" writings or activities emanated from these outlier communities.

A People, Chosen, Apart

After Bar-Kokhba, the Jewish academies moved north into the Galilee, some into Babylonia, this time as voluntary refugees, again to meet their fellows now flourishing by the calm waters of the rivers. From the days of Rabbi Hillel I, and Shamai, Herod's rule, 37 BCE-4 CE, the thrust of the pharisaic community was to help the people in the villages and on the farms obtain an understanding of the ancient writings in terms of the Hellenistic/Roman challenges to ordinary moral and community life. More and more, these *Rabbis* (Aramaic for "teacher") were tested for their intellectualism in revising many of the stern community principles that were at the base of a Torah written by a wandering, struggling, fighting, wilderness tribe of that ancient era of constant want.

The Hellenistic in the time of Herod was not a period of poverty for the masses, rather of great, if ill-distributed wealth. Also, it was a time when the international culture reflected the Greek enlightenment. This reality had an impact on the Jewish consciousness, especially the Pharisaic/Rabbinical leadership that survived the destruction of the Temple incurred by Roman Emperor Titus (70 CE) and then sixty five years later the complete destruction of the homeland by Hadrian, after Bar Kokhba and Rabbi Akiba. The implicit message: stay out of politics, cultivate the new studies by the Soferim/Tannaic Rabbis, the commentaries, elucidations, moral writings.

The Sadducees, Essenes, Qumran communities had now disappeared along with the Temple, later, even the holy city of Jerusalem Yet the Jews could not completely flee from life as it was being rebuilt around them. An example of this still worldly attitude of the leaders of the Jewish community was the work of Rabbi Gamaliel II. A noted controversialist, if leader of the Yavneh Academy, c.90-110 CE, he also is said to have run an academy for the cultivation and teaching of Greek wisdom. In fact, the secular language of the region was Greek, the Romans allowed for the retention of the ancient Alexandrian importation. And, of course, Greek literature represented the acme of scientific, philosophical, medical, historical, dramatic/poetic knowledge, and human civilizational enhancement.

The general atmosphere in the Jewish world was an acceptance of the inevitability of the consequences, in military victory or defeat, of that unique vision that Moses had received from the LORD. The wisdom of God, communicated through Moses, would forever constitute a minority belief. The commitment was now to be taken by this people, chosen by God to keep the sacred truths alive in a hostile, corrupt, if dominating world.

That is, until the arrival of the Messiah, to the Jews and then to the rest of mankind, eternal salvation. National identity and political independence were perhaps not that critical to the retention of the deeper truths of the faith. After all, the wise judge Samuel, over a thousand years earlier (c.1050 BCE) had warned the Israelites about the dangers of ceding their tribal independence for kingship. The Israelites, fearful of the military power of a foreign element, the Philistines, did not listen.

They had learned the extreme price of their claim for exceptionalism from Roman political and military hegemony. Too, they were learning that the high wall of scriptural discipline that had separated them from the Gentile world, despite the allure inspired in the outside world by their commitment to obedience to their LORD, was now being undercut. The Christian sects under the leadership of the followers of Paul, executed in Rome, c.62 CE, were proselytizing among the masses, requiring a much less rigorous set of prerequisites and disciplines for membership in this community of belief. The growth of Christianity was both electrifying and dismaying to Jewish Rabbinical orthodoxy.

The Rabbis had to teach the loyal Jews once more that the deep wisdom of the Torah, the Prophets, the Writings, *TaNaK*, were not dependant on kings, armies, or mysteries of ritual, rather on the Holy written and oral words of God as interpreted for the modern mind by the scholars of the academy. The injunction to the Jewish people, now totally in *Diaspora*, was to turn to the Academies (Yeshivas), the books, to study, contemplate, and pray.

From this time (c.150 CE), the long era of exile begins. The story of the evolution of the Jewish mind is an oft-told tale, at the least in chronicling the external events. The many writings that accumulated with regard to interpretation and explanation of the holy writings, on what it meant to be a Jew; to bear both the burden of obligation and the glory of their covenant with the LORD, to undertake this high responsibility, needed intellectual integration. In Sepphoris, (Galilee) the wealthy scholar, Judah Ha Nasi (the Prince), organized and integrated the Mishnah (Repetition), c.200 CE, thus far the most systematic explanation of Torah law (*Halakhah*) Other writings were integrated and presented to the people by scholars also from the Galilee, Usha.

This was a period of mild Roman recognition of the Jews as a people. The dynasty of Roman Emperor Septimus Severus hailed from North Africa and Syria, and clearly was sensitive to the law-and-order opportunities offered in treating the various religious sects with an unusual gentleness. In fact, his son, Caracalla, otherwise a ferocious acquisitor of power, gave Roman citizenship to the entire Empire, in part, for tax purposes. But he also allowed the Jews back into Jerusalem, c.212 CE. For this, a successor, Alexander Severus (222-235 CE) was derided as "archisynagogus" by Christian and pagan religious authority.

Shortly after, other, more concrete and historical exemplars of interpretation over the Law and Jewish tradition began to be accumulated in Palestine and in Babylon. In the latter case, the Jewish communities had increased in size, and with them quite active and prosperous academies of learning. The Parthian and then the Sassanian ruling classes were beyond the reach of strengthening Christian polemics, no less the Roman legions. By the beginning of the 6th century CE, the extensive Babylonian Talmud (Study) had been completed. Because of Christian Roman harassment in Galilee, the truncated, so-called Jerusalem Talmud had earlier been completed, mainly in the town of Tiberius.

As an example of the redirection in the nature of late-Roman, early-Medieval and eastern Judaism, is given in the Kallah, a twice-yearly convention of scholars, advanced students, at the various academies (Yeshivas), in Babylonia, in that seventy-mile-long enclave of Jews along the central stretches of the Euphrates River, from Nehardia and Pumbeditha in the north to Sura in the south. This area was now known to the Sassanians of the region as "Israel." From the mid-third century, c.250 CE, ever larger assemblages came to discuss special points of concern over the interpretation of Torah law, to debate, concur or disagree, and then to decide what was to be included in the Talmudic dialectics. Off times, not enough homes or inns could be found to accommodate these eager internationally attracted disputants, as to the evolving and contemporary meaning for ritual, festival, and moral practice of the ancient books.

No over-arching bureaucratic system directed any Jewish community or its individual members. The rabbis were or were not graduates of these academies. What mattered was their learning and moral uprightness. Most earned a living by their own toil. Shelomo ben Yitzhak—Rashi, 1040-1105 CE—the greatest expositor and commentator of the Babylonian Talmud, in Troyes, France, was self taught, earned his living, as a seller of wines. But he founded an academy in that city to teach others. Only the patriarch of the Jewish community in its relation to Roman rule or the Exilarch, representative of the community to the then-ruling powers, Sassanian or Muslim, commanded a higher standing, economic or social, in the community. For example, he remitted Jewish tax obligations; likewise, his official position became the vehicle for the transferal of the returned beneficence of the powers-that-be.

As Christianity became the official religion of the Empire, after c.325 CE, the situation of the Jews under Rome became untenable. The Jerusalem Talmud's seemingly abbreviated nature can be attributed to the rapid series of oppressive and discriminatory legislation from Rome that impinged on even the most minute life cycle freedoms of the Jews. In the east, beyond Rome and Byzantium, under Muslim rule, the Jews found, as they had found earlier in the Yehud, under Persian rule, a highly indulgent political climate. Here they could further their economic lives, teach their children Jewish law and practice, and freely intermingle with the ruling domain. The academies continued in Babylon until Babylon itself began its millennial decline, from c.1000 CE, and on into the modern era.

The entire force of Jewish life was now centered on a concentration of mind, body, and community of belief, in a study and practice of the Laws of Jewish life. From the 1st century CE, this had demanded increasing levels of education for all Jews, and from an early age. The Talmud, a veritable encyclopedia of interpretation and debate was the focus of a study, perhaps even a substitution for the mental gymnastics of the ancient Greek educational disciplines. Here, especially along the Euphrates River, these Jews poured their minds and hearts into a learning focused on their righteous relationship with their God, and the complexities of life to be lived in a disciplined and law-like manner, to fulfill this covenant of special merit and obligation.

They were thus alone in a world of power. The strength of their lives, their tenacity, was cemented by literate study, and personal and family discipline.

Bibliography, Chapter 5

Ackroyd, R. 1968. *Exile and Restoration*, Philadelphia: Westminster.

Ahlstrom, G. W. 1986. *Who Were the Israelites?* Winona Lake, Ind: Eisenbrauns.

Albright, W. F. Archaeology and Religion of Israel, Garden City, N.Y.: Doubleday.

Anderson, G. W. 1975. Understanding the Old Testament, Englewood Cliffs, N.J.: Prentice Hall.

Applebaum, S. 1979. *Jews and Greeks in Ancient Cyrene,* Leiden: Brill.

Avery-Peck, A. J., and Neusner, J. eds. 2002. *The Mishna in Contemporary Perspective,* Leiden: Brill.

Barclay, J. 1996. *The Jews in the Mediterranean Diaspora*, Edinburgh: Clark.

Bickerman, E. J. 1955. "The Historical Foundation of Post-Biblical Judaism," in Finkelstein, L., ed. *The Jews, Their History, Culture, Religion*, Vol. I., N.Y.: Harper and Bros.

Bickerman, E. J. 1962. *From Ezra to the Last of the Maccabees*, N.Y.: Schocken.

Birnbaum, E. 1996. *The Place of Judaism in Philo's Thought*, Atlanta: Scholars Press.

Coats, D. W. 1988. *Moses*, Sheffield, Eng: Sheffield Academy.

Collins, J. J. 1999. *Between Athens and Jerusalem*, Grand Rapids, Mich.: Eerdmans.

Collins, J. J., and Sterling, G. E., eds. 2001. *Hellenism in the Land of Israel*, Notre Dame, Ind.: Univ. of Notre Dame Press.

Coogan, M. D., ed. 1998. *Oxford History of the Biblical World*, N.Y.: Oxford Univ. Press.

Daiches, D. 1975. *Moses: The Man and His Vision*, N.Y.: Praeger.

Danby, H. 1933, tr., "Introduction," *The Mishnah*, c.200 CE, Oxford, Eng.: Oxford Univ. Press.

Dotham, T., and .Dotham, M. 1992. *People of the Sea*, N.Y. Macmillan.

Feldman, L. 1993. *Jew and Gentile in the Ancient World*, Princeton, N.J.: Princeton Univ. Press.

Finkelstein, I., and Silberman, N. 2001. *The Bible Unearthed*, N.Y.: The Free Press.

Finkelstein, L. 1938. *The Pharisees*, Philadelphia: Jewish Publication Society.

Finkelstein, L., ed., 1955. *The Jews: Their History, Culture, and Religion*, 2 vols., Garden City, N.Y: Doubleday.

Freud, S. 1939. *Moses and Monotheism*, N.Y.: Knopf.

Friedman, R. E. 1987/1997. *Who Wrote the Bible?*, San Francisco: Harper.

Friedman, R. E. 1999. *The Hidden Book in the Bible*, San Francisco: Harper.

Glatzer, N. N. 1937. *Geschichter der Talmudischen Zeit*, Berlin: Schocken Verlag.

Gottwald, N. K. 1979. *The Tribes of Yahweh*, Maryknoll, N.Y.: Orbis.

Gottwald, N. K. 1985. *The Hebrew Bible, A Socio-Literary Introduction*, Philadelphia: Fortress.

Grabbe, L. L. 1992. *Judaism from Cyrus to Hadrian*, Minneapolis: Fortress Press.

Grant, M. A. 1984. *History of Ancient Israel*, N. Y.: Scribner.

Gruen, E. 1998. *Heritage and Hellenism*, Berkeley: Univ. of California Press.

Hengel, M. 1974. *Judaism and Hellenism*, 2 vols., Philadelphia: Fortress Press.

Isserlin, B. S. J. 1998. *The Israelites*, London: Thames and Hudson.

Itzkoff, S. W. 2004. *A Nation of Philosophers*, Who Are the Jews? Vol. II Ashfield, Mass.: Paideia.

Itzkoff, S. W. 2004. *Soul of the Israelites* , Who Are the Jews? Vol. I, Ashfield, Mass: Paideia.

Johnson, P. 1987. *A History of the Jews*, N.Y.: Harper.

Johnson, S. R. 2004. *Historical Fiction and Hellenistic Jewish Identity*, Berkeley: Univ. of California.

Klausner, I. 1929. *Jesus of Nazareth*, N.Y.: Macmillan.

Levins, L. I. 2000. *The Ancient Synagogue: The First Thousand Years*, New Haven, CT.: Yale Univ. Press.

Maimonides, M. 1975. (1168 CE), *Commentary on the Mishnah*, F. Rosner, tr., N.Y.: Feldheim Publishers.

Malter, H. 1921. *Saadia Gaon*, Philadelphia: Jewish Publication Society.

Marrou, H. I. 1956. *A History of Education in Antiquity*, N.Y.: Sheed and Ward.

Mazar, A. 1990. *Archaeology of the Land of the Bible, 10,000-526 BCE*, N.Y.: Doubleday.

McCarter, P. K., Jr... *Ancient Inscriptions*, Washington, D.C.: Biblical Archaeological Society.

Meeks, W. A., ed. 1993. *The Harper-Collins Study Bible*, N.Y. Harper-Collins.

Mendelson, A. 1988. *Philo's Jewish Identity*, Atlanta: Scholars Press.

Neusner, J. 2001. *Readers Guide to the Talmud*, Leiden: Brill.

Porten, B. 1968. *Archives from Elephantine*, Berkeley: Univ. of California Press.

Raphael, C. 1985. *The Road from Babylon: The Story of Sephardic and Oriental Jews*, London: Weidenfeld and Nicolson.

Redford, D .B. 1992. *Egypt, Canaan, and Israel in Ancient Times*, Princeton, N.J.: Princeton Univ. Press.

Rivkin, E. 1978. *A Hidden Revolution*, Nashville: Abingdon.

Sanders, N. K. 1978. *The Sea Peoples 1250-1150*, London: Thames and Hudson.

Schiffman, L. H. 1985. *Who Was A Jew?*, Hoboken, N.J.: Ktav.

Seltzer, R. M., ed. 1989. *Judaism, A People and Its History*, N.Y:. Macmillan.

Shanks, H., ed. 1999. *Ancient Israel*, Washington, D.C.: Biblical Archaeological Society.

Smelik, K. A. D., ed. 1991 Writings From Ancient Israel: A Handbook of Documents, Edinburgh: University of Edinburgh Press.

Stager, L. 1995. "The Impact of the Sea Peoples, 1185-1050 BCE", in T. E. Levy, ed. *The Archaeology of Society in the Holy Land*, N.Y.: Facts on File.

Steinsaltz, A. 1989. *The Talmud*, N.Y.: Random House.

Sterling, G. E.2001. "Judaism between Jerusalem and Alexandria," in Collins, J. J., and Sterling, G. E., eds. *Hellenism in the Land of Israel*, Notre Dame, Ind.: Univ. of Notre Dame.

Tcherikover, V 1999. (1946). *Hellenistic Civilization and the Jews*, Peabody, Mass.: Hendrickson.

The Holy Bible, Authorized King James Version, London: Harper and Brother.

The Holy Scriptures, Masoretic Text, Philadelphia: Jewish Publication Society, 1965.

Weber, M. 1952, (1917-18). *Ancient Judaism*, N.Y.: The Free Press.

Weigall, A. 1923 *The Life and Times of Akhenaton*, N.Y.: Putnam.

Wellhausen, J. 1957 (1885). *Prolegomena to the History of Ancient Israel*, N.Y.: Meridian.

Young, J. D., ed. 1981. *Ugarit in Retrospective*, Winona Lake, Ind.: Eisenbrauns.

6

Maturation of Jewish Intelligence

Reprise

The intelligence that propagated civilization was created on the borders of the Pleistocene (Ice Age) glaciations, sometime after 200 KBP. There were other *taxa* of *Homo,* including *Homo sapiens,* and their genetics still exist, usually highly interbred with the now-dominant form of *Homo sapiens sapiens.* This new intelligence flowed beyond the mere practicalities of discerning the causal relationships between, for instance, weather, animal migrations, seasonality and the sun, upon which survival depended. This art of making a living was well in hand in terms of the hunting/collecting environment of these Ice Age *Homo sapiens sapiens.* Cro-Magnon flourished economically and demographically, the genes wandering far and wide into the northern and southern domains of other humans, borderline *sapiens.*

We recognize the Cro-Magnon's art as a highly cognitive effusion, issuing from a great brain abuzz beneath that huge eggshell-thin skull. So, too, were their tools the tribal/band social structure that made their life organization possible, refined and specialized. The Cro-Magnons were not primitives, merely naïve sojourners on a planet that they would long struggle to understand. They and we still pursue the causes and their effects, the need for a map of relationships that could work practically for the goals we envision. This human brain was ever active trying to decipher the puzzlements of human experience. It could never stop, not for the Sumerians, the Greeks, the Jews, and other peoples then and now who shared this originating brain power.

The Jews were no different from other ethnics during these early civilizational millennia. The intellectual elite, the judges, prophets, priests that created the Torah (c.900 BCE and after), shared the rich heritage of intellectual achievement of the then-ancient civilizational traditions, from Egypt in the south, to the northern valleys and beyond. It is no mere coincidence that Homer's poetry personified for the Greeks their Mycenaean heritage, just as the writers of the "J" and "E" tradition for the Pentateuch spoke to the role of Moses, the returnees from Egypt, as well as both the southern and northern Canaanite tribal traditions. The terms, 'Apiru and Shasu, appear in the Egyptian records for Canaan and the wilderness; so, too, do the Biblically named Canaanite tribes of the children of Jacob.[1]

Once the tribal memory had been translated into national consciousness, necessitating a written documentation of history, tradition, belief, the inevitable deteriorations associated with nationality, political and personal morality appeared. The Temple itself, enunciating political and economic privilege, functioned little differently for the Israelites than they did for other Near Eastern peoples. The small cadre of intellectuals, the prophets and scribes who kept the Mosaic faith, testify over and over again, that, except for a few kings, here Josiah, King of Judah, the corruptions were perennial, the masses themselves falling into the primitivism of idol worship, child sacrifice, all the ancient abominations of priestly tithing and feudal subjugation.

This state of popular consciousness was raised by the Hasmonean intervention to save Judea from Hellenic dilution of the faith, led by the aristocratic infatuations of the Sadducees. The puzzling seeming schizoid infatuation was paralleled by the scrupulous Sadducean Pentateuchal orthodoxy. However, it was the expanding scribal and pharisaic commitment to the Oral Law, the necessity to reinterpret the Torah in the light of then modernity that became the lever for a massive conversion to Judaism throughout the Hellenistic Diaspora, during the rule of both Macedon and Rome. The translation of the Torah plus many other prophetic and moral/historical documents into Greek by Hellenistic influenced Jewish thinkers helped to reveal this religion of "God-Fearers" to a world now disinclined to merit the ancient pagan pantheon as symbols of devotion and worship.

Thus a new class of leaders began to take a leading role in introducing this religion to the world. The Hasmonean kings/priests were little better than the Seleucid Antiochans in their seduction by Hellenism. Also, they were corrupt and brutal. Thus, the Pharisees ("to stay apart") began to compete with the Temple priesthood and their Sadducean employers for the loyalty of the minds of the ordinary Jew. The Temple had turned into an enormous magnet for the international wealth of Jewry. The Pharisees, by contrast, were locally ensconced as teachers, scribes, leading discussions in the *synagogue*, the *proseuche*, from Alexandria, Ephesus, Cyrene, even Rome.

Marginalization

Rome received a morale boost in the rule of the so-called Antonines: Nerva, Trajan, Hadrian Antoninus Pius, Marcus Aurelius, 98-181 CE. They were unusually uncorrupted. Trajan and Hadrian were especially competent military leaders. Trajan, though he fought their revolutionary movements throughout the Empire, even had a good word for the Jews in their perennial clash with the anti-Semitic majority of Alexandria. Hadrian, a committed Hellenophile was disgusted by Judaic practice, especially circumcision. He put down with especial viciousness the widespread revolts of the Jews that began at the end of Trajan's rule, *e.g.*, Bar Kokhba, 135 CE.

With the Judean homeland destroyed, the Jewish Diaspora began to assume a millennial climate of its own. Over a period of sixteen hundred years, c.150-1750 CE, the Jews largely separated themselves from the allure of Roman, Christian, Islamic modernism, perhaps in reaction to their near absorption by Hellenism. Indeed, they continued to give unto Rome, but ever more as a minority religion of the East. Christianity expanded by lowering the high bar for membership, the Jewish Sabbath, dietary rules, male circumcision, strict rules of worship, increasing studies of the Holy Writings. The Judaic reaction was ever more absorbed in the complex legal adjudications of the Tannaim and the later Talmudic Amoraim commentaries, leading to the completion of the Babylonian/Palestinian Talmuds, in Hebrew and Aramaic. In this way, they were increasingly cut off from the Roman masses of the Western Empire, and to an extent to the east.

Christianity also absorbed into its rituals and the Mass many of the emotional attractions of the mystery religions, the costumes, incense, clerical hierarchy. It opened its arms to all, made the Old Testament an ancillary preparation for the coming of the Christ, no longer cultivating the teachings given by God to Moses. The ties of history, tradition, even ethnicity that Judaism held out to the proselytes, became more and more barriers for membership and allegiance to successive generations of the devoted. Jewish weakness was revealed as the Jews physically fought Roman power, in a vain reach for independence and national self-determination.

Thus, Jewish populations contracted, many turning to Christianity. From the days of Ptolemy I, c.300 BCE, and before, the Jews had dispersed to the far corners of the world. There, the faithful, bound ever more closely to a sense of ethnic/historical solidarity, carried, as did their Babylonian exile precursors, the Holy Writings, in all their multifarious forms, in Greek, Aramaic, and Hebrew.

Wherever they did migrate, they now also needed to be competent in the indigenous language of the host people.

There were moments under Rome when the full force of the state against the Judaic institutions was lifted, no overt oppression, times of quiet. Increasingly, however, from the 4th and 5th centuries CE, Roman Christian emperors imposed increasingly harsh restrictions on the Jews, economic, involving land and slave ownership, banning inter-marriage into Judaism, always heavier confiscatory taxation for the privilege of living a Jewish life in an alien land. As the Church began to exercise dominating power over Rome and Byzantium, the ultimate sanctions were rarely imposed—convert, else move on or die. The Jews were recognized as distinct from heathens in general. They still shared a holy tradition of writing, belief, a heritage. Both Jesus and Paul arose from Jewish roots. The Popes often offered Vatican protection.

Instead of sharing in the rewards of power that derived from political, military dominance, the Jews had to find ways of surviving as an economic and social unit. They had to be always on the alert to new ways of earning a living, given the marginalization of their social roles. They also, at the price of death itself, had to preserve their community of learning and belief. The Talmud, as their core document of modernity, became central to their intellectual life. As their relationship with Hellenism, science, philosophy, intellectualism in general, withered under the first Christian and then Islamic waves of conquest, the Holy Books, now including the Talmud, after, c.500 CE, alone became the focus of Jewish learning, from the earliest minutes of a male's life.

Moments of Reprise

There were two periods of relative emancipation for the Diaspora Jews:

Babylon: The first period involved the Babylonian Jewish communities along the Euphrates River, southeast of the Abbasid capital of Baghdad. They were tolerated and flourished under the Persians, tolerated under the Macedonian/Roman hegemony, and began to flourish under Parthian and the Sassanian Persian rule, after Hadrian's withdrawal, c.118 CE. Co-existence with Islam was especially fruitful from the later 7th century. The status of the Jews withered after the decline of the entire area, from c.1000-1100 CE, because of concubinage, industrial slavery from Africa, polygyny, and then fundamentalism in belief and thought.[2] In the mid-11th century, c.1050, the Seljuk Turks came out of the Central Asian plains to occupy Baghdad.

Before this the Jews were reserved a special status, second to Muslims, but ahead of Christians. It was there that the Exilarch distributed the wealth of the enterprising Jewish community to the Caliph, he in turn providing the Jews with his personal protection. It was there that the Jewish academies created the Babylonian Talmud, and aspired to a high rabbinic intellectualism. From Fayum in

Egypt in the early 10th century, Saadia ben Joseph immigrated to study in the academies along the shores of the Euphrates. In 928 CE, he was appointed Gaon, or leader, educational and administrative, of the Yeshivah of Sura. He became the intellectual light of Jewish Babylon, unusually productive as a scholar, unusually polemical and controversial. He communicated in his writings the mental ferment that was then obtaining in the Islamic schools *mu'tazilah*, the boundaries of reason and faith. Although he was not a philosopher in the secular sense, his openness to reasoning, balanced by considered belief in the totality of holy writings, was a flash of light that was perceived westward across the Mediterranean.

Spain: Jewish colonies had existed in Spain from the days before Julius Caesar. The Jews had been expelled from Republican Rome as a "pernicious cult" in 139 BCE, after which many must have wandered west in search of more hospitable domiciles. Much later, the Athanasian Christian Visigothic kingdoms, c.586-711 CE, were extremely hostile to this growing colony, burdening them with extreme restrictions, economic and religious, including forced conversion or expulsion. When the Islamic Moors, Berbers, and Arabs invaded Iberia at the beginning of the 8th century, the Jews quickly allied themselves with the newcomers. The emancipated conditions of their brethren in the rest of the Muslim world quickly told on their allegiances. They flourished in Muslim Spain.[3]

Even as the Christians re-conquered the peninsula, taking Toledo in central Spain in 1086 CE, and then the rest of Spain (except for Granada) by the early 13th century, the Jews flowed north, surviving the fundamentalist Almohavid invasion from North Africa, mid-12th century. (Maimonides and family fled to North Africa and then to Egypt -1165 CE). These Christian rulers, feudal warriors, now welcomed the Jews, with their urban skills, into the towns of the north, Barcelona, Toledo, Gerona, Burgos, Tudela, Saragossa, Leon. For several centuries, the Jews carried on their mostly Moorish traditions in the north, but enjoyed both economic and religious privileges that continued their prosperity.[4]

Until the heavy hand of the friars started coming down on them, provoking the masses into a frenzy over Jewish privilege with the Catholic aristocracy, and thus Jewish prosperity amidst separation, Spain was branded deeply into the Jewish consciousness. It was a new Canaan, and they set down deep roots.

Before, the Spanish Muslims, mostly converts from the indigenous population of Visigothic Christianity, had enthusiastically taken to the international culture that both Arabs and Jews had communicated from the eastern Mediterranean. This beautiful land seemed to stimulate poetry, philosophy, even science, amid a flurry of economic development. The Jews moved into positions of power throughout the south, centering in Cordoba and Lucena. The latter, with an important Jewish academy, was thought to have a population whose majority was Jewish. But the Islamic political leadership was weak, fractured by its distance from the Arabian and Mesopotamian centers of power, often dependant on northern European mercenaries to fight against descending feudal orders.

The reaction began when the Christian Council of Zamora in 1313 CE imposed the badge on all Jews. Anti-Jewish codes were put into effect in Castile in 1348 CE, banning Jews from the workings of government, prohibiting conversion of Muslims to Judaism and Jews to Islam. There had been sporadic attacks on Jews since Toledo, 1280-81 CE. In general the attempt to separate the Jews from the Christian population, servants, employment of Jewish physicians, began after c.1300 CE. But covertly, when opportunity beckoned, Jews in high places converted to Christianity, becoming bishops, cardinals, and sometimes attaining high office in government.

George Sarton, historian of science, estimates that in the hey-day of Spanish science, 1150-1300, there was a total of 85 scientists worthy of international historical recognition for their achievements, 35 Jews; 30 Muslims; 20 Christians. Thus the Jews contributed 41 percent of this scholarly tradition. Salo Baron estimates that in 1300 CE, the Spanish population, including, Muslim Granada, was 5.5 million; Jews—150,000, or 2.5 percent of the population. (It is probable that there were more Jews in Spain at that time than Baron estimates, when converts to Islam and Christianity are included {authors note}.)[5]

Throughout the 14th century and into the 15th, as the Renaissance was opening up in Europe, including regressive Christian Spain, the important role of the Jews in Spanish life became a great issue for the Spanish masses led by the Dominicans, Jesuits, and Franciscan friars. Under great pressure, large numbers of Jews had converted; the Spanish called them *"marranos,"* *e.g.*, pigs. Jews never wrote their religious, poetical or philosophical works in Spanish, only Arabic or Hebrew. When Spain was Christianized, they reverted from writing in Arabic to Hebrew, later, in the 15th century, writing their colloquial works in Ladino, a version of Spanish Castilian, with Hebrew suffixes and vocabulary. The Hebrew Bible was translated into Ladino only after the expulsion from Spain, indicative further of the Jewish attachment to their lives and culture on the Iberian Peninsula.

Wanderings

The expulsion in 1492 by Ferdinand (partly Jewish heritage) and Isabella under the pressure of the Church, took place as Columbus, (Charles Singer hypothesizes that he was a Genoese Jew himself), witnessed and recognized their ships departing from Spain.[6] He was then leaving for the New World. Approximately 150-200,000 Jews left, for Portugal, North Africa, Ottoman Turkey (Istanbul-Constantinople) where large Jewish populations from the Near East and North Africa had already migrated. Thessaloniki in Greece would shortly become a largely Jewish city. (In 1913, its population still included 61,439 Jews,

45,867 Turks, 39,957 Greeks, 10,626 other.)[7] In the early 16th-century, Jews (many Spaniards) were expelled from Portugal, and migrated to the same areas as Spanish Jews. The Dutch voluntarily, after their independence from Spain, 1581, took in many of these wandering victims of the Inquisition, (Spinoza, 1632-1677). Also, all Muslims were expelled, c.1615, from Spain and Portugal.

In Rome, at the end of the 15th century, subsequent to the Spanish expulsion, members of the tiny Jewish ghetto, then being deluged with refugees, requested of Pope Alexander VI, that he limit the number of these immigrants, giving him a bequest of 1000 ducats. "The pope, however, refused to comply and demanded instead another 2000 ducats to permit the petitioners themselves to remain."[8]

Clearly the one hundred and fifty to two hundred thousand Jews who refused to surrender their religious beliefs were the tough ones. During a period of one hundred fifty years of intense discrimination against Jews, certainly two or three times this number capitulated and converted, or at least pretended to, until caught and forced to make the ultimate decision, truly commit to Christianity, abandon the faith of one's ancestors, leave or truly depart from this comfortable and beloved world. Iberia had been home for the Jews for over fifteen hundred years. Before the 15th century Inquisition, Spain and Portugal were the only parts of Europe where Jews were allowed to own land and ply agriculture. Much Jewish blood still remained on the Iberian Peninsula.

Patai and Wing claim that in Valladolid, Spain alone, at least 15 percent of the population on the basis of anthropometric analysis appears to be Jewish![9] Salo Baron, eminent modern scholar, lectured in Columbia University about the Inquisitional Court's certificates of Christian purity, the *limpieza*, wherein one could attest to having no Jewish (*converso*) blood in one's ancestry. One sixteenth Jewish ancestry was enough to be disqualified—a herald of things to come under the Nazi German rule.[10] The Bernals, Abraham Nunez, and Isaac de Almeida, scholars, poets, were burned at the stake in Spain in 1655. *Conversos*, they were discovered and accused; hundreds of others were thus uncovered and burned by the Inquisition in the 1640-1650s.[11]

The Sephardic Jews of Holland quickly prospered under Dutch openness to a new world of economic and social progress, most importantly their liberation from the Spanish Catholic yoke, hinting at future results for the Jews when Enlightenment tolerance would be extended elsewhere. It is not well known about Jewish fate in those Muslim nations that offered them haven from the Christian Inquisition.

However, in 1534, an Italian traveler, Benedetto Ramberti, wrote his impressions of Constantinople/Istanbul, which in 1453 had fallen to the Ottoman Turks: "There are in the city besides Turks, countless Jews, or Marrani expelled from Spain; these are they who have taught and who are teaching every useful art to the Turks; and the greater part of the shops and arts are kept and exercised by these Marrani. There is a place which is called *Bezestan*, where they sell and buy all sorts of cloth and Turkish wares, silks, stuffs, linens, silver, wrought gold, bows, slaves, and horses; and in short all the things that are to be found in Constantinople are brought there to market: this, except for Friday, is open every day."[12]

Lyber, the author of the book containing this quotation, who was a doctoral graduate of Harvard and then a Professor of History at Oberlin College, personally commented on Ramberti's description: "This statement and the following one are certainly exaggerations," meaning that an American Christian such as Professor Lyber, writing in 1913, could not believe that the Jews, most arriving shortly after 1492, could have become so quickly (1534) prominent in the economic life of Turkish/Islamic Constantinople![13]

Beyond Babylon, until c.1050 CE, and Spain, 700-1300 CE, the Jewish experience in Islam was spotty and subject to fits of peace and prosperity, other times terrible degradation. In his family's flight from Spain, c.1150 CE, Maimonides found refuge with the Kurdish Sultan of Egypt, Saladin, himself carrying on a bitter war with the Crusaders in Palestine. The remnant Jewish community was allowed to carry on in peace. But the culture of Islam, here, across North Africa, in Babylon, was in decline, corrupted by wealth and a religious culture of sexual weakness and indulgence.

Jewish populations regressed in their creative output, more and more resembling their Arab neighbors, weak in intellectual as well as economic power, only a few families rising above the sadness. This decline was now essential to the power positions of the Muslim overlords, now able, in an increasingly dynamic northern European world, to be able to retain that aristocracy of status that heralded their best days under Islam.[14] The state of Jewish persecution, degradation, is best illustrated by the cultural and social condition of the North African, Yemenite, Arab mid-East Jews that were flown into Israel from 1949 CE.

The North: The political stabilization initiated under the Carolingians based in Aix-la-Chapelle (Aachen) by Charlemagne and his sons, c.800 CE, required economic advancement. Here, the Jews, already in residence and flourishing in the north of the Roman Empire during the 4th and 5th century (Romanesque architecture in Trier along the Moselle River) were welcomed, including a colony of invited Jews from the Italian town of Lucca, to stimulate the development of this backward region. Naturally, there were soon a number of thriving communities with their accompanying academies.

The city of Mainz was the center of northern Judaism during the following several centuries. This peaceful coexistence with their Christian neighbors ended with the First Crusade, 1096 CE. These Jewish communities, including Speyer Trier, and Worms, along the Rhine, were attacked. The killings and destruction dispersed the Jews; some drifted west into France. Rashi was then teaching and developing his commentaries on the Old Testament and the Talmud for the guidance of these French communities, only recently being re-discovered. Others fled east into the German domains, the beginning of the tradition of Yiddish as the vernacular of European Jewry.

Earlier, about 1000 CE, during the good times, Rabbi Gershom of Mainz, head of the academy in that city, called together a conclave of rabbis from the relatively prosperous region, this before the slaughter of 1096, CE. The decision was to revoke the privilege of polygyny among the Jews, and to give women the equal right to initiate divorce, more in keeping with orthodox Roman/Christian traditions. The tactic of defensive life in a potentially hostile environment required prudential actions by the vulnerable minority to institute laws for the guidance of their own behavior which would not be a red flag of remembrance to Christians that the Jews were originally from the distant Oriental east.

The history of the *Ashkenazim* (the "German" Jews) in Europe (with the exception of the Jews of southern France and Italy, they coming under the protection of and supervision by the Papacy), from that time, is one of rare toleration, mostly intolerance, reflected in economic regulation, land-owning strictures, intermarriage bans, periodic deportations, physical attacks, *pogroms*. This violence often originated in the instigation of myths about Jewish religious practices, *e.g.*, using Christian children as sacrificial victims. Other anti-Semitic policies involved the beginning of ghettoization, in Venice, 15th century, the periodic driving of Jews ever eastward into Poland. And thus the Jews wandered, searching for a home where they could be useful as business people, craftsmen, traders, bankers (usury, a Church prohibition for Christians).

The court Jews thus developed in this atmosphere of constant persecution, their skills provided to the uneducated ruling elites. Thus did they flourish in Poland before that nation was conquered and then divided up in the late 18th century between Austria, Prussia, and Russia. Many Jews then fled east into the vale of settlement established by Catherine of Russia as a limited zone for Jewish immigration. These events occurred simultaneous with their Enlightenment release from subjugation in the West.

The one area of life that Christian authorities allowed for the Jews was self-education. The Talmud was the great purveyor of intellectual life to this people. True, at times, 1242 CE, after a debate between Jewish rabbis and scholastic philosophers, including Albertus Magnus, Louis IX, in Paris had all copies of the Talmud burned. Because the Talmud is often disputatious in its commentary on the Law of Holy Writ, as well as containing much legal interpretation, it can be considered an ongoing encyclopedia of Jewish thinking on important contemporary issues of moral and community life. The original writings of the Torah had their origins in the often mystifying contexts of Biblical life, 15th to 10th century BCE.

Thus Jewish education in the Yeshivahs of the Ashkenazim, while often rote Hebrew learning in the early stages, at the advanced secondary and higher educational stages of Talmudic analysis, became a great intellectual chess game in which disputation, argument, analysis, imaginative insinuation, all played important roles in deciding who were the intellectual "winners." These worthies gained great eminence but minimal social privilege within the Jewish community; marriage to the daughter of a middle-class merchant, else the daughter of an eminent scholar. This social hierarchy of competitive achievement could take place amongst the Jews, beyond the ken of the external power centers of the Christian world. It was a free enterprise race within the Jewish community with little tangible material gain.[15]

Ethnic Membrane

Marginalization is the first step in creating an ethnic identity. The two elements (marginalization and identity) can and do, however, work in tandem with each other. Certainly ethnic identity arises without the element of marginalization. The Sumerians, Egyptians, Greeks, in their originating environments lived together without external pressures that could have isolated them from a majority group. Their ethnicities grew from their unique environmental and historical experience as tribal and then national entities. They spoke self-created languages, worshipped gods that mirrored their own psychic equipment, even when borrowing religious elements from other peoples at a distance. Over time they developed an historical sense of being together, suffering together, sharing the rewards of triumphs, associating in the fields with their crops, else out on the battlefield against the stranger.

In the case of the Jews, marginalization was part of a later phase of their historical experience. It intensified their long standing historical consciousness, gave it a new chapter of reality. It sent them in new directions, and, as we have learned, forced them to invent a powerful internal discipline that became a shaping force, high human, civilizational intelligence.

The first seeming recognition of ethnic identity is reflected in the teachings and writings of Ezra and Nehemiah, as given in the Old Testament. They arrived in the Persian province of Yehud, c.450 BCE, some eighty to ninety years after the first returnees from captivity in Babylon, under Persian auspices. Ezra and Nehemiah discovered that these several thousand, c.5,000-10,000, descendants of the returnees, over this time period, had themselves lost the zeal that imbued the first group of priests and scribes who sought the rebuilding of the Temple. The task had itself lagged, the city of Jerusalem still open to the world, now needing new walls and reconstruction. The Jewish returnees and the indigenous people of the land, having now lived in Jerusalem and the Yehud a longer period than they had under restrictive Babylonian rule along the Euphrates and in the homeland, had fallen into degenerate ways, including marrying women of foreign religious ideals.

Of course, Samaria had earlier been repopulated by the Assyrians with non Israelites, and Ezra and Nehemiah had great suspicions about these so-called believers in the Book. The Samarians, rebuffed in their desire to help in the reconstruction of Jerusalem, carved off from the Persians their own provincial administration, eventually to become religious Samaritan dissidents. Essentially they still were Jews, for they worshipped the Pentateuch, even without the prophetic writings. Politically, they gradually grew apart from those who recognized the special role of Jerusalem in the fixing of Jewish identity.

On close inspection, the urging of Ezra and Nehemiah to give up these foreign wives, allowing the essentially polygamous Jews to keep their Jerusalemite wives, was an attempt to maintain the purity of worship of the Jews of the "land," in harmony with the now-evolving holy writings of the Babylonian Diaspora. Both elements were here in Jerusalem to be developed apace, now under the auspices of Ezra and Nehemiah and other prophetic thinkers. Without corrupt Israelite kings needing to make political deals with surrounding non-believers, this new ethnicity of belief could hew true to the original Mosaic teachings.

The monotheistic belief system of the Jews, especially that which had carried them forth during the Hellenistic Diaspora, after the Hasmonean revolt and purification, was persuasive with large non-Hellenistic populations who felt the Greek theophany to be foreign to their experience. Even Greeks and Romans as time went on saw in this "God-fearing" religion a more philosophical and morally pure system of belief, all quite attractive. And if they did not subscribe to the full panoply of orthodox practice—circumcision, ritual food and Sabbath disciplines—they still became associated with Judaism. One could no longer see the religion as an ethnicity of belief, rather an international religion, as Christianity was to become.

Toward the end of the 2nd century CE, a new stage of ethnic awareness began to be formed around Judaism. The Jews had lost their homeland, were being persecuted in all the foreign domains. Increasingly a new book of belief was needed to clarify their way forward. Now the writing was ever more in Hebrew, the secret and endogamous language of a people that would live together as they wandered the earth in search of peace. They maintained a special relationship with their transcendental God. They were comforted in the belief that a Messiah who would some day lead them into a world purer than the earth, and then eternal bliss.

They would now have to demonstrate their "chosenness," atone for the sins that had led to this new alienation, the wanderings that were mandated by the loss of their Temple, their city on Mount Zion. A new ethnicity was in the making. Bound together by Holy Writings, encased in language, ritual, and tradition, the membrane of community inbreeding of Jew with Jew, *marginalization*, was transforming this community of belief. A set of powerfully centripetal writings was being cemented into a moral system of social behaviors that set the Jews apart from all others in the world of man.

The memory of the times when the Jews were still engaged and competing with other sects, including the Christian schismatics, in proselytism, was still alive when Roman authority, under Christian guidance, 4th century CE, had closed the door to intermarriage. Except for special times of prosperity and privilege, for the Jewish elite, intermarriage became a rarity, and the role of the mother of the children began to be critical in defining Jewish descent. This Talmudic *halakhic* (law) ruling came about because, conversely, in times of great impression, forced concubinage, enslavement of Jewish women would sometimes result in the birth of a child. At the least, the child of a fully Jewish woman would be half Jewish.[16] This could not be surely known of the children of a Jewish male married to a non-Jewish woman. In general, as with all peoples during these times, most marriages took place within the extended family, also allowed between cousins.

The long tradition of Jewish international correspondence goes back to the Babylonian academies (Yeshivas) both during the Sassanian Persian control of the area, and then to the international sway of Islam. The so-called *"responsas,"* letters, petitions, even contributions to these varied centers of Jewish learning, were transmitted as petitions for guidance over difficult points of law and custom in Jewish religious or daily life. The evidence takes us back to the appeals of the Elephantine Jewish military community near Aswan in Upper Egypt, writing to both the authorities in Samaria and Jerusalem for directions as to the proper ritual methods for celebrating the high holidays as well as requests for monies to help rebuild their "Egyptian Priest destroyed" temples, c.410 BCE.

Clearly, the differing political, cultural contexts in which Judaism developed and diverged did not create a chasm between these Jewish communities, in Lucena (Spain), Mainz, Rome, Pumbeditha (Babylon), Fustat/Cairo (Maimonides). The Babylonian and Ashkenazi Jews were clearly two extensions of one branch. They threw themselves completely into the internal dialectics of Talmudic interpretation. In the case of the Babylonian and Galilee scholars, it was a rush to save Judaism from a foreign modernity, to resist the Roman Imperium, as well as the challenge of the Christians. Later the Ashkenazim were under a continuing if varied political and national press undertaken by a universal Christian oppression. The Rabbis dug deep into the inner resources of the Jewish mind, binding the small Jewish enclaves into a religio-legalistic Talmudic embrace, for survival.

To the south, the Iberian, south France and Italian Jews were seduced by the philosophy, poetry, science that had come down from the Greeks through the Islamic intellectual community. The Islamic world had been shaped by the small in number, if determined Arab desert fighters. But the contemporary 7th-century masses and educated were still longing for the ancient easy-going Mediterranean culture, free of Christian or Islamic Puritanism. The Muslims flourished intellectually and economically, the Jews early on joining in this momentary emancipation, 700-1100 CE. Here, first the Jews and then the Christian intellectual communities had joined in a pre-Renaissance indulgence pursuing the meanings of the secular mind.

The only serious conflict between Jew and Jew occurs at the very end of the medieval encasement, at Bordeaux in France, c.1760. Here a community of Portuguese Jews, 200 families, that had arrived and prospered from the 1550s, resented the immigration of Ashkenazi Jews, Germans and Avignonese, the latter once (12th-13th centuries) linked to Spanish cultural circles, now clearly reflecting new movements of Jews, these speaking Yiddish. The plea given by J. Pereira and I. de Pinto, on behalf of the Iberian Jews to have this community of Ashkenazim expelled, was successfully acted upon by Louis XV.[17]

The Hidden Defense

From the standpoint of an analysis of the bond of ethnicity as it evolves from a defensive tribal profile, people wandering together, protective of their integrity of identity and humanity, to a more aggressive, perhaps expansive profile as it finds a geographical home, ethnicity now shows an entirely different face. At one time in history, the ecological world of humans was empty. There was room for many languages, religious visions, cultural profiles. The lands filled up, wanderers abandoned a more ecstatic experience of life for the more prosaic—sit and work.

Creative, civilizational ethnicities, those which broke new soil in the vision of human life, often succumbed to the worst in human behavior. Think of the Sumerians of the first Royal Dynasty at Ur, c.2950 BCE. Evidence is that the Sumerians with their vaunted monomaniacal vision of efficiency surged far beyond the struggling discipline earlier (Uruk) required to perfect their economy, the first richly civilized style of life. Under the leadership of Uruk, they were in full civilizational posture and comfort, with soaring ziggurats, personal jewelry, the public arts, a world-extended system of trade and wealth building, serious schooling for the cultivation of a written heritage. Now needed were the educated literati for both the economical and legal side of civilization, as well as a world still immersed in mythology and poetry.

The Royals quickly created a class-structured system, in which wealth and autocracy pushed the old egalitarian and democratic Uruk heritage, c.4500-3000 BCE, firmly beyond memory. They were now responsible for that amazing series of sacrificial "Royal Tombs" in which dozens of certainly loyal royal attendants of the king seemingly voluntarily, drank poison to accompany the leadership beyond this world to the next. The wealth that had been so arduously achieved had quickly degenerated; man had succumbed to his worst instincts and fears.

The same general degradation occurred in Athens. Athens' first great achievements were focused on industrialization and democracy. Of all the Greek states, it was open to the intellectual. Following came its active leadership against Persia, after, the design and planning of the Acropolis, the theatre. Finally, the philosophy and science which Pericles invited to its shores.

Then, under the stress of the war with Sparta, 431-404 BCE, it was corrupted by its slaughter of the innocents on the island of Melos, 415 BCE. Melos, an island in the Aegean had originally been a colony of the Peloponnesians, most often allies of Sparta. In the war, because of the dominance of the Athenian navy, Melos declared its neutrality. Pericles, dying during the plague of 430 at the beginning of the war, was succeeded by an Athenian leadership intent on survival. It demanded the capitulation of the Melians. When refused, the Athenians invaded, killed all the males, and sent the women and children into slavery. Two years later, 413 BCE, when themselves defeated by Sicilian/Greek Syracuse, the captured Athenian warriors were tossed into the Syracusan stone quarries as slave labor; most died.

And, of course, ethnicity and nationality outgrow themselves as they expand into international political holding corporations, as did both Macedonian Hellenistic Greece and then Rome. So, too, with universalistic Islam, bursting from its Arabian desert womb into the public arena of a world of cruel wars, human subjugation and degradation. And on and on into the modern world.

With the Jews, after c.150 CE, it was different. Here, a new ethnicity was created out of a central religious vision. Nationality was surrendered, and with it the Jewish warrior fighting for his land. War and nationhood vanished for almost two millennia from the Jewish mental structure and thus from Jewish experience. This was now a "free floating ethnicity" balancing on a delicate edge of survival, as alien guests, else wandering in search of a momentary port of call. In exchange, they cultivated, protected and enhanced the essence of their ethnic integrity, the Jewish mind.

The Jews had to survive by searching for opportunity wherever it might lie. No army, but a new form of warfare, always defensive. The Jew had to fight in secret, first a covert socio-economic life, "don't challenge the powers that be"— *e.g.,* monogamy, Western chivalry toward the female. Ever alert to the need to move on if necessary. Second, they created an emphasis on cultivating mobile skills (usury) that would be useful everywhere in the Christian world. The Jews' mind was strong in its Biblical and Talmudic core, yet still capable of satisfying the needs of host powers everywhere: medicine, trade, banking/money, lending, crafts. If they would burn the holy books here, other Jews elsewhere would provide new copies. The Torah, the Bible, the Talmud, for the Jews, a mobile education.

Indeed, learn the language, the behaviors of the majority in the new home, appease the powers, serve them. To survive, be smart, wise, opportunistic, make them need you—in Spain, for the Muslims, become part of the warrior leadership, for the Christians, they need your medical, craft, agriculture, linguistic, international trading skills. In Germany, be the court Jew, in Poland, create politically autonomous Kahals, serving the feudal oppressors.

The wandering Jew never had to suffer slavery or feudal labor at the hands of Muslim, Jew, or Christian, as did the indigenous Christian or Islamic slaves and serfs. While they were excluded from the basic land-owning economics of employing agricultural back labor, they were allowed into money-lending or banking, disciplined trade, skilled crafts, always requiring brain power.[18]

Never would the most intellectual be proscribed from marriage or child rearing. Christian intellectuals, whose only recourse was entrance into the Church, thus often left no offspring. It is important to note that this did not preclude their brothers, sisters, cousins, who did not enter the Church, from having large families, thus preserving their lineage of accomplishment. Researchers estimate that, for example in Saxony, up until 1850, when national social welfare policies were instituted, the wealthier peasants had a survival rate of their children from marriage of twice that of the lowest social echelons of the peasantry.[19]

Jews were often allowed to run their own law courts, for internal adjudication, often, as in defensive cultures, extremely harsh on their own. Internally, an unknowing but extremely rigorous eugenic rule was covertly applied. Salo Baron paraphrases an ancient Rabbinical injunction: "To the future bridegroom: One should always sell everything one possesses in order to marry the daughter of a scholar; if one does not find a scholar's daughter, he should marry the daughter of the great men of the generation (the communal leaders); if he does not find a daughter of great men, he should marry the daughter of the archisynogogi (lay head of the synagogue); if he does not find the daughter of the archisynogogi, he should marry the daughter of charity supervisors; he should marry the daughter of elementary teachers; but he should never marry the daughter of the people of the land, (*am ha aretz*/illiterates)."[20]

In the case of the Diaspora Jew, often barred from owning land, the injunction against the people of the land refers only to the lowest caste of Diaspora

Jew at the periphery of competence and community orthodoxy. Terms used in Yiddish, *schlemiel, nebbish schmendrik schlemazl, chochem-etz* (literally "idiot-savant"), reflect self-deprecation, but also point to real individual distinctions. On the other hand, the injunction was to marry your daughter to the smartest, most able person, here, to the rabbi or Yeshivah/Talmudic scholar, even if he could only work part-time for a living. His wife, a *"balabusta"* (Russian for female home competence) would also run the business. In general the smartest had also to be fecund; no incompetent children wanted in the community. The greatest compliment one could make to an Ashkenazi parent about a child—he/she has *"eine yiddisher kaeppele,"* a Jewish brain.

In the *shul*, the teachers were often uncouth, brutal, at all grade levels in the cycle of learning, allowing little freedom. The consequent appearance of a more Dionysian form of Ashkenazi Judaism, represented by the Hassidic movement of the mid-18th century in Eastern Europe, a reminiscence of Kabbalistic mysticism of late medieval Spanish Jewry, represented an emotional release from the Talmudic rigor and inflexibility that had held the Jewish community together for so many centuries. Hassidism also came to influence at the time of the Enlightenment, an opening door for the Jews to reenter the world community.

The Permeable Membrane

The question is often asked, are the Jews a race? Most say no.[21] The Jews of the Mid-East and North Africa became increasingly vulnerable as these civilizations slipped into neo-slavery and non-competence under Islam. The increasingly bitter forms of fundamentalist Islam subjected the Jewish communities to continued degradation, loss of autonomy, and subject to the disease of late-medieval Islam, slavery, concubinage, polygyny. With this came unlimited autocracy. Jewish women were enjoined to keep the children born out of wedlock, rape, seduction, marriage and rejection by Muslim men and their communities. Rarely would an Islamic male join the Jewish community in marriage.

Because of the Jewish complicity in the enslavement of sub-Saharan blacks, and then their subsequent manumission, in keeping with the practice of the Muslim overlords, the Jewish communities approached the levels of interracial amalgamation that took place in Islam. The entire geographical extant of Islam took on the relative backwardness of sub-Saharan Africa, in consequence, subjugation not only by Turkish and Kurdish invaders, but eventually by European colonialists. In short, enough of the genetics from the Arab world entered the Jewish communities that the latter suffered the evolving modern malaise of Islam, itself saved only by the West's discovery of oil under the desert.

In the Sephardic world, the original invasion of Iberia in the early eighth century, was led by Berber recruits to Islam. The Berbers were then largely post-Cro-Magnon invaders of North Africa, having many of the physical characteristics of north Europe, hair, eyes, facial structure, complexion. The Arab invaders, too, were Semites descendants of the ancient post-glacial wanderers. The ongoing degradation of industrial slavery had not yet undermined their culture and competence.

By the time the Almohad fundamentalists reinvaded Spain from Morocco, mid-12 century, most of Spain was under northern Christian control. Many Jews who could not flee north into the Christian provinces, or like Maimonides' family, leave Spain altogether, surrendered their religion; many were slaughtered. By this time, the levels of Jewish genetic integration with the Iberian Muslim rulers had been completed.

Thus, much Jewish genetics could have remained in southernmost Spain under this fundamentalist Islamic regime. But soon the Muslims were ousted by the Christian north, except for the enclave around Granada. The Jewish renaissance in Spain under Islamic rule had by then shown its full force of intellectual and creative power. It now shifted to the Christian provinces. Here there was less opportunity for cultural assimilation.

In the early stages of life in Christian Iberia, the Jews wrote their internal religious and other literature in Arabic. Later, as this became dangerous, they switched to Hebrew. They were also well versed in Spanish, the language of the ruling classes. This vernacular became the *lingua franca* of Jews all across the Mediterranean. And surely there was here, too, a continual if covert sharing of genes with the dominant community.

Evidence is that more Jewish genes entered the Christian community of Iberia, by conversion, than Christian genes entered the Jewish community, surreptitiously. At any rate, the demands of a Jewish community, long an elite force within Muslim Iberia, for the retention of their sense of *"hidalgo,"* a minority aristocracy of the intelligent, successful, and chosen, required that all members of the Spanish/Portuguese Jewish communities live up to a standard, higher in material things and social graces than the Ashkenazim to the north. The Ashkenazim, as noted above, were no less rigorous in their internal selectivity of membership. In contrast, the Iberian Jews had a heritage of material wealth and aristocratic pretense dating back to the 8th century, including their early usefulness to the Christian conquerors.

Among the Ashkenazim, it has long been noted, since we have seen large numbers of north European Jews become available for anthropometric research, the Jews are extremely variable. Part of this variability of appearance is due, of course, to the propinquity of location and relationship with their neighbors, French, Germans, Poles, or Rumanians. As Patai and Wing have outlined in detail, only a small number of non-Jewish genes need have entered the Jewish gene-pool each generation to have had, over time, an enormous impact on the physical attributes of the Ashkenazim.[22] It is also quite likely that the scattered indigenous movement, over time, of the Jews from the southeast to the north-west, brought with these small-scale migrations a variety of genetic heritages. In ancient times, the peoples of Canaan, Syria, even Egypt retained many of the traits associated with contemporary northern peoples, blond/red hair, blue eyes, for example.

Thus it is quite possible that this diversity of characteristics, c.150 CE, of the Jews of the Middle East and North Africa, as well as southern Europe, was maintained as the Jews entered northern Europe in small numbers. Most Ashkenazim would argue that they can recognize a Jewish face and Jewish mannerisms. Whether or not these reminders of a heritage are merely part of their East European heritage, including the resident non-Jews, and their own characteristics, is an open question.

What clearly holds from subsequent events is that the Jewish communities of Iberia and Europe were allowed to retain their inner eugenic discipline. Clearly, the constant pogroms and slaughter of Jewish communities, while momentarily horrific in their impact on Jewish life and consciousness, did not effectively impede the general evolution of Jewish communal competence, until the *Holocaust.* For example, the horrific, internationally condemned pogrom in Kishinev, Western Ukraine, now Moldova, in the first decade of the 20th century, saw the populace's killing of about fifty Jews

One could argue that Christian Europe while engaging in its never-ending wars, caused generations of its finest young men to be slaughtered. Then, its second sons were sent to the monastery. One can thus hypothesize that with all the weight of prejudice and violence directed at the Jews, the Christians suffered much greater intellectual debilitation.

Yet, the level of creativity that emerged from these Christian communities from the 13th century onward into the modern era is barely second to the genius shown by the Greeks in the Hellenic and Hellenistic eras. The Greek genius may have been gradually undercut by bloody internecine wars, starting with the Peloponnesian conflict of 431-404 BCE. European medieval Christianity, too, suffered its own feudal wars of *hybris*. Then consider the brutal battles among the Renaissance cities. Add the horrific wars of religion in the 16th century and beyond. Consider further, the revolutionary slaughters in France, the Napoleonic wars, and on into the 19th century, now including North America. Finally, the most horrible century in the history of humankind, the 20th.

Would it be impolite, as we enter a debilitated 21st century, to posit a near suicide of a civilization?

Endnotes, Chapter 6

[1] See Itzkoff, S. W. 2005. *Who Are the Jews*, Part 1, "Soul of the Israelites," Ashfield, MA: Paideia.

[2] Goitein, S. D. 1955. *Jews and Arabs*, N.Y.: Schocken, pp. 50*ff*, 184*ff*, 212*ff*.

[3] Chouraqui, A. N. 1968. *Between East and West,* Philadelphia: Jewish Publication Society, p. 86*ff*.

[4] Baer, Y. 1961. *A History of the Jews in Christian Spain*, Vol. 1, Ch. V, Philadelphia: The Jewish Publication Society, p. 186*ff*.

[5] Patai, R. 1977. *The Jewish* Mind, N.Y.: Scribner, p. 125.

[6] Singer, C. 1955. "Science and Judaism," in *The Jews*, ed. by L. Finkelstein, N.Y.: Harper and Bros., pp. 1063-1054.

[7] *Enciclopedia Italiana*, 1949.

[8] Abrahams, I. 1932. *Jewish Life in thee Middle Ages*, 2nd ed., London: Edward Goldstone, pp. 433-434; Patai, R., *The Jewish Mind, op. cit.*, p. 153.

[9] Patai, R., and Wing, J. 1989. *The Myth of the Jewish Race*, Detroit: Wayne State.

[10] Hilberg, R. 1996. *The Politics of Memory,* Chicago: Ivan Dee, p. 60.

[11] .Patai, R., *op. cit.*, p. 230.

[12] Lyber, A. H. 1913. *The Government of the Ottoman Empire in the Time of Suleiman the Magnificent*, Cambridge: Harvard Univ. Press, p. 241.

[13] Lyber, *op cit.*

[14] Goitein, S. D. 1970 *A Mediterranean Society, Vol. 2 The Community*, Berkeley: Univ. of California Press; Goitein, S. D. 1988 *A Mediterranean Society, Vol.5, The Individual*, Berkeley: Univ. of California Press.

[15] Abrahams, I. 1934. *Jewish Life in the Middle Ages*, 2nd ed., Chs. XIX, XX, London: Edward Goldstone.

[16] B. Yeb. 23a, 45a; Maimonides, *Yad haHazaqua*, Issure Bi'a 15.3; *Shulhan 'Arukh, Even ha Ezer*, 4:19, p. 117; Patai, R. and Wing, J. P. 1975 *The Myth of the Jewish Race, op. cit.*

[17] Patai, *The Jewish Mind, op. cit.*, pp. 227-228.

[18] Bottecini, M., and Eckstein, Z. 2005. "Jewish Occupational Selection: Education, Restrictions, or Minorities," *Journal of Economic History*. December; Bottecini, M., and Eckstein, Z. 2006. "From Farmers to Merchants: A Human Capital Interpretation of Jewish History," forthcoming.

[19] Weiss, V., and Munchow, K. 1998. *Ostfamilienbücher mit Standort,* Leipzig. Neustadt/Aisch: Degener.

[20] Baron, S. 1942. *The Jewish Community*, Vol. 1, Jewish Publications Society of America, p. 124.

[21] Herskovits, M. J. 1955. "Who Are the Jews? In L. Finkelstein, ed. *The Jews*, N.Y.: Harper and Bros., pp. 1151-1171; Patai, R., and Wing, J. 1989. *The Myth of the Jewish Race, op. cit.*

[22] Patai, R. and Wing, J. 1989. *The Myth of the Jewish Race, op. cit.*

7

Enlightenment, Emancipation, Assimilation

Talmudism Reconsidered

Modernity is a slippery concept. It connotes a superiority of this life over the past; it implies a learning curve upward in dealing with human experience that had not been before attained. We view the Renaissance, then followed by the Enlightenment, as periods of modernistic advance over the so-called Dark Ages. This followed the collapse of the Western Roman Empire, and the medieval period dominated by the Catholic Church and the feudal political structure of Christianized Europe.

It is clear that we look upon the entrance into the mainstream of European and world history, during the Enlightenment, after 1750, of the Jews, as a progressive, a modernistic step forward. This is because we see their encapsulation during the Dark Ages and the medieval as a retrogressive imprisonment, a time when the destiny of this people was dependent upon the momentary good will of the ruling authority, the local nobility, often a local bishop, though rarely even of the Papacy itself.

"During the Middle Ages the Jewish communities no longer contemplated battle. The medieval Hebrew poets did not celebrate the martial arts. The Jews of Europe were placing themselves under the protection of constituted authority. The reliance was legal, physical, and psychological."[1]

The implication is one of surrender and apathetic reception of the good or evil that was imposed upon this people by the powers-that-be. The further implication is that the Jews struggled mightily to survive economically, finding every empty niche, banking, loan-sharking, peddling, that remained open to them, if only to nourish their families, and thus survive. The Talmudic education here evolved from the post-exilic Babylonian Diaspora, c.200-500 CE, and its further evolution at the hands of Ashkenazi scholars such as Rashi, c.1100 CE, who furthered this development of Jewish Law, *Halakha*. Here it emphasized the endogamatic preservation of Jewish ritual, ceremony, family life.

The development of the European Talmudic academies, the *Yeshivoth*, served the function of creating the wisest teachers, rabbis, who might both internally adjudicate and lead the Jewish communities scattered over the face of Christian Europe in their attempts to survive as practicing Jews. Here a different form of knowledge accumulation occurred than was traditional in the classical Hellenic and Hellenistic worlds, perhaps even different in its emphases from that of the great Spanish Jewish scholar, Maimonides. When living in Egypt under Muslim rule, Maimonides attempted to extend the vision of the ancient Asiatic Talmudists into an accommodation with the growing awareness of the larger world of Greek knowledge as it was being rediscovered in this late-medieval era, the Mediterranean world of c.1200 CE.

The later reaction against Ashkenazic Talmudism was that it had become casuistic, scholastic, preoccupied with the splitting of hairs about the meaning of the Holy Writings as applied to life within the Jewish community. Talmudic disputation became a type of chess game where one could argue about the most subtle and ingenious meanings from the ancient texts, and the earlier Talmudic sages that none before might have intuited. This was a game of finding subtle meanings within the textual traditions of the past, rarely relevant to the world external to Jewish existence. Thus, the later Jewish disdain for a self absorbed world, even in raw survival. The Ahkenazim were maintaining this experiential autonomy of knowledge making, even while the Renaissance was opening up to the outside gentile world, a revolutionary vision of life and experience.

"The Polish Jewish schoolmasters…with rod and angry gesture, instructed Jewish boys in tender youth to discover the most absurd perversities in the Holy Book, translated into their hateful jargon, and so confusing the text with their own translation that it seemed as if Moses had spoken in the barbarous dialect of Polish Jews.…the neglect of all secular knowledge, which increased with every century, had reached such a pitch that every measured oddity, even blasphemy, was subtly read into the verses of Scripture."[2]

From a perspective of an additional century, however, one can better appreciate the role of Talmudic study, a universal preoccupation and discipline for all Jews in the period before the *Haskala*, the Enlightenment emancipation. It created, in the first place, an elite that was independent from, perhaps even higher in status than the role of those few ambitious and chance taking Jews, who took on the Christian world in the open economic areas of life. As noted in the previous chapter, the highest levels of Jewish attainment involved the subtle hair-splitting, chess-game dialectics of the Yeshiva scholar. And to him the brightest young wives from the wealthier families were offered. And there were many children who were born to these "house" intellectuals, they, completely irrelevant to the outside world.

But more. This world lived through these Talmudic "games," the stuff of their moral and social existence. These created meanings allowed for a dynamic that was internally rich in social movement and advancement, even without the tangible wealth to show for it.

In short, materialistically deprived, it was a culture steeped in symbolic and fluid attainments, even if the knowledge, the grist of these attainments, had nothing to do with the dynamics of material events in the external world of feudal, national, religious wars, the power plays of secular and Christian life. As long as the knowledge structure of Christian thought was not in advance of the Talmudists, as their several famous debates in Spain, Paris, and Rome, seemed to have shown, this Talmudic world remained happily inured to the events of the outside.

One could compare the Talmudic socio-cultural world with that of the Catholic Church. Here monks, priests, Bishops, Cardinals, and the Pope played a hierarchical game of positional status, hardly related to the material dynamics of economy, trade, craft, even agriculture. Yet the power shifts, the political, military, and social impact of the dynamics of Church hierarchy and power were enormous. Today the same status games, mostly impotent, are played within the secular Academy.

Within the bounds of Talmudic Judaism, the power, leadership, hierarchical positioning of religious knowledge, became the fuel of this society, marching in place, going nowhere materially or politically, no less militarily, rather, just impacting on the internal redactions issuing out of the ever growing commentaries, disputations, analyses that made up an infinitely expanding literary and intellectual heritage, the Talmud.

But this situation gradually ended, as the Renaissance in Italy and then elsewhere in Europe opened up wholly new dimensions of knowledge applications with which neither Christian nor Jewish scholasticism could compete. Clearly, the situation in Spain, in which the Jews had, until shortly before the expulsion, attained remarkable influence throughout the tenure of the Muslim and Christian rulers, had traditionally signified a path for ethnic survival. Here they were always on the leading edge of modernity, of trade, craft, finance, literature, science. Eventually, Christian Spain began to come into its own as the

Moors were expelled from the peninsula. The modernity toward which the Jews aspired, withal their religious scholarly, educationally centripetal domains, burned on the various Catholic orders that feared the fires of Renaissance innovation and secular motivations. These wealthy, literate, influential Spanish Jews, and the hidden *conversos*, could destabilize their influence and power

It is not coincidental, that the opportunistic ruling cliques of Spain sent Columbus on his way west, 1492 CE, at the same time that the Jews were being sent on their way North, East, and South. The world even then was bubbling with the new technological and intellectual innovations of the Renaissance. Economies were percolating, trade expanding, a world opening up even as the Portuguese explorers, many armed with the maps created by Jewish scholars, e.g., Abraham Zacuto and Joseph Vecinho, were guiding them around Africa to the spices, textiles, the richness of the unexplored East. It is no coincidence that the Hanseatic German, Nicholas Copernicus, 1473-1543, and the heretical German theologian, Martin Luther, 1483-1546, were contemporaries, movers in the astronomical/scientific and religio/political sense. The world was on the move toward a new cultural and historical ethos.

Entrance to Modernization

As we have noted in Chapter 6, the expelling of the Jews from Spain and Portugal, this pushed hard during the *Inquisition* by the various orders of Friars, was precipitated by the power that both the orthodox Jews as well as the *conversos* in Spain had attained over the several centuries before 1492. So too in the next decades in Portugal, before those indigenous and refugee Sephardic populations were expelled from that country.

We have also noted in the previous chapter the success quickly attained by the Sephardic Jews who fled to the Ottoman lands. Everywhere these Jews landed they were in the forefront of modernization. When Gutenberg invented the movable type printing press, c.1450, the Jews of the continent were quick to use this technology for their own purposes, both commercial and communitarian. Patai reports that "…in Cremona, (Italy), the Inquisition destroyed at one time 12,000 books which were in possession of the eighty Jewish families in the city. This astounding figure indicates the extent of Renaissance Jewish bibliophilism, for some Jews it became a veritable passion."[3] Hundreds of Jewish scribes made their living in Italy. At end of fifteenth century many Jewish printing presses were in operation, even translating into Yiddish.

The sense of movement in the European world was felt in the Ashkenazi north as well. Amidst the economic poverty there were a number of Jews who survived better than most on their commercial and banking efforts, areas which the Christian feudal system had done little to develop. "In The Middle Ages the Jews carried out vital economic functions. Precisely in the usury so much complained of by Luther and his contemporaries, there was an important catalyst for the development of a more complex economic system. In modern times, too, Jews have pioneered in trade, in the professions, and in the arts. Among some Jews the conviction grew that Jewry was 'indispensable.'[4] The theory grew amongst the Jews, even in an environment of expanding hatred: "One does not kill the cow one wants to milk."[5]

Thus we have in the sixteenth century Reformation awakening in the German north, a Luther expatiating on the Jews, perhaps expressing subliminally his own precarious political position: "…they hold us Christians captive in our country. They let us work in the sweat of our noses, to earn money and property for them, while they sit behind the oven, lazy, let off gas, bake pears, eat, drink, live softly and well from our wealth. They have captured us and our goods through their accursed usury; mock us and spit on us, because we work and permit them to be lazy squires who own us and our realm; they are therefore our lords, we their servants with our wealth, sweat, and work:…Moses could improve Pharaoh neither with plagues nor with miracles, neither with threats nor with prayers; he had to let him drown in the sea.."[6]

As we pass through the 15th century, the beginnings of Jewish self-doubt appear, in part precipitated by the impact on Jewish life by the Inquisition, in part by the increasing dynamic of modernity, inventions thrown off by Italian Renaissance mercantilism and enterprise—the compass, astrolabe, telescope, the printing press, also the advances in architecture and engineering—*viz.*, the cathedrals in Florence, the Vatican. Add to these gunpowder and the cannon, now the rifle, all in the fifteenth century, and, of course, the increasing pace of exploration and discovery, ultimately the expansion of the world's self-envisionment.

In Italy a series of rabbis and other Jewish writers began to look seriously at the world of Jewry and the Talmudic and other Jewish traditions:[7] Azariah de Rossi, c.1511-1578, Mantua, wrote *Light of the Eyes*, a critical analysis of Judaic religious tradition. This work was vigorously attacked by rabbis in that century. Later, in the 18th century, this work was held up as a forerunner by Enlightenment Ashkenazim. Leon de Modena, c.1571-1648, co-Rabbi of the Venice ghetto, wrote *The Fool's Voice*, which attacked Jewish traditionalism, argued for the reform of Judaism's legal structure, *Halakha*, dietary laws, ritual in synagogue, Sabbath observances.

Perhaps the most influential Jewish/Italian writer of this period was Simeone Luzzatto c.1583-1663, co-Rabbi with Leon of Modena of the Venice ghetto. His *Discourse on the Status of the Jews*, in Italian, was an apologetic for the usefulness of the Jews to modern states. Later, these arguments would be used by John Tolland, 1714, in England, arguing for the naturalization of the Jews.

Luzzatto distinguished between different groups of Jews, the Talmudic scholars, followers of the Kabbala, Karaites, also different nationalities of the

Jews from Venice, Constantinople, Poland, Damascus, Germany, etc, yet a common character. Luzzatto: The Jews were: "…a nation of timid and unmanly disposition, at present incapable of political government, occupied only with separate interests, and caring little about public welfare. The economy of the Jews borders on avarice, they are admirers of antiquity, and have no eye for the present course of things. Many are uneducated, have no taste for learning or the knowledge of languages, and in following the laws of their religion, they exaggerate to the most painful degree. But they have also noteworthy peculiarities— firmness and endurance in their religion, uniformity of doctrinal teaching in the long course of more than fifteen centuries since their dispersion; wonderful steadfastness which leads them, if not to go into dangers, yet to endure the most severest suffering. They possess knowledge of the Holy Scripture and its exposition, gentleness and hospitality to the members of their race—the Persian Jew in some degree suffers the wrong of the Italian—strict abstinence from carnal offenses, extraordinary carefulness to keep the family unspotted, and skill in managing difficult matters. They are submissive and yielding to every one, only not to their brethren in religion. The failings of the Jew have rather the character of cowardice and meanness than of cruelty and atrocity."[8]

The third writer of note, also of Venice, Isaac Cardozo: 1604-1681, wrote *Distinctions and Calumnies of the Jews*, in Spanish. Born of *converso* parents in Portugal, he escaped to die in Venice. In this work he also tried to explain and rationalize the various accusations brought against the Jews. Clearly, for Sephardic intellectuals, so long willing to take the risks of life in Spain or Portugal, as Jews, in exchange for the heritage of a benign life style, as well as their fixed historical claim to life in Spain, the results of expulsion weighed heavily on their sense, as Jews.

Life for these Jews in Holland was different. The Northern provinces of the former Spanish principate, had thrown off Catholicism for a Protestant commitment. Being burghers and business people, clearly given in their mental allegiances, to the new knowledge, the exploration of the world and its economic possibilities was a lure. The arrival of a few thousand alien Jews, hardly decades after a declining Spain had been forced out of Holland, was a beneficent event for both the Dutch and the Sephardim.

By 1670, the height of Jewish Sephardic influence, there were in Amsterdam, c.4,000 Jewish families, by then mostly poor Ashkenazim The Sephardic Belmonte family, Jacob and Israel, 1570-1629, Moses, 1619-1647, Isaac Nunez, d. 1705, all poets, historians, ambassadors, printers, illuminated the community. Portugese/Dutch Sephardic Jews, writers of poetry such as Reuel Jesurum, 1575-1634, David Jesurum, died c.1650, also were glorified by this community.

Menasseh ben Israel, 1604-1657, Rabbi, printer, poet, Kabbalist, was sent to England from Holland to successfully advocate the admission of Jews to

Cromwell's England As part of the mission his *Vindiciae Judaeorum;* was published in London, 1656. Daniel Levi de Barrios 1625-1701, a *converso* escapee to Amsterdam wrote in Spanish: *The Triumph of Popular Government*, an extolling of the rich cultural contributions of Sephardic scholars, poets, and Jewish Sephardic institutions in Holland, this, the product of a free society.

A modern Jewish scholar phrases the role of Jewish intellectuality and culture in the first great free society in Europe. "The Dutch Sephardic interlude of the seventeenth century can be taken as a prime example of the cultural-historical law which can be formulated as follows. Whenever the Jews enjoyed even a modest measure of liberty in the midst of a gentile society whose culture they found attractive, they experienced a cultural upswing both in Jewish learning and in many of those fields in which their neighbors excelled. This law operated in all the great Jewish-Gentile historic encounters...and it again proved valid in seventeenth century Holland."[9]

Such a situation had been true of the hostile Hellenistic with its attractive Hellenic philosophy, the acquiescent, intellectually interesting, but not culturally or religiously attractive Muslim/Mesopotamian Islamic world, stimulus for the expansion of Talmudic education. On the other hand, for the Jews of Spain and Portugal, there was a magnet in the medieval Spanish Arab/Christian exploration of ancient Greek philosophy, poetry, and science, and its stimulus for mystical Kabbalistic studies. By contrast, the non-existent Christian culture in the northern Ashkenazim domains, parallel with the encapsulation and dependency of its Jews, only allowed for the continued self development of Talmudic *Halakha*.

The great stain on the Jewish community of Holland during this period was, of course, Baruch Spinoza, 1632-1677. He was excommunicated from the Jewish community, its synagogue, (so too the tragic Jewish dissenter Uriel da Costa who killed himself in 1640), when he was twenty three, before any of his writings had been published. They feared his heretical thinking, not wanting to endanger their position with Dutch religious leaders. Spinoza was able to read the rich literature available in Holland at this time, which the Dutch churches did nothing to censor. Spinoza was therefore influenced by René Descartes, Giordano Bruno, Thomas Hobbes, also Sephardic Jewish philosophers Maimonides, Gersonides, Hasdai Crescas. Little did the Jewish/Sephardic leadership realize how quickly the breezes of intellectual liberty would make themselves felt in this newly dynamic world of Europe north.[10]

Ashkenazim

The 1474 alliance of the Polish nobility with Lithuania was significant for this domain of Jewry. The Polish nobility needed the expertise of Jewish traders, craftsmen, those with financial skills. The so-called *Kahals*, Jewish self-governing communities living within the Polish and Lithuanian towns became under the protection of the nobility, who needed these skills, amongst a population that was completely illiterate and under the forceful feudal thumb of this nobility. Poland now stretched deep into the Ukraine, and the Yiddish speaking populations, in the following centuries trickled east ever in search of security and opportunity. As time went on the Jews themselves divided into two dialectical groups of Yiddish speakers, the so-called *Litvaks* (Latvians/Lithuanians) of the north, and the *Galizianer* (Galicians) of the south, the latter coming ever more under Hapsburg, Austro-Germanic control.

The Germans proper, ever ambivalent about these Jewish populations within their midst evicted, then invited, then evicted once more, this wandering, alien race. The spewing hatred of Luther, quoted above, in the mid-16th century gives evidence of the tenuous condition of the *Ashkenazim*. Throughout this period the condition of the Jews in the eastern Germanic and western Slavic domains were more stable.

The famous Jewish cemetery in Prague gives evidence of the long existing and moderately affluent Jewish community in this city, periodically undergoing religious contention, the Protestant revolutionary vying for control against Catholic orthodoxy. In eastern Germanic cities such as Leipzig, Dresden, Dessau, even seemingly far removed Eisenstadt, today in Austria, there is evidence of large medieval in origin, Jewish populations. The latter city, home to an 18th-century Hungarian vassal of the Hapsburgs, the Esterhazy, was home to the Austrian/Hungarian composer Haydn. It, too, passed back and forth from Hungarian to Germanic control.

In 966, "Jews and other legitimate merchants" were mentioned in the earliest Vienna archives. By 1300, an early observer stated that more Jews resided in Vienna than in any other German city. In 1421 the Viennese destroyed the Jewish community, demanding, "Baptize or die." Most ran. By the mid-1600s, five hundred Jewish families were living in the Leopoldstadt section of Vienna. Many had S*chutzbriefe*," *i.e.,* they were protected Jews. In 1664, the Jews were again expelled from Vienna. They were back in 1693, with a noted businessman/financier, Samuel Oppenheimer, their leader, he deemed essential for the running of the Habsburg enterprise.[11]

The year 1648 was a pivotal one in European history. The Treaty of Westphalia, finally brought peace to Central Europe, by dividing Europe into religious zones of dominance, Catholicism and Protestantism. At the same time, surging Russian nationalism brought on the Cossack Revolts which marked the beginning of the end of Polish ascendancy in Eastern Europe, and of course once more, the onset of vicious pogroms against the Jews. A little over thirty years later, a Christian army led by Polish nobility, 1683, turned the Ottomans back from the gates of Vienna. All three events had their implications for the Ashkenazim.

Peace and economic stability brought a measure of prosperity to the German states in the Protestant north and to the Habsburg domains in the south. David Sorkin develops the evolving relationship of the Jews in the German states as a parallel process of modernization, first the indigenous Protestant elites of the north, then the more advanced mercantile and craft elements in the indigenous German/Jewish populations. The explosion of new knowledge from the end of the 15th century to the mid-17th century had led throughout Europe, but especially in Protestant Germany, to the founding of new universities: Halle, founded 1694; Gőttingen, 1736; the Berlin Academy, 1700; also the Bavarian Academy, 1759.

Jews were allowed to resettle in Berlin, 1671; in Anhalt-Dessau, 1672; in Kurhessen, 1653. They were previously allowed in Frankfurt-am-Main, all of Hesse, and in southeastern Germany (Dresden, Leipzig, Kassel, Brunswick, Halle) after they had had been expelled from the rest of Germany in the 1570s. In Brandenburg, after the Protestant/Catholic Peace of Westphalia, 1648, gradual tolerance for the Jews was introduced. In 1664, for example, fifty families recently expelled from Vienna were allowed to resettle there. These were merchant families, typical of events in all the German principalities, Court Jews, *Schutzjuden*. Because of their necessary service to the state they were given the same rights as Christian merchants, in Prussia, 1761. Full political participation of the Jews in Prussia began to be put into effect in the 1790s. By the first half of the 18th century Jews in future Imperial Germany, not Austria, numbered 60-70K, half at the level of petty trade, begging, "thievery." These *Bettlejuden/Trodeljuden*, were expelled from Prussia in 1750.[12]

The above population figures for Jews in Germany represented the impact of a flood of Jews from the east into modernizing Germany, especially Prussia in first half of 18th century. Chief Rabbis in Frankfurt, Hamburg, were all Polish. Many had *Schutzbriefe*, letters of protection from local princes. Their conservatism within the Rabbinate was maintained throughout the century, in Germany. Moses Mendelssohn, originally from Dessau in the east of Germany, led the Berlin *Aufklarung* in the mid-18th century. He had arguments with local Rabbis over the fixed dates between death and burial, much greater conflict over his translation of the Pentateuch into German using Hebrew orthography. However, his various commentaries, gradually led to larger demand for internal liberalization within the structure of Judaism itself. This trend eventually led to Reformed Judaism, at the same time, massive conversion.

Enlightenment—Aufklärung/Haskala

This period, dating from approximately the last quarter of the 17th century to the cusp of the 19th, was preceded by two and a half centuries of Renaissance and scientific advances over the given structure of ideas, meanings, and the political/intellectual hierarchy of medievalism. A world that was statically engraved in the minds of the intellects as well as the masses had been breached. For almost a thousand years a theological view of man and nature related to an omniscient god towering above man, was interpreted in his laws and day-to-day guidance by priests, mullahs, rabbis, Protestant ministers. These latter, taking their legitimacy from the holiness of the Papacy, the Koran, the Talmud, the Bible, had now been challenged.

The new forms of mathematical, cosmological theorizing, using the ancient Greek scientific writings as their take off point, had been joined by a multifarious experimentalism in the technology of life, as well as the search for distant lands of wealth by instruments: the compass, telescope, astrolabe, microscope, the printing press, maps of the skies and the lands, the unencumbered mind searching for knowledge out of reach of the old sources of religious authority.

The shock of realization that the mind could go beyond the given knowledge of the world, the work of Copernicus, 1473-1543 (Hanseatic German/Pole), Brahe, 1540-1601 (Dane), Kepler, 1571-1630 (German), Galileo 1564-1642 (Italian), culminating in the research of the Englishman, Newton (1642-1727) opened the door to a new world of meaning far beyond the stars and the land. Man on earth could also be interpreted in terms of secular knowledge, Thomas Hobbes (1588-1679, England), author of *Leviathan*. The old holy injunctions concerning man's place in the world, no longer bore the same kinds of powerful experiential fruit in a European world that had, unaided, discovered new wealth and ways of living far beyond what existed under the thumb of the religious/feudal regime.

The art, architecture, mercantilism, of the Renaissance was added to by the explorations overseas, new middle-class wealth and power, from craft, manufacturing, finance, agriculture, tobacco, rum, coffee, even the African slave trade, all came to challenge the feudal agricultural order. The days of the power of church, aristocratic monarchical dominance was waning. So, too, with Talmudic, rabbinical authority.

There is no question but that the intellectual elite of gentile Europe had erupted out of all the hidden crevices of European society. The continent was experiencing a torrent of social and economic change. And with this alteration in European life, so, too, was there an impact on the Jews.

It is agreed that the fire-storm of Reformation spread for reasons beyond the special corruptions of Papal practice, having the purpose of filling the coffers in Rome with northern gold. The move to emancipate these northern principalities from Papal control had its roots in the new economies of the Renaissance north, and the wish to explore their own political and economic futures out of control of Catholic interdict. This all occurred in the first half of the 16th century, while the horizons of European vision were expanding beyond the home continent.

For the Jews these horizons did not exist. They were to be encapsulated for two more centuries. But it must be proposed that these winds of change penetrated not merely north to the German states and west to Holland and Britain, but also into the darkness of what would be the Jewish *Pale*, the lands to the Slavic east. Thus can we partially explain the Hassidic movement that broke out in mid-18th century, simultaneously with both the Christian *Aufklärung* in Western Europe, and the first throbbings for political and economic emancipation for the Jews in these same western domains.

The origin of the Hasidism is rooted in the East European mystic tendencies, including the Russian dissenting sects. It was founded by Israel Ba'al Shem Tov, in the mid-18th century, in Podolia and Volhynia, Poland. Raphael Patai glorifies the movement, as a *dionysian* response to the Talmudic elite which dominated the *Kahals*, the Jewish community governments set up by the Polish nobility—Poland from the 15th century occupied large portions of White Russia, Ukraine, Lithuania, until the 1772 partition by the great powers.[13]

"Hasidism represents one of the most significant and most original phenomena not only in the history of Judaism, but also in the history of the development of religions in general…It did not aim at the improvement of the tenets of the faith or at a reform of religious practices; what it endeavored was something greater and deeper: the perfection of the *soul*. By means of exerting a powerful psychological influence Hasidism succeeded in creating a type of *believer* which valued the ardor of feeling higher than the observance of rites, piety and religious fervor, higher than speculation and *Torah*-study."[14]

The summary impact of the Hassidic movement, coming at the time that it did, was an undermining of the Talmudic educational authority at the very moment that the scientific and mercantile movements were opening up for the Jewish mind an even more powerful realm of reality and possibility.

Emancipation

Perhaps the most significant figure among the *maskilim*, those most influenced by the Enlightenment, and most eager to translate the potential alteration in the status of the Jews, first by the reshaping of Judaism itself, into a congruency with the new world, then, to be liberated in consonance with the views of the enlightened, was Moses Mendelssohn, 1729-1786. Hailing from one of the more tolerant German towns in the southeast, Dessau, educated by teachers who themselves had migrated from Poland, Mendelssohn, burdened with significant physical deformities, transcended his time.

From 1755 Mendelssohn was publishing a journal containing historic literary and philosophical articles, *Preacher of Morals*. His first efforts were in the direction of ridding Jewish education of "Talmudic casuistry," in favor of teaching the Talmud literally, teaching the Hebrew Bible and the Hebrew language, more so than Yiddish. Here he was in harmony with the Sephardic educational tradition, which for long had included secular sciences, mathematics, and vernacular language learning as part of their curriculum for all the young.

In fact, the lack of historical awareness in the traditional German and Eastern European Jewish education revealed itself in the fact that the first publishing in the north of Maimonides' *Guide for the Perplexed*, was in 1742.

The Marquis d'Argens, a French nobleman who was to become a Chamberlain to Fredrick the Great of Prussia, had been impressed with the abilities of the Sephardic Italian Jews. In the Enlightenment spirit he had written in 1737, *Lettres Juives*, arguing for their inclusion in civil society, seeing their "bad" qualities as a product of their exclusion and unjust treatment, and noting the outstanding intellect of the Sephardi-Italian Jews whose "decisions on matters of the mind are often of much greater value than those of the best academicians" To the King of Prussia, Frederick the Great, d'Argens appealed for Moses Mendelssohn to be given the status of a protected Jew and allowed to live in Berlin.

David Sorkin views the work of Moses Mendelssohn, Naphtali Herz Wessely, and David Friedlander as assisting in the task of bringing the Jews into the mainstream of German and Enlightenment society.[15]

This was part of a movement that was penetrating into the heart and minds of progressive intellectuals of the time. John Locke, in 1689 had written *Letter Concerning Toleration*, which argued for Jews to be allowed the civil rights of residents, along with the maintenance of their synagogues. John Tolland as earlier noted had translated Luzzatto's *Discourse on the Status of Jews*, c.1660, and had subsequently published anonymously in 1714, his own, *Reasons for Naturalizing the Jews of Great Britain and Ireland....*" British Parliament passed the *Jew Bill*, 1753, allowing for the naturalization of the Jews, but popular outcry caused its immediate repeal.[16]

This antagonism against Jewish emancipation was not merely a response from the anxious masses, afraid of and thus hateful of a foreign element being added to the new national stew.

Voltaire, in Volume VII of his Historical Writings (Geneva 1756) on the Jews: "...raging fanaticism would someday become deadly to the human race."[17] The bad moral condition of the Jews, gave rise to cruel, fanatical, cannibalism, unrestrained barbarism. The Jews were given to atrocities and sexual immorality, intercourse with animals. They sold their own sons and daughters into slavery, they were dishonest and greedy, strove for dominance over the whole world. Even the Biblical writings, Voltaire felt, were plagiarisms from the Greeks (1771).[18]

Montesquieu, in his *Lettres Persanes* (1721), although dubbed by David Sorkin as having an image of the Jew more positive than Voltaire, Holbach, and Diderot, the other French Enlightenment savants, still proclaimed: "Wherever there is money there are the Jews."[19] Also, the writings of the Rabbis representing the spirit of slaves, fashioned the continuing low taste and low character of the Jews, Montesquieu, writing prior to 1748.[20]

Even Immanuel Kant, 1725-1804, the greatest philosopher of the 18th century and the personification of the Enlightenment worship of the scientific ethos of Isaac Newton, still, in his late-18th-century writings, could find little in the contemporary Jew to justify his membership in the national state. He makes a distinction between the rational and the crafty man. Kant's example of craftiness, cunning, slyness made of the Jews, a "nation of deceivers" who use their special command of language for their economic advantage. Kant associates little or no virtue with the image of the eastern (Polish) Jew. Indeed, the Eastern Jew becomes the model for the rapaciousness and destructiveness of the Jew. The language of the Jews in this context becomes the measure of their craftiness, not their intelligence.[21]

Moses Mendelssohn was well aware of this hateful opposition to the emancipation of the Jews. Thus, in his introduction to his German translation of Manasseh Israel's *Vindiciae Judaeorum* (1656):

"It is remarkable to observe how prejudice has taken on the shape of all centuries in order to oppress us and to place difficulties in the way of our civil acceptance. In those superstitious times it was the sacra which {they said} we wantonly desecrated, crucifixes which we pierced through and made bleed; children whom we secretly circumcised, and tore apart for the delight of the eyes; Christian blood which we needed for sacrificial feasts, wells which we poisoned, etc.; unbelief, stubbornness, secret arts and devilishness of which we were accused and because of which we were tortured, robbed of our property, driven into misery, even when not actually executed—Now {that} times have changed, those calumnies no longer make the desired impression. Now it is precisely superstition and stupidity which are attributed to us; lack of moral sentiment, of taste and refined manners, inability in the arts, sciences, and useful crafts, especially those in the service of war and the state, unconquerable inclination to cheating, usury, and lawlessness, which took the place of those cruder accusations, in order to exclude us from the number of useful citizens and to push us away from the motherly bosom of the state."[22]

One of Mendelssohn's first, if controversial achievements as a leader of the German Jewish community had been the above noted translation into German of the Pentateuch, written in Hebrew script, with Hebrew commentary. One of his last writings was a plea for the granting of rights to Jews in the name of tolerance and the secularity of the state: *Jerusalem, Or, On Ecclesiastical Authority and Judaism*, 1783: Berlin.

Naphtali Herz Wessely (1725-1805), of Sephardic Portuguese origins, from Copenhagen and a follower of the Italian scientific Talmudist, Joseph Delmedigo, 1591-1655, was a sympathizer of the Mendelssohnian program. Wessely wrote in Hebrew, *Words of Peace and Truth* (1782-Berlin). It consisted of a new scientific course of study for Jewish youth. The Sephardic Jewish world, the Portuguese Jews of Trieste in Italy, Italian Rabbis of Venice and Ferrara responded positively. Wessely was condemned by Polish and German Rabbis, especially for his endorsement of Hapsburg Emperor, Joseph II pending "Toleranzpatent" proposals for Jewish integration in the Austrian domains. Here, compulsory education including secular subjects for all Jewish children.[23]

In Germany, at the behest of Moses Mendelssohn, the Christian historian Christian Wilhelm von Dohm (1751-1820), wrote in 1781 *On the Civic Improvement of the Jews*: The Jews had wisdom and intellect, were assiduous and persevering, but addicted to material gain and usury. This was the result of persecution and forced isolation. Von Dohm argued that the solution was to educate them and bring them within the circle of the state, abolish restrictions on their participation. Sorkin sees von Dohm as the key to the German Enlightenment's acceptance of the Jew as more than a protected Court Jew. "The Jew is more than a Jew."[24]

Even earlier, 1762, a truly revolutionary mind, Jean-Jacques Rousseau (1712-1778) wrote as follows: "The Jews present us with an outstanding spectacle: the laws of Numa, Lycurgus, and Solon are dead, the far more ancient ones of Moses are still alive. Athens, Sparta, and Rome have perished and all their people have vanished from the earth; though destroyed, Zion has not lost her children. They mingle with all the nations but are never lost among them; they no longer have leaders, yet they are still a nation; they no longer have a country and yet they are still citizens."[25] Rousseau further urged that there be created, a separate Jewish state, with schools and universities where they could speak and argue without danger.

Alsace-Lorraine contained many Yiddish-speaking Jews when Louis XIV took it over in 1681. Abbé Henri Gregoire (1750-1831), on October 1, 1789, spoke to the French National Assembly: "Fifty thousand Frenchman arose this morning as slaves, it depends on you whether they shall go to bed as free people." The French revolutionist Robespierre: "Jewish vices are rooted in the lowly status to which you have reduced them.....It is our misdeeds as a nation, which we must atone for by restoring to them those inalienable human rights of which no human power may deprive them....Let us restore them to happiness, to a fatherland, to propriety, by restoring to them the dignity of human beings and citizens."[26]

In 1782, the *"Toleranzpatent"* of Emperor Joseph II of Austria was officially enunciated, the beginning of a long and arduous release of the Jews from their segregation in the German world, but also demanding of the Jews the dissolution of their institutions.

In 1796, Dutch Jews submitted a petition to their States general asking for Jewish Emancipation. The Rabbinate of both communities, Sephardic and Ashkenazi vigorously opposed this move, which was granted in the same year. The Rabbis saw emancipation as the beginning of the end, the disintegration of Judaism.

The ideal of *Haskalah* and *Aufklärung* was the virtuous man, an educated person. This ideal purported to keep Judaism still within the bounds of religious authority and piety. By the 1770-80s *Haskalah* had become politicized, it connoted emancipation, *e.g.,* Joseph II *Patent of Toleration*, 1782, (Austria).Then in the 1790s, assimilation began to be a factor in West European Jewish life. Usually it meant the attenuation of Judaic practice. However, in the broadest sense, the impact of the Enlightenment on Catholicism and Protestantism was similar, a deep change of human allegiance and man's relationship to religion. The United States Constitution of 1787, and the Bill of Rights, powerfully reflected this change.

Assimilation

The price of the *Aufklärung* for the emancipation of the Jews was high, assimilation. Mirabeau (1749-1791) wrote favorably about Moses Mendelssohn; also, in a memorandum to Frederick the Great in 1788, he maintained that the Jewish desire for citizenship and equality argued that they were ready to surrender their separatism.

Count Stanislas de Clermont-Tonnerre (1757-92), in France in 1789: 'Every Jew must individually become a citizen; if they do not want this, they must inform us and we shall be impelled to expel them. The existence of a nation within a nation is unacceptable to our country.'

However, the opposition to the assimilation of the Jews went deep. Immanuel Kant, as noted above, was among the doubters: "All separatists, that is, those who subject themselves not only to the general laws of the country but also to a special sectarian law, are exposed through their eccentricity and alleged chosen ness to the attention and criticism of the community, and thus cannot relax in their self-control for intoxication, which deprives one of cautiousness, would be a scandal for them."[27]

Again, Kant on the Jews: Judaism consisted of laws and rituals whereas true religion was based on morality alone. "Pure moral religion means the death of Judaism." Michael Meyer explains Kant's Enlightenment perspective: "If Jews wanted to be genuinely religious, as a modern philosopher understood religion, they would have to leave Judaism behind, for it was inseparable from its laws, which rendered it necessarily heteronymous, eliminating the moral freedom which Kant regarded as essential to an enlightened faith."[28]

During this late-18th-century time-frame, the Lithuanian Jewish Council sent representatives and money to Warsaw to forestall the dangers to halakhic Judaism that the *Haskala* represented.[29] From c.1775, this opposition from the orthodox grew increasingly passionate as the *maskilim* increased in number and broke down the membrane of Judaic separatism. These East-European opponents of the Berlin *Haskala*, however, did not necessarily want to exclude scientific education.

Exemplars: 1. Ezekiel Landau, 1713-1793, Chief Rabbi of Prague and Bohemia, opposed Mendelssohn's translation of the Bible into German, Wessely's view of Jewish education, and the Berlin "rabble" in general. 2. Elijah, Gaon of Vilna, 1720-1797: not a Rabbi, advocated science; he hated the Hasidim, opposed the Berlin *Haskala* and its philosophy, which he felt threatened Judaism. 3. Rabbi Moses Sofer (Schreiber) of Pressburg/Bratislava, 1762-1839, whose Talmudic and moral status in Europe was at that time the highest, advocated a program of Jewish education in which the youth would learn the sciences, astronomy, anatomy, even modern music. But, he emphasized, 'do not mingle with the Gentiles, for a people dwelling alone can always sanctify and cleanse itself from the defilement of intermingling.'

In the Russian domains, after the division of Poland, 1770s, all assimilationist writings were condemned by the Talmudic schools, especially by Rabbi Herschel Josefowicz of Chelm. Life for the Jews, however, showed no betterment in the East European expansion of the powers of the czars.

The trickle of Jews migrating east to west grew into a flood. The great Jewish philosopher, Solomon Maimon, 1754-1800, came out of Poland, an impoverished student studying the Latin alphabet. Hungry to learn German, eager to abandon Yiddish, his goal was to learn of the knowledge of the Enlightenment. In Maimon's words, he was: "...like starving persons suddenly treated to a delicious meal." Maimon, and Mendelssohn's own associate, David Friedlander, became converts to Christianity, as were the parents of Karl Marx, they from a long line of rabbis.

The key event in this transition of the Jews from the emancipation of ghetto life to the full intellectual, political, and economic freedom, came with Napoleon's radical reforms, now in early-19th-century, Paris, 1806-1807: Here was gathered an Assembly of Jewish Notables and the Grand Sanhedrin of Jewish religious leaders in France. Decided for all Jews were a set of principles setting forth a new relationship between the Jews and the state: Here, a general accommodation between non-Jew and Jew, in equality of treatment. But also mandated was the Jewish accommodation to the laws of the state or nation. The state would validate the exception of religious sanctification or blessing of intermarriage between Jew and Gentile.

Raphael Patai, the most serious commentator on these events of the 18th and early-19th century, contrasted the *Haskala* (assimilation/Enlightenment) movement in the Germanic north in the 18th century, with the earlier Renaissance and post-Renaissance Italian Jew. The latter had remained true to their Judaic heritage. They did so despite enormous pressure to convert, from the Church. But then they faced the old enemy, not science or capitalism.

Four out of Moses Mendelssohn's six children converted, and all of his grandchildren, including Felix, the composer, became nominal Christians.[30]

Further, Patai discusses the efforts of Mendelssohn, representative of the Jewish/German *Haskala*, the Enlightenment, and the *maskilim*, the Enlighteners who argued for an integration into the national state, and openness to the new knowledge. As with the domino effect the process went from 1. *Enlightenment*: new knowledge, new intellectual allegiances, dedication or fealty. 2. *Emancipation*: the struggle for full political, economic, religious educational rights, adherence to secular law. 3: *Assmiliation*: the Jews as merely one national religious group among others, not holding themselves apart in the legal, social, moral, cultural sense. This led to vast intermarriage rates in Germany, then in Austria, France, England, finally and to the shock of the Orthodox, often by the liberal emancipated Reform Jews, a full transfer of loyalty to the nationally dominant religion, and then, *conversion.*[31]

The lure of assimilation was powerfully demonstrated in the evidence. Solomon Volkov sees over three-quarters of Jews in Germany living below the middle-class standard in the 18th century, whereas three-quarters of them lived above the middle-class standard by the end of the 19th century.[32]

There here existed an inner enticement for…"enlightenment, emancipation, assimilation". From the 1780s Jews gradually began to publicly show their new found wealth in the salons of their majestic homes: Berlin banker family names: Ephraim; Itzig; Cohen; Mayer; Mendelssohn; Herz; von Arnstein (Vienna); von Eskeles(Vienna); Varnhagen (Berlin); Lippmann (Vienna); Koenigswarter (Vienna-Paris); Rothschild (Frankfurt-Paris); Straus (Paris). Many of the women of these families were converts, all ran famous intellectual and artistic salons.

The German philosophical follower of Kant, Johann Gottlieb Fichte (1762-1814) could assert in 1793, that he was against granting Jews emancipation. Jewish ideas, he asserted were as obnoxious as French ideas. A little later, 1808, he would modify slightly these thoughts. The only way in which he could concede giving rights to Jews would be "to cut off all their heads in one night, and to set new ones on their shoulders, which should not contain a single Jewish idea."[33]

Thus would begin the 19th century. Little would the Jews realize in the century to follow the looming price that they would pay for this freedom to compete, play the game of their gentile neighbors. A world was on the move, the future now undefined by supra-human authority, only by human ingenuity, intelligence, and weakness.

Endnotes, Chapter 7

[1] Hilberg, R. 1985. *The Destruction of the European Jews,* Vol. I, 3nd ed., New Haven: Yale Univ. Press, p. 22.

[2] Graetz, H. (1817-1891). *History of the Jews*, Philadelphia: Jewish Publication Society, 5:292-301.

[3] Patai, R. 1977. *The Jewish Mind,* N.Y.: Scribner, p. 166.

[4] See Hugo Bettauer, *Die Stadt ohne Juden*—Ein Roman von Übermorgen, Vienna, 1922; in Hilberg, *op cit.*, pp. 27-28.

[5] Stowasser, "Zur Geschichte der Wiener Geserah," *Vierteljahrschrift für Sozial und Wirtschaftgeschichte,* 16 (1922):106

[6] *Luther, Martin, 1543, Wittenberg, Von der Jueden und Ihren Luegen, p.* Aiii, in Hilberg, Vol. II, 3rd ed., *op. cit.,* p .409, quoted in Hilberg, 1985. *The Destruction of the European Jews-* Vol. 1, 2nd ed., New Haven: Yale Univ. Press, p. 16.

[7] Patai, *The Jewish Mind, op. cit.,* pp. 225-227.

[8] Graetz, Heinrich. *History of the Jews,* Reprint, Philadelphia: Jewish Publication Society, 5:83-84 167.

[9] Patai, *The Jewish Mind, op. cit.,* pp. 229-235.

[10] Bodian, M. 1997. *Hebrews of the Portuguese Nation,* Bloomington: Indiana Univ. Press.

[11] Berkley, G. E. 1988. *Vienna and Its Jews*, Cambridge, Mass.: Abt Books, p. 29*ff.*

[12] Sorkin, D. 1994. "Jews, the Enlightenment, and Religious Toleration—Some Reflections" *The Jews in European History*, ed. by Wolfgang Beck Cincinnati: Hebrew Union College Press, pp. 39-56.

[13] Patai, *The Jewish Mind, op. cit.,* pp. 180-181.

[14] Dubnow, S. 1931. *Geschichte des Chassidismus*, tr. Patai, Berlin: Judischer Verlag, I-67-68—.

[15] Sorkin, D. 1994. "Jews, the Enlightenment, and Religious Toleration—Some Reflections, *op. cit.,* pp 39-56.

[16] Patai, *The Jewish Mind, op. cit.,* p. 236*ff.*

[17] Patai, *The Jewish Mind, op. cit.,* p. 251.

[18] *Ibid.*

[19] Montesquieu, *Works* I-218-219.

[20] Patai, *The Jewish Mind, op. cit.,* p. 252; Sorkin, "Jews, the Enlightenment, and Religious Toleration—Some Reflections," *op. cit.,* pp. 39-56.

[21] Gilman, S. L. 1996. *Smart Jews*, Lincoln, Neb.: Univ. of Nebraska Press, p. 15; Kant, I. *Anthropology from a Pragmatic Point of View*, tr. by V. L. Dowdell (1978), Carbondale: Southern Illinois Univ. Press, pp. 101-102.

[22] Tr. by R. Patai, 1977. *The Jewish Mind, op. cit.*, p. 244.

[23] Sorkin, "Jews, the Enlightenment, and Religious Toleration—Some Reflections," *op. cit.*, pp. 48-49.

[24] .Meyer, P. 1963. "The Attitude of the Enlightenment towards the Jews," in "Studies on Voltaire and the Eighteenth Century," 26 1161-1205; Hertzberg, A. 1970. *The French Enlightenment and the Jews.* N.Y.

[25] *Encyclopedia Judaea*, 14: 352-353; *Emile*, 4:268.

[26] Mahler, R. 1971. *A History of Modern Jewry,* London: Valentine, Mitchell, p. 33.

[27] Patai, *op. cit.*, p. 445; Kant, I. 1789 *Anthropolgie*, Part 1, Bk.1, Par. 29.

[28] Kant, I. (1798) 1838. "Der Streit der Facultäten," in *Sämtlicher Werke,* 10, Leipzig, p. 338; Meyer, M. 1994. "Should and Can an 'Antiquated' Religion Become Modern?" in *The Jews in European History*, ed. by Wolfgang Beck, Cincinnati: Hebrew Union College Press, pp. 62-63.

[29] Salo Baron, quoted by Patai, *op. cit.*, p. 253.

[30] Patai, R. *The Jewish Mind*, pp. 178-179.

[31] Weyl, N., and Possony, S. T. 1963. *The Geography of Intellect*, Chicago: Regnery, pp. 116-119; Patai, R., *op. cit.*, p. 260*ff.*

[32] Volkov, S. 1994. "Jews and Judaism in the Age of Emancipation: Unity and Variety," in *The Jews in European History*, ed. by W. Beck, Cincinnati: Hebrew Union College Press, pp. 73-92.

[33] Dawidowicz, L. S. 1975. *The War against the Jews, 1933-1945*, N.Y.: Holt, Rinehart and Winston, pp. 26-27; Johann Gottlieb Fichte, *Reden an die deutsche Nation* (1808).

8

Dilemmas of Intelligence and Power

The Jews in Two Civilizations

There are interesting parallels between the circumstances of Philo Judaeus of Hellenistic Alexandria, c.40 CE and Moses Mendelssohn, c.1780 CE in Berlin. Philo was a wealthy son of a line of prominent Alexandrian Jews, at a time when the Jewish communities throughout the now Roman Hellenistic world were still at peace with the universal civilization. Approximately one hundred and fifty years after the Jews first encountered the Greek civilizational world, they had to fight (Judah Maccabeus—166 BCE) for the right to practice their Biblical and Prophetic traditions even after accepting a veneer of Hellenism. Two hundred years after this accommodation, accepted by Rome, Philo was himself in Rome pleading with the representatives of a mad emperor, Caligula, that the emperor not place representations of himself as supreme god, in the Jewish temples, and thus demand worship over Jehovah.

Philo was perhaps the greatest philosophical mind to arise from the Alexandrian Hellenistic environment, a center of Hellenic/Hebraic culture, far beyond the reach of Jerusalem, still the holy outpost of Judaism, and itself also under siege from the edicts of Caligula. The Roman governor of Judea and Jerusalem knew that Caligula would bring down upon Rome a ferocious war, by attempting to place exemplifications of himself into the holiest Temple of the Jews. Fortunately for the peace of this civilization, the Praetorian Guard had had enough of Caligula's madness and assassinated him, placing a more compliant Emperor, Claudius, on the throne. The crisis was over, the Jews would be at peace with this military civilization for another generation. They then would revolt in an attempt to reassert their influence and numbers. We see from 135 CE, the gradual dissolution of the powerful Jewish element in Hellenistic Civilization.

Only the Christian philosophical/theological successors to this Jewish element in Roman culture would study the writings of Philo. The Jews would recede into their enclosed Talmudic interpretive succoring of the ancient Biblical writings. Earlier infatuations with Hellenistic civilization would gradually wither. In truth, the power of Rome and the populist accommodations of Christianity to the mystery religion cravings of the masses signified no loss to Judaism. There was nothing in Judaism's rejection of the Hellenistic, nor its withdrawal from the Christian and Islamic successors to Rome that connoted religio-philosophical inferiority. What the Jews abandoned was the political, military independence that was once theirs.

Philo had not requested entrance or assimilation into the Roman world, merely that the old balance between religion and state be retained. The Hellenistic Jews were then content with maintaining their freedoms (emancipation) within the Roman world. They would attend to their own Enlightenment within the *Proseuche* and *Synagogue* of their officially recognized communities. No assimilation needed here.

When Moses Mendelssohn was arguing with his own Jewish constituencies in the Yiddish/German speaking world of the 18th century, it was clear that a new civilization was being born, secular, scientific, experimental, but also deep in intellectual and moral meanings. Mendelssohn argued for emancipation, politically, economically, socially. But he also argued for the international nature of the Enlightenment, in many ways similar to Philo's integration of Greek and Judaic thought. Philo wrote in Greek, hardly knew any Hebrew.

Mendelssohn wanted to trade Yiddish for German with Hebrew as the holy script. But more, he wanted the Jews to renounce an enclosed historical past and enter into a new rising world of universal power, one that brought into the shadows not only traditional Talmudism, but also the entire panoply of Christian and Islamic thought. Here the historical contrast between the two figures is sharp.

In a sense, to this prescient thinker, Mendelssohn, the playing field for the Jew had been leveled by science and the Enlightenment. To Philo, the Jews entreated with the Roman Hellenistic power to be treated as co-equal with all competing faiths and political arrangements. To Mendelssohn, the entreaties had to be directed both to the Jews, for them to emerge from isolation, and then to the powers that be, to allow the Jews into this new world in which, by legal and philosophical right they now required emancipation.

But the magnet also seemed to require assimilation, often conversion in recognition of the still powerful political role of Christianity. As noted in Chapter 7, four of Mendelssohn's six children converted, all of his grandchildren, including Felix, the composer, and Philip Veit, one of the greatest 19th-century portraitists, were nominal Christians. Portentially, the parents of Karl Marx, themselves children of a long line of Rabbis in Trier, an ancient founding city of the Roman and then the Yiddish Rhineland, converted, for the opportunities that membership in the local Church conferred upon them. This now included the marriage of their son, Karl, to a daughter of the local Protestant aristocracy.

Out of Confinement and Poverty

The writers, who rounded out the Hebrew Bible in the Hellenistic Age: the *ketuvim* (Writings) Pharisaic thinkers such as Rabbis Hillel, Zakai, Akiba, all 1st- and 2nd-century sages, now including Philo; finally in c.200 CE, in Galilee, Judah Ha-Nasi, the greatest of the *tannaim* (teachers), and the redactor of the *Mishnah* (Repetition), the first part of the Talmud, can all be considered products of the Greek Enlightenment. Even without the complex politico/military claims for Jewish sovereignty, these leaders of Judaism were products of an emancipation that allowed the Jews to live and think as they were wont. Bar Kokhba, allied with Reb Akiba, during his revolt, 132-135 CE, dictated his written communications to his comrades-in-arms, in Greek.

Then, under the Spanish Muslim, then Christian rule, which in their most benign periods allowed the Jews that freedom to think (see Chapter 7 on Sarton's analysis of Jewish scientific achievement), a peak was reached in the thought of the Spaniard, Moses Maimonides, he, inspired by both the classical Greek writers plus the Greek-influenced Arabic philosophical tradition. So, too, 19th and then 20th century Jews would flee the ghettos and *shtetls* to make their contributions to this open world of intellectual and material opportunity.

We have already enumerated, in Chapter 7, the Jewish banking families in Berlin, Vienna, and elsewhere that had early developed out of the freedoms given to the *Schutzjuden*, the protected Jews needed by the ruling classes of the German, Polish, even the French establishments. By 1800 the banking houses of Arnstein-Eskeles and Hertz-Leidersdorf plus Prague wool merchant Lamel helped subsidize the war against Napoleon for the Hapsburgs.[1]

In 1800 there were approximately 2.5 million Jews in the world. In Berlin, 1816, with a population of c.200,000, there were c.3,400 Jews. In 1849, the population of Berlin had risen to c.412,000, with c.9,600 Jews. By 1895, the German population of Berlin had increased 307 percent, the Jews 798 percent. By 1925, Germany had a population of c.56 million, the total German Jewish population was 564,379, with 172,672 or 30.6 percent of Germany's Jews living in Berlin: By 1930 the world's Jewish population had soared to c.16 million.[2]

As they ran from the oppressive life of ghetto and *shtetl*, they came armed with the literacy of the Talmud. They alone of the people of Europe came as a classless ethnicity, even the especially wealthy few did not rule over the common working Jew. The rich Jew usually attended synagogues with his fellow communicants. And he owed his fellow Jews the philanthropic help that being a member of the synagogue required. The Jews did not use their intellectual skills to remain as peasant farmers. Rather, along with all capable and ready minds they searched opportunity to rise up economically and socially. Here in the new world of science, technology, industry, finance they were beckoned to use their ready intelligence to avoid the poverty that might once more leave them defenseless. Here against the always oppressive *goyim,* as well as the inevitable disasters of nature.

A not atypical example from Prussia: Meyer Kauffman, a Silesian Jew who worked in the garment trade, opened with his wife Philippine, in 1824, a drapers shop in Schweidnitz. Ever alert to opportunity, in 1841, Meyer opened a second shop in Breslau. Hearing about new mechanical inventions in the trade, he traveled to London in 1851 to attend the Exposition. There, he and his wife purchased 200 mechanical looms and opened a large textile factory back in their homeland. They were on their way to becoming large-scale manufacturers, capitalists.[3]

As noted in the previous chapter, by the late 19th century over seventy-five percent of the Jews in Germany proper lived above the middle-class standard. A century earlier, as the iron gates of the ghettos were being opened, exactly the reverse percentages were the rule.[4] In this late-19th-century period, seventy eight percent of the Jews were in commerce, industry and the professions. By the dawn of the twentieth century, most Germans were still on farms/villages.[5]

Karl Wittgenstein is an Austrian exemplar of this gradual growth of Jewish power and wealth, seeking out opportunities, as with their fellow Christian entrepreneurs. Wittgenstein's father was a small-time merchant in Bohemia. Karl was able thus to travel widely in Europe and then in America, always with his violin, becoming acquainted with newer industrial techniques, especially in the production of steel. Returning to Austria he became a literal whirlwind of enterprise, building a vast industrial complex of iron and steel mills, taking a significant role in the practically wholly Jewish, Austrian railroad system. Wittgenstein and his Jewish associates were also deeply involved in textiles, sugar refining, meat packing drilling for oil in Galicia. By the end of the 19th century the Jews owned all but one of the leading banks in Vienna, most of the fashionable clothing stores along the *Ringstrasse*.[6]

By mid-19th century, having taken advantage of the secular schools and universities just being opened to them, they were ever more deeply involved in science, invention, secular literature and the arts. Example: Siegfried Marcus in

1864 built the first internal combustion machine. In 1875, he was driving the first automobile through Vienna's streets.[7] The Herschels, father and son, F. W. 1736-1822, J. F. W., 1792-1871, left Germany to pursue a more opportune life in England, and made great contributions to scientific astronomy, as well as to philosophy. Ludwig Boltzmann and Heinrich Hertz, somewhat later, remained in Germany, their epochal research to be followed in physics by Albert Einstein.

The Jewish medical tradition stretches back deep into the Muslim era. In 1881, when Freud was beginning his medical career, Jews already made up sixty percent of Vienna's doctors. By 1900 a majority of University clinical chairs, medical directorship of city hospitals were in Jewish hands. Jewish researchers: Bela Schick, Josef Breuer, Emil Zuckerkandl, Sigmund Freud, Alfred Adler, Otto Rank, Karl Abraham, Heinrich von Neumann, Karl Landsteiner, Oscar Lowi.

Theodore Billroth was one of the few accomplished non-Jews. Quite ambivalent in the early part of his career about the Jewish dominance of medicine in Austria, he was married to a Jewess, and his own personal doctor was Josef Breuer.[8] In Prussian Germany to the north, such Jews as Robert Koch, Paul Ehrlich, August Wasserman were making their contributions to the nation that had opened its gates.

The Austrian Empire's per capita income was by mid-19th century only 40 percent of Germany's, because of the impoverished Eastern Provinces, including Poland, Ruthenia, Ukraine. Fifty million lived in the Empire, 5 percent were Jews.[9] In Germany the Jews never made up more than one percent of the population. By 1900 there were 147,000 Jews in Vienna, 9 percent of the population. The percentage of Jew in Berlin at this time was not as high, even though they represented such a high proportion of the German Jewish population. Berlin was growing rapidly at the turn of the 20th century and continued to expand. In contrast, the dismemberment of the Austrian Empire after World War I caused the Jewish population of Vienna to decline by 1925.

However: "We should note that throughout Europe during the nineteenth century the Jewish population increased at twice the rate of the non-Jewish population. This remarkable growth resulted not from a greater birth rate but from reduced infant mortality, Jewish communities had lower rates of illegitimacy, venereal disease, and alcoholism, those favorable factors plus the greater status accorded to mothers and the greater care lavished on children, and the increased charitable or communal aid given to the needy, enabled a much higher proportion of children to survive."[10]

To give this estimate tangibility, we must again set forth some approximate population estimates. The world population in 1800, when the Jews were at c.2.5 million, was c.700 million people. The Jews then were approximately 0.36 percent of world population. By 1930, when the Jews had increased to approximately 16 million, the world population had also increased, to 2 billion. Thus the Jews were now at 0.8 percent of the world population. During this interval, 130 years, the greatest increase in world population was registered in Europe and North America, both for the Jews and the indigenous populations. Thus the increase of the Jews relative to their Christian European *Landsmen* was tangibly twice as rapid.

The Europeans in general were descendants of the ancient Cro-Magnons, as were the West Asians, and the Vedic Aryans who migrated south into India. Despite the often oppressive conditions of life, serfdom, debilitating wars wounding the small elite Christian aristocracy, this population gave us the Renaissance, the Enlightenment, and the great discoveries, scientific and cultural that drew the Jews so powerfully into their midst. Sadly, in the Asiatic West under Islam, massive slave trading had changed the nature of the demographic balance. These people were now infused with the hereditary and cultural heritage of Africa below the Sahara. Their once cultural advance over Europe had disappeared, perhaps forever. The fate of the Jews of the Arab/Islamic world was not dissimilar. Except for a few who were able to deal with the elite, and remain aloof from the "attractions" of slavery, concubinage, polygamy, their cultural/intellectual descent was also palpable.

The Jews of the Ashkenazic world were now different from both their brethren in the ancient Asiatic and North African homelands, but also different in extent if not in kind from their European Christian neighbors, often oppressors. This difference was in the Talmudic family structure and education, the massive ethnic defense/marginalization the Jews had been obligated to erect. Ironically the Jews, as they emerged from this cocoon of protectiveness looked back with denigration on this supposedly outmoded cultural ethos.

Heinrich Graetz (1817-1891), author of the definitive multi-volume *History of the Jews,* was a Yeshiva student in Eastern Europe before he was able to study European languages and secular knowledge. He was admitted to the University of Breslau at the late age of 25. On Moses Mendelssohn: "The incarnation of his race...stunted in form, awkward, timid, stuttering, ugly, repulsive in appearance,...Jewish race deformity...{yet} thoughtful in spirit."[11] Graetz on his home language, Yiddish: "The consequence of the debasement of language, {here} the German and Polish Jews had lost all sense of form, taste for artistic beauty, and aesthetic feeling...{Polish Jews were} barbarous...an aversion to civilization."[12]

Graetz on Talmudic study: "The perverse course of study...had blunted their minds to simplicity. They had grown so accustomed to all that was artificial, distorted, super cunningly wrought, and to subtleties, that the simple, unadorned truth became worthless, if not childish and ridiculous, in their eyes.

Their train of thought was mostly perverted, uncultivated, and defiant of logical discipline."[13]

However, Graetz is ambivalent. On Moses Mendelssohn's significance: "As if touched by a magic wand, the Talmud students, fossils of the musty schoolhouses, were transfigured, and upon the wings of the intellect they soared above the gloomy present, and took their flight heavenwards."

Graetz again, on Talmudic study: "…the acumen, quick comprehension, and profound penetrativeness which these youths acquired in their close study of the Talmud rendered it easy for them to take their position in the newly discovered world. Thousands of Talmud students…became little Mendelssohns; many of them eloquent, profound thinkers. With them Judaism renewed its youth…In a very short time a numerous band of Jewish authors arose who wrote in clear Hebrew or German style upon matters which shortly before they had no knowledge…They found their level in European civilization more quickly than the {Christian} Germans, and—what should not be overlooked—Talmudic schooling had shaped their intelligence."[14]

Because of the large Eastern European territories that the Austrian Empire controlled during the period before World War I, the large Jewish population in the Eastern provinces saw Vienna as their "city of dreams." Indeed, so did Beethoven and Brahms, themselves from the Protestant Germanic north. While Austria might have been poorer than Germany on the per capita statistics cited above, 40 percent of the per capita wealth of Prussian Germany, Vienna was still an extremely wealthy capital city. And thus Jewish abilities, not only in the medical and other sciences, migrated to Vienna, but also the arts and humanities.

> Philosophers: Felix Brenatano, Edmund Husserl, Martin Buber, Ludwig Wittgenstein, Moritz Schlick, Rudolf Carnap.
>
> Composers: Gustav Mahler, Karl Goldmark, Arnold Schoenberg, Johann Straus, Oscar Straus, George Fuld, Emmerich Kalman, Franz Schrecker, Alexander Zemlinsky;
>
> Journalists: Theodor Herzl, Karl Kraus, Eduard Hanslick, Hans Habe.
>
> Authors: Lorenzo da Ponte, Richard Beer-Hoffman, Felix Salten, Arthur Schnitzler, Hugo von Hoffmannsthal, Stephan Zweig, Hugo Bettauer (The City without Jews)—assassinated 1925), Franz Werfel, Hermann Broch, Ernst Waldinger, Elias Canetti, Arthur Koestler, plus a great non-Jew, with a Jewish wife, Robert Musil.
>
> Photographer: Phillip Halsman.
>
> Painter: Richard Gerstl—suicide at 25.
>
> Economists: Ludwig von Mises, Paul Lazarsfeld;
>
> Theatre: Max Reinhardt, Eric von Stroheim, Josef von Sternberg, Fred Zimmerman, Billy Wilder.

Performance: Fritz Kreisler, Emanuel Feuermann, Erica Morini, Josef Hoffman, Bruno Walter, Felix Weingartner, Erich Kleiber, David Popper, Josef Wolfstahl, Artur Schnabel.

Political: Otto Bauer (aide to Seipel), Victor Adler, Robert Stricker, Nahum Goldman.

Harry Zohn writes: "In 1898 the Jewish writer Jacob Wasserman, a native of Franconia, came to Austria; he was to spend the rest of his life there. He found the banks, the press, the theatre, the literature, and the social organizations of Vienna in Jewish hands. As with {Theodor} Herzl he criticized the Jews for their self serving opportunism, their servility..."

Zohn tells a typical story. Isak Low Hofmann, born 1759, became a cloth and silk merchant; later, in 1835, he became Edler von Hofmannsthal. He had founded the Jewish Community Council of Vienna, but his children were already converting to Catholicism. His great grandson, Hugo von Hofmannsthal, would become a Catholic leader of the Austrian literary world at the turn of the 20th century. Had he been alive, in 1938, he would probably have been a prime target of the Austrian Nazis. Zohn compiled a list of the eighteen greatest end-of-19th-century Austrian writers. Fourteen were of Jewish background.[15]

Peter Pulzer summed it up: "The coming of the Industrial Revolution to Austria was to a large extent a Jewish enterprise...most of the country's bankers and many of its industrialists were Jews."[16] An outsider, William A. Jenks, commented on the anti-Semitism of the day: "There is considerable reason to suppose that the emancipated Jew who tremulously reached out his hand for the trappings of Gentile culture was more hated than the Jew who kept to his ghetto and his orthodoxy."[17]

Racial Hatred

The breath of air that the Enlightenment had introduced into Western European civilization in the preceding centuries came to an end in the 19th century. As we have seen in the raw anti-Semitic late 18th-century enunciations of a powerful mind such as Fichte, these formerly under-the-breath mumblings became increasingly crass as the Jews took advantage of the opportunity to join the great surge forward of the modern scientific civilization that the West had rediscovered.

The new slant on Jewish "evil," was precipitated not from the rare Jewish financier or usurer, epitomized in Luther's rant, or even in Shakespeare's nuanced and equivocal portrayal of the *Merchant of Venice*, Shylock. Increasingly, it became racial or ethnic, directed at the Jews as a people, more so than their religion, once a rival to Christianity. Some examples:

The first German to advocate, explicitly, the extermination of the Jews. Hartwig Hundt, 1819, *The Jew Mirror*: "...the men should be emasculated, and their wives and daughters be lodged in houses of shame. The best plan would be to purge the land entirely of this vermin, either by exterminating them, or as Pharaoh and the people of Meiningen, Wurzburg, and Frankfurt did, by driving them from the country."[18]

The explorations of Europeans, the beginning of colonial occupation of the discovered underdeveloped world had provided new grist for racial comparisons. The most notorious, the French writer, Arthur Gobineau 1853 in his, *An Essay on the Inequality of Human Races* gave us the first exemplar of the superiority of the Europeans, often hinted at in 18th- and early-19th-century Enlightenment writers from Voltaire to Jefferson. The Jews would be compared next.

Karl Eugen Duhring, (1833-1921) wrote the *The Jewish Question as a Racial, Moral, and Cultural Question*: Duhring was, in his own misanthropic ways, a radical genius. He first wrote on physics and scientific issues, a materialist follower of the French philosopher, Auguste Comte, but later mostly on political/economic issues, especially on anarchism. He became blind and gradually withdrew from controversy. Before this he had been fired from his University of Berlin Lectureship in1877 after disputes with the professoriate. This he blamed on the Jews. In general, Duhring was anti-Christian, anti-Jewish, anti-Socialist-Marxist. Friederich Engels, Marx's English/Jewish *Mycaenas* took Duhring's writings seriously enough to write his critique, "Anti-Duhring." To Duhring the Jews were a despicable racial cultural and economic group that was threatening Western civilization with disaster.[19]

In Germany, Wilhelm Marr (1819-1904) became the epitome of the classic anti-Semite, raw loathing without end, *The Victory of the Jews over the Germans*, 1879. This book went through twelve editions. Simply, wrote Marr, the Jews were trying to dominate the Germans; they should be driven out. His subtheme: "The Way to Victory of Germanism over Judaism."[20] Ironically, Marr was the son of a Jewish actor.

Then, Adolph Stoecker (1835-1909), head of the Christian Social Party between 1878 and 1885. He was fervently anti-capitalist and anti-Semitic, dreamed of a more traditionalist Christian world led by Prussian Junkers.

Theodore Fritsch, 1852-1933, *Handbook of Anti-Semitism*, 1896, an enormous success, was developed from his earlier, *The Riddle of the Jewish Success*, 1887.[21] Fritsch's theme was the purification of the *Volk*, the return of the German people to the ancient rural German ethic. His writings and persona strongly influenced both Himmler and Hitler, to the point of stimulating them to incorporate special rituals for the Hitler youth and the SS, intent on bringing back the ancient glories of the Teuton/Nordic heritage. Typical phraseology of Fritsch: "The crooked thinking" of the Hebrew whose "brain is a provocation-machine with a perverse way of thinking...the born bacillus of decomposition."[22]

Following in the path of Fritsch was Otto Boeckel (1859-1923). Boeckel's 1922 *Die Deutsche Volksage* was anti-capitalist.[23] The Jews were blamed for exploiting peasants, rural communities. Boeckel wanted to revoke the emancipation of the Jews, politically, economically.

Also, writing as late as 1922, a writer, following Eugen Duhring: could quote approvingly, "in their entire long history the Jews have never contributed anything to science."[24]

A representative to the Reichstag, Hermann Ahlwardt, speaking before the assemblage to their enthusiastic cheers, March 6, 1895: "If one designates the whole of Jewry as harmful, one does so in the knowledge that the racial qualities of this people are such that in the long run they can not harmonize with the racial qualities of the Germanic peoples....The Jews accomplished what no other enemy has accomplished: they have driven the people from Frankfort into the suburbs. And that's the way it is wherever Jews congregate in large numbers. Gentlemen, the Jews are indeed beasts of prey....We should leave the Jews alone because we have too many laws?! Well, I think, if we could do away with the Jews, we could do away with half the laws that we have now on the books....The Jews operate like parasites....The Jews are cholera germs...Gentlemen, it is the infectiousness and exploitative power of Jewry that is involved."[25]

L. Woltmann, a follower of Gobineau, in 1904, offered a different kind of "appreciation" of Jewish intellect and power, one with which many democratic liberals would agree long into the 20th century: "...the substantially higher percentage of Jews in institutions of higher education cannot be accounted for by superior ability, but can be explained by the 'family hot-house culture.' Jewish pseudo-intellectualism is a sign of the collapse of the race under the strain of the modern." Woltmann certainly was early echoed by modern environmentalists who attribute omnipotence to family culture.[26]

One of the great influences over German views was the writing of Houston Stewart Chamberlain, especially his *Foundations of the Nineteenth Century*, 1900. Chamberlain wrote that Germans would lose their greatness if they did not protect themselves against the Jews, for the Jews were using their unique racial qualities to destroy and conquer the Aryan world.[27] The Jews, he argued, "evidence an absolute ignorance and cultural crudeness that has never made the smallest contribution to a single area of human knowledge and creativity." Kaiser Wilhelm II wanted to use Chamberlain's book in his military academies in Berlin. At the same time, his close military advisor was General Walter von Moessner, "Aide-de-Camp." Moessner, a Jew, won great fame for his heroic cavalry achievements in the Austro-Prussian War, 1867-1868. In World War I, 100,000 Jews fought with the Prussian army; 12,000 died in combat.

One of the more preeminent German intellectuals at the turn of the 20th century, the sociologist Werner Sombart, was the author of *The Jew and Modern Capitalism*. Sombart hesitated in attributing Jewish economic hegemony over the Christians from the Middle Ages to the early 20th century to their higher intelligence. For him, as for Woltmann, this dominance could be laid at the door of tradition, "the pathological qualities of mind required for adaptation to a foreign milieu."[28] Sanford Gilman, despite his own ambivalent views about Jewish intelligence, sees Sombart as a classic intellectual anti-Semite.[29] On the other hand, Nathaniel Weyl sees Sombart as highly complementary of Jewish intellect in 1911, even though in the end he became "an apologist for the Nazis."[30]

It was no different in the south, in Austria, perhaps even worse, with many more Jews as a percentage of the national profile, especially in Vienna. Theodor Billroth, the Gentile Viennese medical professor, who, as noted above was later on friendly terms with his Viennese Jewish colleagues, wrote in 1876, *The Teaching and Learning of Medical Science*. Here he complained that Jewish Galician medical students pursued their studies while selling firewood on the streets of Vienna, "the gulf between German blood and Jewish blood" was too great to be bridged. Later he repudiated these words and ideas.

Karl Vogelsang, editor from 1875 of *Vaterland*, the official Catholic hierarchy newspaper, and Ernst Schneider, a member of Austrian Parliament, led the explosion of the virulent Austrian anti-Semitism of the 1880s. The latter's daughter married a Jew. Schneider: 'put all the country's Jews on a big ship, send it to the middle of the ocean, and sink it. This would end the Jewish problem for good' (c.1888).[31] Father August Rohling, author of *The Talmud Jew*, 1871, claimed that the Talmud described Christians as animals.

Political anti-Semitism made greater inroads into Austrian life than in Germany in spite of Emperor Franz Joseph's long reign of toleration. George Ritter von Schönerer (1842-1921) a powerful anti-Semitic voice from 1879 on: "Our anti-Semitism is not directed against the religion of the Jews, but against their racial peculiarities which have not changed under past oppression or present freedom."[32] Schönerer had Jewish ancestry, his wife, daughter of a rabbi.

Karl Lueger, head of the Christian Social Union, with the Pope's blessing, won the election for Mayor and City Council in 1895. The cry on the streets of Vienna: "Lueger will live and the Jews will croak!" Lueger associated with Jews, used them in his office, ("Who is a Jew, that I decide"), created the semi-socialist model that was later a theme of "National Socialism."[33] Lueger ruled and rebuilt Vienna for over a decade. Both Schönerer, who was a blatant street inciter and Lueger, the suave and handsome politician, were direct sources for Hitler's vision. Except, they emphasized Austrian national ambitions, whereas Hitler later argued for the *"Anschluss."* Hitler calls Lueger "the last great German to be produced by the Austrian Empire."[34] Lueger died in 1910.

The French, though they were shielded by geography from the magnetic surge of the Jews from east to west, did have a heritage of indigenous assimilated Jewish populations, as well as a sprinkling of new migrants throughout the centuries leading up to this 19th-century crisis. Early on, the socialist Pierre Joseph Proudhon (1809-1865): "The Jew is by temperament an anti-producer, neither a farmer nor an industrial worker, nor even a true merchant. He is an intermediary, always fraudulent and parasitic, who operates in trade as in philosophy, by means of falsification, counterfeiting, and horse-dealing."[35] Further, Alphonse Toussenel (1803-1885) in *The Jews, Kings of the Epoch: A History of Financial Feudalism* (1844): "I call by the despised name of Jew every dealer in money, every unproductive parasite living off the work of someone else...note well that not one Jew has done anything useful with his hands since the beginning of time."[36]

Ernest Renan (1823-1892), not to be considered an anti-Semite, was a theorizer, as with Francis Galton (see below). Renan: "...the Semitic race {the Jews} compared to the Indo-European race, represents essentially an inferior level of human nature."[37] To Renan, "...the Jews are a people of the desert, prophetic, not artistic...an inflexible Hebraic genius, all of a piece, like the bare rocks that loom up far off in the desert." Jewish genius: "...the eminently subjective characteristic of Arabian and Hebrew poetry is due to another trait of the Semitic spirit, to its complete lack of creative imagination and to the consequence absence of fiction."[38] True anti-Semitic French authors: Edouard Drumont, Edmund Picard, and Auguste Chirac (1838-1903): parasitism—the Jew constituted its "first and complete incarnation," Paris, 1896.[39]

The theme of Jewish parasitism, enunciated by Ahlwardt, before the Reichstag in 1896, thus had many prior and then enthusiastic contemporary advocates, and throughout European society. In theory, Jewish dominance and power in the abstract disciplines of trade, banking, philosophy, science, medicine, literature, the arts, seemed to argue for "their non-participation in good hard work," *e.g.*, Otto Boeckel's view of the Jews as exploiters of the rural peasantry. This position became the political rallying cry in the Austrian march toward Nazism. In fact, at the anti-Semitic demonstrations in 1923 in Austria, speakers claimed that Jews owned seventy-five percent of the apartment houses in Vienna, and that workers had to surrender three-quarters of their earnings to the Jewish bankers. Julius Streicher of Nuremberg spoke at these rallies urging Austrians to attack any woman who dates a Jew.[40]

Oddly, this theme was also echoed in the writings of the brilliant Englishman, Francis Galton, (1822-1911), first cousin to Charles Darwin. Galton, was one of the seminal scientific minds of the 19th century. In 1884, he wrote, "The Jews are specialized for a parasitical existence upon other nations, and...there is need of evidence that they are capable of fulfilling the varied duties of a civilized nation by themselves."[41] His student, the eminent philosopher/psychologist, Karl Pearson, 1857-1936, later (1924) agreed. "They {the Jews} will not be absorbed by, and at the same time strengthen the existing population, they will develop into a parasitic race."[42]

In France racial detestation of the Jews came to a head in the famous trial, 1898, of Captain Dreyfus for 'traitorous actions'. The world is insufficiently aware of the role of the Catholic Church in France for waging a bitter and underground war against him as a Jew and by implication the accusation that no Jew could be a patriot to the French Catholic nation. Hardly seven years earlier, in 1891, the Grand Rabbi of France, J. H. Dreyfus, had given a sermon in which he attempted to defuse this growing and by now volatile French anti-Semitism. "The French are this elect people of modern times, spreading abroad the blessed notions of liberty, equality, and fraternity. There is a direct parallel between this elect people and the elect people of the ancient world {the Jews}. Against the French there was arranged on the international level the same kind of 'jealousy' for having been divinely chosen which Israel had endured. The one and the other had to suffer in bringing their message to the world around them."[43]

An American Catholic theologian himself describes the leadership of the French Roman Catholic hierarchy in the prosecution of Captain Dreyfus in 1898, as adamant in going against the Jew. Hundreds/thousands of local Catholic priests gave sermons against the Jews and Dreyfus in a move to bolster the position of the Church.[44] In 1998, the 100th anniversary of Emile Zola's successful defense of Dreyfus and subsequent accusation of perfidy toward the governmental authorities, *J'Accuse,* France's Roman Catholic daily newspaper *La Croix*, apologized for its anti-Semitic editorials during the Dreyfus Affair.[45]

Jewish Self-Hatred

Here we begin with classic and not-so-classic exemplars. It, of course, began with a jolt, as noted in the previous chapter, in the writings of Moses Mendelssohn against his Yiddish-speaking, orthodox Talmudist confreres. In the Enlightenment, Jewish self-hatred focused on the ancient vernacular tongue, Yiddish: "A tongue of buffoons, very inadequate and corrupt," from which "a reader capable of elegant speech must recoil in disgust."

For Mendelssohn's close ally, Naphtali Herz Wessely, Yiddish: was "mutilated and confused., desolate and arid." Lazarus Bendavid (1762-1832), was a Berlin follower of Mendelssohn, principal of the Jewish Free School, 1806-1825; author of *Something on the Characteristics of the Jews*, in German. He condemned the Jewish character, argued against religious ceremonial laws. Judaism must become a true natural religion; otherwise, the assimilated youth will remain confused and wayward.

Much later into the 19th century, the theme remained. Isaac Marcus Jost, 1793-1860, an historian of the Jews: The Talmudists "stood outside the present time, living in an imaginary world."[46]

It is well known that the writings of Karl Marx, as noted above, son of converted Jews of a long line of rabbis, married into an aristocratic Christian Rhineland family, are replete with viciously anti-Semitic sentiments.

Writing in the *New York Herald Tribune*, Marx referred to "loan mongering Jews." In another setting on "The Jewish Question": "What is the world religion of the Jew? Huckstering! What is his worldly God? Money!" In an early letter to Arnold Ruge in 1842, Marx asserted that the "the Israelite faith" was "repugnant" to him. He called fellow socialist Ferdinand Lasalle "the Jewish nigger." Throughout his career, Marx equated Jews with the capitalist exploitation of the workers, the plutocratic domination of the Gentile working classes. In this, he mirrored contemporary anti-Semitic opinion, Jews as parasites.

It is hardly possible that Richard Wagner did not know of the rumors, the possible truth, that his biological father was Ludwig Geyer, the Jewish actor who married his mother after the death of her elderly husband, Wagner's ostensible "father." A raving anti-Semite, Wagner was especially provoked by his war to get his operas performed by the Paris Opera, as were the operas of his successful, fully Jewish rival, Giacomo Meyerbeer:

"Our whole European art and civilization, however, have remained to the Jew a foreign tongue; for, just as he has taken no part in the evolution of the one, so has he taken none in that of the other; but at most the homeless person has been a cold, nay more, a hostile onlooker. In this Speech, this Art, the Jew can only mimic and mock—not truly make a poem of his words, an art work of his doings."[47]

The same rationalizations may be attributed to the arch-anti-Semitic madman, Adolf Hitler. Hitler, born in Austria in 1879, arrived in Vienna in 1906. Jews had assisted his family and himself, including art dealers. As with the communist totalitarian V. Lenin, he was probably one-fourth Jewish. His father was the illegitimate child of a servant girl in a family of Jews with young men in the household. This grandmother later married a "Hitler."[48]

Hitler once asked Hans Frank, Governor General of Poland during the Nazi occupation, but earlier, legal advisor to the NSDAP, the "Party" to research the rumors that he, Hitler, had Jewish blood. While awaiting execution at Nuremburg in 1946, Frank made a written confession of this request by Hitler, stating that he, Frank, felt the research confirmed the rumor.[49] Hitler: "...the Jewish people, despite all apparent intellectual qualities, is without any true culture, and especially without any culture of its own. For what sham culture the Jew today possesses is the property of other people, and for the most part it is ruined in his hands."[50]

Classic exemplars of the divided state of mind of the educated Jew of the mid- to late-19th century were a number of French writers, here the brothers Reinach: Joseph Reinach, (1851-1900); Salomon Reinach (1858-1932); Theodore Reinach, (1860-1928). These French Jews were critical of their Judaic past, at the same time fighters for justice and equality for the Jews, and along the way, strong supporters of Captain Dreyfus. Theodore: Reinach: "Hatred, persecutions, legal restrictions have everywhere engendered in the Jews physical and moral decadence, all the vices of oppressed and deprived races." Salomon Reinach: "Talmud, those backward Jews who follow its rules…the inferiority of East-European Jews."[51]

Leon Kahn (1851-1900), editor of *L'Univers Israelite*: The Jew, before, "hypocrisy, cowardice, vice." Now, "liberty, equality, and liberty shall lift him up."

Julian Benda (1867-1956): "The narrowly Hebraic Jew, enslaved by the passion for the small and daily lucre, patient, fearful, thrifty, hard working, blind preserver of a bundle of customs which has lost its justification."[52]

Bernard Lazare (1865-1903) had a short but eventful life. He went through an evolution of thought in which he first saw the need for Jews to rid themselves of all their heritage and be completely absorbed into the French nation. Then his thinking evolved to an appreciation of the Jewish heritage, so much so that he saw the converted Jews: Heine, Marx, Borne, Lasalle, Moses Hess, Robert Blum, Disraeli, as examples of men who yet retained their Judaic "genius" and national character. At the very end of his life, he became an advocate of the French Zionist movement, editor of *Zion,* a friend and rival of Theodor Herzl.

Bernard Lazare: "What things of history has the Jew not felt? What has he not experienced? To what shame has he not been subjected? What pain has he not suffered? What triumphs has he not known? What defeats has he not accepted? What resignation has he not shown? What pride has he not displayed? And all that has left profound traces in his soul, just as flood waters leave their sediments on the valley floor."[53]

In the record of history, there needs be remembered pro-Semitic Jews: Alfred Naquet, member of the French Chamber of Deputies, Camille Dreyfus, editor of *La Nation.*[54]

As early as 1884, Sigmund Zins organized the *Union of Austrian Israelites* to help the youth of the Jewish community who "are more ashamed of being Jewish than anything else. If anti-Semitism must be fought we must begin with Jewish anti-Semitism."[55]

Perhaps the most notorious self-hating Jew was Otto Weininger. Unanimously seen as a brilliant thinker, he wrote as a Doctoral Dissertation: *Sex and Character*, at the University of Vienna in 1902. He was baptized a Christian in 1902, the day he received his doctorate. The next year he committed suicide at age of twenty-three: "The Aryan-like Man, knows extremes of good and evil, of brilliance and stupidity. The Jew-like Woman, is utterly devoid of genius, and hence always mediocre and imitative….the bitterest anti-Semites are to be found amongst the Jews themselves; and their anti-Semitism bears witness to the fact that not even they themselves consider their kind lovable."[56]

So intent were Vienna's Sephardic Jews to distance themselves from their East European Germanic fellow Jews that they placed themselves under the protection of the Sultan of Turkey.[57] The intermarriage rate in both Berlin and Vienna in 1900 was approximately 15 percent. Between 1868 and 1903, 9,000 Austrian Jews renounced Judaism. Gustav Mahler is reported to have converted when, after being considered for the position of music director of the Vienna State Opera, Wagner's widow objected to a Jew conducting her late husband's work. Also Arnold Schoenberg, Karl Kraus, Alfred Adler, psychologist, Victor Adler, head of the Social Democratic Party, Edmund Husserl, philosopher, the industrialist Karl Wittgenstein and all of his children converted to one or another Christian faith, in Austria, almost always, Catholicism.[58]

Arthur Schnitzler cites a friend, Louis Friedman, who vowed never to beget children lest he perpetuate the hated Jewish blood that flowed through his veins.[59] Jewish plutocrats Nathaniel Rothschild and Baron Maurice de Hirsch were virulent anti-Semites, de Hirsch giving $100 million to settle Jews outside of Europe.

Hermann Schwartzwals, a deformed Galician Jew was a brilliant civil servant, and virulent Jewish anti-Semite. He regularly laid wreaths on the grave of the German anti-Semite Eugen Duhring. However when promoted to Imperial Counselor by Franz Joseph, on the condition that he would convert, he refused. He got the job anyway, at the precocious age of 35. Karl Kraus, convert from Judaism, and the most popular pamphleteer in Vienna, became a vicious anti-Semite in his periodical, *Die Fackel*, strongly anti-Captain Alfred Dreyfus. Arthur Schnitzler: "Anti-Semitism became popular in the early 1880s in Vienna only when the Jews themselves took it up!"[60]:

"Franz Kafka's friend Felix Weltsch wrote in the Zionist journal *Self-Defense*, that the Jews must 'shed our heavy stress on intellectual preeminence…and our excessive nervousness, a heritage of the ghetto…We spend all too much of our time debating, and not enough time in play and gymnastics…What makes a man a man is not his mouth, nor his mind, nor yet his morals, but discipline…What we need is manliness."[61]

The "anti-anti-Semites" were ever busy creating lists of defectors, Jewish anti-Semites. Raphael Patai lists them: David Gordon (1856-1922); David Frischmann (1860-1922); Mikha Yosef Bin-Gorion (1865-1921); Yosif Haym Brenner (1881-1922); Abraham Schwadron, (1878-1957); Judah L. Magnes, (1877-1948); Max Naumann, founder of the *Verband National Deutscher Juden*, in 1921. The basis of this self-hatred was the presumably contemptible life of the Jews in the Diaspora.[62]

T. Lessing, 1930, presents another list of Jewish anti-Semites: Paul Ree, Otto Weininger, Arthur Trebitsch, Max Steiner, Walter Cale, Maximilian Harden.[63] Also, Wilhem Marr and G.R von Schönerer, see above. Much later, in our own day, Isaiah Berlin analyzed the special and egregious cases of Jewish self-hate exemplified in Marx and Disraeli. He also referred to the self-hate of Walter Rathenau (Chancellor of Weimar Germany, assassinated, 1922; and Simone Weil (1909-1943), philosophical mystic, converted to Catholicism in 1938, she became a fighter against fascism.[64]

Kurt Grunwals reports that *fin de-siècle* Jews took absolutely no interest in Judaism. As long as their environment did not remind them of their Judaism, it caused them no inner discomfort."[65] Raphael Patai reports on his own observing of a march of the Histradut, Labor Organization's celebration in Tel Aviv, in 1933: Printed on their banners of parade: "A parasitic people had become a people of workers."[66]

We have to view the Zionist movement as a product of the above events, the rampant anti-Semitism of the Gentile community, and the reactive Jewish self-detestation that flowed from their desire to be part of the modern world of French, German and Austrian life, their embarrassment with and resentment of their East European Yiddish/Talmudic past. The *Alliance Israelite Universale* in France, c.1860, *Union of Austrian Israelites*, 1884, and *Centralverein deutscher Staatsburger judischer Glaubens* (CV), 1893, were the leadership institutions which increasingly defended the Jewish community. The CV leadership: Max Bodenheimer, Franz Oppenheimer, Theodor Herzl. The First Zionist Congress was held in 1897.[67] Reinharz sees the Zionist argument as based on its potential for improving the Jewish psychological handicaps of the past: To Theodor Herzl the primary goal was to eliminate Jewish servility, opportunism, lack of dignity, the ghetto mentality. Also leading the movement were Richard Lichtheim, Max Bodenheimer, Kurt Blumenfeld, Sigfried Kanowitz, Adolf Friedmann, Martin Buber.

Theodor Herzl was born in Budapest, 1860, of a religiously liberal Jewish family. He preferred Nordic-looking women, sang Christmas carols at Christmas, fell into a bad marriage; he did not have his son circumcised. He wrote in his diary "If there is one thing I would like to be, is a member of the Prussian nobility." He saw the problem of being a Jew, and his own solution, Zionism, out of his vain attempt to leave it behind. However, he would not convert in order to turn his legal education into a judicial position. He remained a member of the Jewish *Gemeinde,* even though he was not religious. He saw anti-Semitism being turned into a racial phenomenon, "...the modern petrol." Herzl paid for the publication of his revolutionary book, *The Jewish State*, 1896. At the time he was literary editor of the *Neue Freie Presse,* perhaps the most liberal newspaper in Vienna. He was also a frustrated playwright. However, he was always respectful of the religious orthodoxy of many of his members. Herzl had to shift early Zionist conferences from Vienna to Munich because Vienna had no kosher restaurant. After his sudden death in 1904, at the age of 44, the Zionist movement was headquartered in Berlin.[68]

Sub-Surface Realities

In barely one and one half centuries, 150 years, the Jews had emerged from their enforced ghettoization, poverty, a disdained and powerless people, now to a minority which if one takes Gentile anti-Semitism literally, threatened the very power base of the non-Jewish world. Indeed, the Jews had learned and absorbed the institutional structure and symbols of the new civilization. This, the Christian leadership of the Renaissance and the Enlightenment had created.

Yet, they were still Jews, and for many Jews, self-haters. What did it mean? Neither the blatant anti-Semites, nor the Jews themselves understood it. Of course, it had to do with their ability not to be chained to the older Talmudic/Orthodox religious system of meaning. As a consequence of this abandonment of the past, they had sped forward to move into those institutional positions of society that connoted wealth rather than poverty, education, rather than ignorance, to attempt to rise to the top of society, rather than remain at the bottom of the well.

The only meaning with which all Jew haters could come up with was that the lurch for power and materiality seemed to be linked to Jewish enterprise. The grouse was that they were Jews, not Frenchmen, Austrians or Germans, certainly not Christians. Even as alienated, Jewish *Yiddishhkeit* seemed still to radiate a threatening strangeness, power from within the nation that often retained cross-national power alliances, the Rothschild banking/financial system. At the same time bearded black hatted, caftan clad Jews roamed around the pushcarts of the Leopoldstaadt in Vienna. The language of ignorance and hate: Jew, "parasite, falsifiers, fraudulent, mediocre, imitative, huckstering, vermin, bacillus of decomposition, cholera germs." Such terms were always associated with the fear that the Jews were taking over the world, their power and threat was of infinite durability. The anti-Semitic solution, the Jews must be ousted, the nation cleansed of their presence.

This contempt and abhorrence was not understood by most Jews. They wanted to slip unnoticed into this culture of dynamic change, to move silently with it, to explore its creative possibilities for the new. But somehow they could not lose this Jewishness that clung to them. It was almost as if the act of denouncing themselves, their heritage, all that was constituted of this persistent ethnicity/race, might yet allow them the anonymity of creation and success. Exchanging their Judaic heritage for success seemed to be key. Yet the Gentile never allowed them to forget from whence they had emerged.

Success derived from education and perseverance, even if it meant for the medical students to be selling wood on the bridges of the Danube tributaries. The Jew could not stop this striving. He could not act to please the anti-Semite by returning to the stained chains of the ghetto. Perhaps, he would leave, as so many Gentiles wished, to set up shop in the ancient homeland. But would not these Zionists, in effect vindicate the anti-Semitic rhetoric of the hate mongers? Many, many others opted for migration to America, a land of vast spaces, opportunities unlimited, perhaps even welcoming the poorest of Jews. But the thought of emigration was exactly the problem for the Jews of France, Germany, Austria. They were already middle class, competitive with the most educated, sophisticated of their Gentile neighbors. Already, they were contributing, often dying for the nations to which they had now sworn allegiance. They coveted this allegiance, in exchange for being emancipated from the "deformities" and burdens of the past.

Could this threatening situation have been defanged through some higher understanding, a new agreement on principle? How far assimilation, if even after many generations, often religious conversion, they were still "outsiders"? The lessons learned long ago from the Spanish Inquisition should have told them that even after conversion, the Jew in them would still constitute the burr for loathing and threat.

Endnotes, Chapter 8

[1] Berkley, G. 1988. *Vienna and Its Jews: the tragedy of success*, Cambridge, Mass.: Abt Books, p. 32.

[2] Melson, R. 1992. *Revolution and Genocide,* Chicago: Univ. of Chicago Press.

[3] *Florida Holocaust Museum,* "Anti-Semitism," n.d.

[4] Volkov, S. 1994. "Jews and Judaism in the Age of Emancipation: Unity and Variety," in *The Jews in European History*, ed. by W. Beck, Cincinnati: Hebrew Union College Press, pp. 73-92.

[5] Klemig, R. 1984. *Jews in Germany under Prussian Rule*, Berlin: Bildarchive Preussischer Kulture Besitz; Richarz, M., ed. 1991. *Jewish Life in Germany,* Bloomington: Indiana Univ. Press.

[6] Janik, A. and Toulmin, S. 1973. *Wittgenstein's Vienna*, N.Y.: Simon and Schuster, pp. 169-174; Berkley, *op cit.,* p. 36.

[7] Berkley, p. 5.

[8] Berkley, p. 37*ff.*

[9] Berkley, p. 29*ff.*

[10] Berkley, p. 35.

[11] Patai, R. 1977. *The Jewish Mind,* N.Y.: Scribner, p. 468.

[12] *Ibid.*

---

[13] *Ibid.*

[14] Patai, *op. cit.*, quote of Graetz, pp. 469-470.

[15] Harry Zohn, Foreword in Berkley, xiv-xv; in Berkley, *op. cit.*

[16] Berkley, pp. 69-70.

[17] Berkley, p. 66.

[18] In Graetz, 5:532, *History of the Jews*—quoted in Patai, *op. cit.*, p. 252.

[19] Berkley, p. 64.

[20] Marcus, J. R. 1934. *The Rise and Destiny of the German Jew*, Cincinnati: Union of American Hebrew Congregations, pp. 26-36.

[21] Leipzig: Hammer Verlag.

[22] Fritsch, Theodore. 1923, 1927. *The Riddle of Jewish Success,* Leipzig; Patai, p. 457; also see Weiss, J. 1996. *Ideology of Death,* Chicago: Ivan Dee.

[23] Berlin: Teubner.

[24] Kahn, F. 1922. Die *Juden als Rasse und Kulturvolk,* Berlin: Welt Verlag, cited p. 226; in Gilman, S. 1996. *Smart Jews: the construction of the image of Jewish superior intelligence,* Lincoln, NB: Univ. of Nebraska Press, p. 45.

[25] In Hilberg, R., 2003. *The Destruction of the European* Jews, Vol. 1, New Haven: Yale Univ. Press, pp. 17-19.

[26] Gilman, *op. cit.*, p. 46; Woltmann, L. 1904. "Rassenpsychologie und Kulturgeschichte," *Politisch-Anthropologische Revue* 3: 350-357.

[27] Berkley, p. 108.

[28] Gilman, *op. cit.,* pp. 47-48.

[29] Gilman, p. 50.

[30] Weyl, N. 1989. *The Geography of American Achievement,* Washington, D.C.: Scott-Townsend, pp. 242-243.

[31] Berkley, p. 85.

[32] Berkley, p. 94.

[33] Dawidowicz, L. S. 1975. *The War against the Jews, 1933-1945,* N.Y.: Holt, Rinehart and Winston, p. 11.

[34] *Mein Kampf.*

[35] Patai, *op.* cit., p. 456; Silberer, Edmund. 1948. "Proudohn's Judeophobia," *Historica Judaica,* April 1948, 10(1):67.

[36] Patai, *op cit.* p. 456

[37] Renan, Ernest. 1858. *Histoire generale et systeme compare des langues semitiques*, Paris: Im-premiere Imperiale.

[38] Gilman, S., pp. 49-50.

[39] Patai, p. 471.

[40] Berkley, p. 159.

[41] Patai, p. 457, in Weaver, T., ed. 1973. *To See Ourselves: Anthropology and Modern Social Issues,* Glenview, Il: Scott-Foresman, pp. 211-212.

[42] Patai, p. 457; Weaver, T., *op cit.*

[43] Dreyfuss, J. H. 1891. in *Sermons et allocations*, 2 vols., Paris: L. Kahn, 1908-1913, 1:277-283; Patai, pp. 330-333; see Ch. 7, Fichte's 1793 comparison of the Jews and the French.

[44] Carroll, J. 2001. *Constantine's Sword,* Boston: Houghton Mifflin, pp. 457-459.

[45] *Time Magazine*, June 26, 1998, p. 20.

[46] Patai, p. 466*ff.*

[47] Gilman, pp. 44-45: Wagner, R. 1912-1929. *Richard Wagner's Prose Works*, tr. by W. A. Ellis, London: Kegan Paul, 3:84-85.

[48] Berkley, pp. 109-110.

[49] Dawidowicz, *op. cit.,* p. 6.

[50] Hitler, A. Mein *Kampf*; Gilman, pp. 48-49.

[51] Patai, p. 473.

[52] Benda, J. 1900. *Dialogue à Byzance*, Paris, pp. 71-73.

[53] Patai translation, p. 476.

[54] Patai, p. 471*ff.*

[55] Berkley, p. 82.

[56] Patai, p. 463; Abrahamsen, D. 1946. *The Mind and Death of a Genius,* N.Y.: Columbia Univ. Press, p. 183*ff.*

[57] Berkley, p. 48.

[58] Comas, J. 1951. *Racial Myths,* Paris: UNESCO, pp. 27-32.

[59] Berkley, p. 55*ff.*

[60] Berkley, p. 58.

[61] Pawel, E. 1988. *The Nightmare of Reason: A Life of Franz Kafka,* London: Collins Harvill, p. 205; Gilman, p. 23.

[62] Patai, pp. 459-459.

[63] Lessing, T. 1930. *Der Judische Selbsthaas,* Berlin: Zionistischer Bucher-Bund.

[64] Berlin, Isaiah. 1970. "Benjamin Disraeli, Karl Marx, and the Search for Identity," London: *Jewish Historical Society of England,* Transaction, 1968-9.

[65] Berkley, p. 53.

[66] Patai, p. 359.

[67] Reinharz, J. 1994. "Jewish Nationalism and Jewish Identity in Central Europe," in *The Jews in European History*, ed. by W. Beck, Cincinnati: Hebrew Union College Press, pp. 93-122.

[68] Berkley, p. 49*ff.*

9

Destruction

The Discovery of High Jewish Intelligence

A philosopher friend of the Jews, Friedrich Nietzsche, *Human, All Too Human*: "The Jews have produced the noblest human being (Christ), the purest sage (Spinoza), the mightiest book and the most efficacious moral code in the world…In the darkest periods of the Middle Ages, when the cloud banks of Asia had settled low over Europe, it was the Jewish free thinkers, scholars, and physicians who, under the harshest personal constraint, held firmly to the banner of enlightenment and intellectual independence and defended Europe against Asia."[1]

It is interesting to note the ambivalence of Francis Galton (1822-1911) to the issue of the Jew in England, mid-19th century. As quoted in Chapter 8, in a letter of 1884, his derogation of the possible contribution of the Jew to high British civilization was a typical ethnic slur, from the vantage point of an English aristocrat. But in this case, an intellectual aristocrat, as with his cousin Charles Darwin, both grandsons of Erasmus Darwin, himself a prescient biological scientist, philosopher, one of the most distinguished of that turn of the 19th-century men-of-letters who brought the British Enlightenment to its peak accomplishments.

Galton's views were of a *class*. Perhaps he had written those comments about the Jews being parasites after his photographic study of Jews in the East End of London, made for comparative anthropological study. He did make similar analyses of Africans, including highly controversial comments about female Hottentot anatomy, and African Negro intelligence, in general.[2]

Earlier, in 1869, Galton had commented on the presence of genius in Jews and Italians, "both of whom appear to be rich in families of high intellectual interest." Galton, on his decades later photographic trip to Bell Lane School in London: Jews: "…children of poor parents, dirty little fellows individually, but wonderfully beautiful, as I think, in these composites"…in the adjoining Jewish quarter, "cold scanning gaze of man, woman, and child.…There was no sign of diffidence in any of their looks, nor of surprise at the unwonted intrusion. I felt, rightly or wrongly, that every one of them was coolly appraising me at market value, without the slightest interest of any other kind."[3]

Note the typical *Merchant of Venice,* Shylock, caricature, of Jewish eyes being poised on the market value, or the commercial dimension to his visit. Why, Francis Galton, must have wondered, in their impoverished condition, did they not appraise him with scientific "anthropological" analysis, rather than, 'how many pence might he be good for?'

Joseph Jacobs, an English Jew (1854-1916), who used much of Galton's research for his own analyses of Jewish intelligence, did see those Jewish ghetto eyes as reminiscent of an incipient Spinoza, rather than a Shylock.[4] However Galton did raise the comparative analysis of human intellectual ability out of its colloquial, humanistic and sociological level of discourse into mathematical, statistical measurable status, as predictive scientific principle. Even the issue of human genius could now be subject to hard data analyses.

Jacobs did this for Galton's own research. Using the statistical analyses that Galton had introduced in 1869, *Hereditary Genius,* Jacobs found that the average Jew has about 4 percent more ability than the average Englishman. Jacobs: "the weaker members of each generation have been weeded out by persecution which tempted or forced them to embrace Christianity and thus contemporary Jews are the survival of a long process of unnatural selection which has seemingly fitted them excellently for the struggle for intellectual existence."[5] Darlington, a more contemporary British Christian botanist and evolutionist saw the definitive shift in Jewish intellectuality and literacy as emanating from the Babylonian Captivity when their intellectuals took over the guidance and leadership of the religion, especially as they returned to Jerusalem, and separated from the *am ha aretz.*

At roughly the same period as Galton, 1874, the Louisiana physician Madison Marsh would comment on the 'fact' of the Jew's 'high average physique…{as being} not less remarkable than the high average of his intelligence."

Marsh was trying to argue for the hygienic practices prescribed in the Bible. Yet it was the first time that an American intellectual would make such an observation on contemporary Jewish intelligence, and report his research to a scientific publication.[6]

The debate that was being raised in France toward the end of the century over the rising influence of Jews on French culture had an unusual question set forth by Anatole Leroy-Beaulieu {a non-Jew} "...whether there is a Jewish genius or spirit, that is to say, whether in letters, science, or politics the Jew is characterized by a national genius or a national spirit different from that of the nations among whom he lives."[7] "...The nervousness which we have already noticed in them predisposes them to the most vibrating of the arts, that one which has most sway over the nerves" {Music}[8] "I have heard Germans urge this intellectual precocity of the Jews as a reason for debarring their children from the schools and colleges attended by other children, 'The struggle' they {the Germans} said 'between the sons of the North, the pale Germans with their blond hair and sluggish intellects, and these sons of the Orient with their black eyes and alert minds, is an unequal one.'"[9]

Sander Gilman notes Mark Twain's always insightful perspective on human experience. "Mark Twain's 1898 comment that the 'Jew's contribution to the world's list of great names in literature, science, art, music finance, medicine, and abstruse learning' is ' way out of proportion to the weakness of his numbers'...attributed the hatred of the Jews to the 'average Christian's inability to compete successfully with the average Jew in business."[10]

This period, the turn of the 20th century, saw one of the key transitions in the study of human ability, the creation of tests for predicting mental functioning and educational potential. In France, c.1900, Alfred Binet and his colleague, Theodore Simon, (both Jews), first developed a series of tests to attempt to predict which children would start school at a disadvantage, and thus would need extra tutoring assistance. The purpose at first was completely heuristic. Its success led to the development of the I.Q. score and the science of mental testing.

Key to the progress of this program was the development in England, in 1904, of the theory of the general factor in intelligence. Charles Spearman, in working with a number of ability tests, found a correlation in those tests that seemed to call for reasoning, cognitive processing, as compared with tests that seemed merely to show more surface structure, memory or perception skills, talents. He called it the "g" factor, denoting general intelligence, proposing that there is in mental functioning a locus of cognitive activity, here the source of scientific, literary, mathematical achievement.

In 1914, the numerical concept of I.Q., using a ratio consisting of educational age divided by chronological age, an average ratio equaling 100, set the norm for Europeans. This research was developed in Germany by the Jewish psychologist, Wilhelm Stern. The mental testing movement had moved into high gear.

Throughout the world the concept of human intelligence rose up from its anecdotal social (ethnic/national), vocational, and professional references to become a more universal and abstract scientific tool for the study of human behavior. Scholars would have to think of intelligence not merely in terms of its moral resonance but from a more generic perspective. Thorstein Veblen, the American social thinker, was early amongst this group of intellectuals to attempt to integrate the scientific with the sociological and historical points of view.

Veblen: "Men of Jewish extraction continue to supply more than a proportionate quota to the rank and file engaged in scientific and scholarly work....a disproportionate number of the men to whom modern science and scholarship look to guidance and leadership are of the same derivation." They differ from the gentiles "in distinctive traits of temperament and aptitude...Only in contact with Gentile cultures did the Jews achieve true greatness as "creative leaders in the world's intellectual enterprise" Among great men of science there have been many "renegade Jews."

Thus the Jew becomes a disturber of intellectual peace and is likely to become intellectually an alien. Spiritually, however, "he is more likely to remain a Jew, for the heart-strings of affection and consuetude are tied early and they are not readily retied after life {The record is clear about} that massive endowment of spiritual and intellectual capacities {of which the Jews} have given evidence throughout their troubled history, and not at least during these concluding centuries of their exile."[11]

The awareness that human intelligence is a discrete and malleable dimension in the variability of the species gave a great push to the eugenics movement, which early on became tinged with a strong liberal/socialistic ethos. A leading American eugenicist, Thurman Rice, in 1929, wrote as follows: "The chosen people of Israel are the most spectacular and successful of all experiments in human race culture...In every line of progress the Jew stands at or near the head of the list and has done so for forty or more centuries. In science and medicine, in philosophy and literature, in music and art, in statesmanship, business and finance, investigation will show that a large percentage of men at the top are Jews. There is no better argument for the universal practice of the principles of eugenics than the marvelous success of the Jewish race, the only race of importance to have a history of progress extending over a period as long as a thousand years."[12]

In 1921-22, in California, Professor Lewis Terman of Stanford University began his longitudinal study of young "genius" and their ontogenetic destiny. One hundred thousand youngsters were tested; about fifteen hundred were accepted with a mean I.Q. of 150, average I.Q. of Europeans, 100. It was clear from the very beginning that the number of those even admitting to four Jewish grandparents was out of proportion to the expectations, by at least twice. This research was communicated to academic communities throughout the world, to Germany also, which was then under Weimar democratic rule.

Ernst Kretchmer, who was doing research into the national/racial profile of Germans with respect to their high talents, did not include Jews specifically in his study. However, one prescient comment slipped out in this 1919 research. "There is a kernel of truth about claims of genius, even one would suppose, about claims regarding Jewish superior intelligence."[1314]

Two important textbooks were distributed to social science and psychology students in this era, and then into the early Nazi period, the latter without censorship, even with approval. Neither was incompatible with Nazism, the authors being full-blooded *Aryans*:

Hans Guenther, in 1930, tried to explain Jewish success in the modern world by their need to struggle to survive using their abilities in areas like commerce and finance, urban skills that were reserved for them when barred from traditional agricultural and social/political ways of life. The parasitism thus forced upon them, their need to learn to get along with majorities formed their ethnic character. This circumstance of living as a minority amongst foreign peoples, thus to adapt and survive, produced their prudent demeanor, adroit speech, versatile calculations, a special intelligence required in predominantly urban environments, trading in merchandise, money transactions. Thus is explained "the considerable average intelligence which distinguishes the Jewish people."[15]

Fritz Lenz, lead author of the most influential textbook on heredity and eugenics, translated into English, 1931, to be used in American colleges. It was later used in the *Third Reich*. His book had a very odd perspective on Jewish intelligence for one so favored by the Nazis. "...Next to the Teutonic, the Jewish spirit is the chief motive force of modern Western Civilization. The emancipation of the Jews has had an effect like that of one of the waves of Nordic blood upon the Indo-Germanic civilization. Were it merely through the diffusion of Christianity as one of the main roots of western civilization, the Jewish spirit has been decisively effective in universal history....Jews and Teutons are alike distinguished by great powers of understanding and by remarkable strength of will; Jews and Teutons resemble each other in having a large measure of self-confidence, an enterprising spirit, and a strong desire to get their own way—the difference being that the Teuton is inclined to seek his ends by force, the Jew rather by cunning."[16]

Conclusive Evidence

The Armistice ending World War I saw the Jews in a new state of assimilation in all the European states. They had participated as warriors for the national governments wherein they lived. Also, they had emerged even more fully from the ghetto/Yiddish/Talmudic world of their forefathers. Much of Eastern Europe was now made up of independent nations, Poland, Hungary, Yugoslavia, Czechoslovakia, Rumania, Bulgaria, the Baltic States. The education of the Jews, as citizens of their respective nations was now clearly centered not in the *Schule* or Yeshiva, but rather in the respective national public education systems leading up to the secular universities of the world.

As Louis Marshall, president of the American Jewish Committee stated to a 1919 Carnegie Hall audience of its members: "For the first time, the nations of the world recognized that, in common with all other peoples, we are entitled to equality in law…It has now become an established principle that any violation of the rights of a minority is an offense not only against the individuals but against the law which controls all the civilized nations of the earth."[17]

The great issue following World War I was legality and toleration, even hope that the issue of Jewish intelligence would no longer rear its controversial head.

Yet, the debate continued Some contemporary critics have noted that in contrast to the claim that the Jews in the *shtetl* married for intelligence, the scholar often marrying the daughter of the most successful businessman, most Jews in the post-emancipation period, after 1750, married within their social class. Here, the rich marrying with the rich, the poor, within their own circles.[18] This is probably true for the advanced nations of this period. However, after a thousand years of encapsulation it is also true that by the time of the 18th century and beyond, the nature and capabilities of Ashkenazi Jewish intelligence had already been fixed in all 18th-century Jewish sociological strata.

By the early 20th century, Jewish intelligence and achievement as entertained by higher social circles no longer elicited ethnic slurs, embarrassments. There was even a self-developing Jewish enclave in Palestine under the Mandate to Britain. Most important, Jewish intelligence had become a factual element in the universal language of science, in the study of human achievement. It could be interpreted in quantitative, mathematical parameters, placed in the context of all human ability and educated achievement. This was a structure of meaning that presumably barred ethnic or historic slurs, a concept subject to universal analysis, prediction, confirmation or falsification.

To the educated, the growing reality of powerful Jewish intellection, as it poured out onto the face of Europe and the Americas, could no longer be the mere intuitive stuff of anti-Semitic poison. I.Q. supposedly told a very different story about the Jews and their relationship with their gentile neighbors, if only one would listen, read and study. From 1901, the Nobel Prizes, which had been awarded in increasing percentages to Jews by Christian arbiters in Sweden and Norway, had public significance. There now seemed to be the germ of recognition, that in the 20th century a unique value was being placed on the Jewish mind, for the enhancement of Western Civilization itself.

By 1985, when one could argue that much of Jewish potential had been placed before the world, in terms of the betterment of all of human existence, the Jews, then about 13 million in total world population, out of the five billion humans on the planet, had won 16.8 percent of awarded Nobel Prizes, 91 out of 540.. Of the total awarding of Nobel Prizes, there is a consensus that many more German Jews (*conversos*) would have been discovered had their ethnic heritage been more closely analyzed. One example, Lise Meitner, a *converso* to Christianity, who fled the Nazis, was later overlooked for her work in nuclear fission, in favor of colleague, Otto Hahn, who quietly remained in Germany during the Nazi period.[19]

We must consider the fact that the Jews during these periods were subject to extreme discrimination in their admittance to all European and American colleges and universities. Further, the destruction of 6 million European Jews during the *Holocaust* meant that had this event not occurred, Jews could have even more demonstrated their intellectual significance, contributions now not made, to Western Civilization.[20]

Envy, Madness, Power—Germany

Prussian power grew throughout the 19th century. The defeat of Austria, 1866, the simultaneous unification of the German states under Prussian rule, then the defeat of France in 1871, all paralleled by the expansion of German research, science, and industry, by the end of the century catapulted this nation into a position of world leadership. She was even then dabbling in colonial expansion, becoming an important naval power.

World War I was a crushing blow to the egotism of this nation/culture which had produced some of the greatest literature, music, scientific and technological advances that Western Civilization had experienced. To be a German once signified membership in the most advanced nation/people of the world. The Jews had contributed much, and they were rapidly becoming Germanized, ever intermarried into the indigenous elite.

The heavy penalties of Versailles, the humiliation of defeat, inflation and unemployment undermined the new Weimar Republic. The final economic blows came with the depression of the early thirties. It was a time ripe for irrationality, the search for scapegoats for this come down populace from national eminence. Adolf Hitler came out of the war with a vicious Jew hatred. "If at the at the beginning of the War {World War I} and during the War, twelve or fifteen thousand of these Hebrew corrupters of the people had been held under poison gas, as happened to hundreds of thousands of our very best German workers in the field, the sacrifice of millions at the front would not have been in vain."[21]

It is fair to quote Lucy Dawidowicz on the general symptomatics of this threatening post-World War I anti-Semitism: "The Germans were in search of a mysterious wholeness that would restore them to primeval happiness, destroying the hostile milieu of urban industrial civilization that the Jewish conspiracy had foisted upon them."[22]

A nation that had militarily surged to the top of the power equation, in population and industrial wealth would not so humbly step back from its victorious peers. Weimar democracy sputtered, and its enemies roamed the streets of Germany. The German "Free Corps," the war veterans' organization sang "Mow down Walter Rathenau, The goddamned Jewish sow."[23]

With Hitler as one of its leaders the NSDAP *(National Socialist German Workers Party)* was founded and named in March 1920.

The communist and left-wing socialists had founded parties, along with Catholics and diverse right-wing groups. The reality of the Soviet Union, with the part Jew, Lenin and the full Jew, Trotsky feeding its international ambitions, infiltrated the German and Austrian political environment.[24] In counteraction, a failed Bavarian *Putsch* by the Nazis in 1923 put Hitler in jail for a year. *Mein Kampf* (1924) was written during this incarceration. In the 1923 elections the Nazis had gained approximately 800,000 votes. Their Jew-hate, nationalistic irredentism gained them increasing support from the lower middle classes who were suffering most from the economic crisis of the 1920s.

In the 1930 election the NSDAP garnered 6.5 million votes. In November 1932 they obtained 14 million votes out of a total of 45 million. This close-to-33 percent share, compared with the Socialist 20 percent, the Communist 17 percent, the Catholic Parties 15 percent, the Right Wing DNVP, 9 percent. The anti-Semitism even within the German bureaucracy was boiling. In October, 1932, before Hitler took power, Minister Von Gayl, Reichs Interior Minister, was considering a twenty year residency before eligibility for citizenship for *"Anhorigen niederer Kultur,"* i.e., Polish Jews.[25]

Hitler forced Hindenburg to order a new election in March 1933, because of the turmoil, the unclear majoritarian outcome of the November, 1932 election, and the 'threat of a Communist revolt'. The burning of the Reichstag on February 27, 1933 helped Hitler's party get 44 percent of the March vote. The Enabling Act of March 23 helped by Catholic Centrist parties, allowed Hitler dictatorial powers, and sent fifteen thousand radicals and Jews to the concentration camps in Dachau, near Munich, Oranienburg Camp, outside Berlin.

By July 8, 1933, Hitler had been able to suppress all other parties. Germany was now a one party state. Goebbels had met with Hitler on March 26, 1933 to organize a boycott of Jewish business...Goebbels: "...perhaps the foreign Jews will think better of the matter when their racial comrades in Germany begin to get it in the neck."[26]

"While anti-Semitism among the Germans was certainly extensive, it was not, except for a relatively small number, very intense….the typical German was only a lukewarm anti-Semite, although this may sound ridiculous in view of the Holocaust, evidence exists…Even after years of subjecting the Germans to constant anti-Semitic propaganda, Hitler complained that they were still 'insufficiently enlightened about racial matters and so the SS has to carry the main burden'…Their limited anti-Semitism combined with their almost innate love of legality and order, made most, though certainly not all, Germans look with disfavor and even disgust on the street violence against Jews which accompanied Hitler's assumption of power. Moreover, when the Nazis organized a boycott of Jewish stores for April 1, 1933, it failed miserably. In at least one district, purchases at Jewish stores actually increased."[27]

Goebbels was one of the most eager and ambitious of the anti-Semites among the Hitler entourage. He announced a book burning day in Berlin for May 10, 1933. Here he would announce and celebrate the end of "an age of exaggerated Jewish intellectualism."[28]

When the Nazis took over in 1933 in Germany there were examples of outrageous behaviors including the arrest of the above noted 15,000 potential enemies of Hitler. But German legality still had a small voice and by 1935, most were free and only one Jew remained in Dachau. The annexation of the Saar, by plebiscite, took place in 1935 and the military takeover of the Rhineland in 1936, also showed no outbreaks against the Jews of the areas.[29]

Yet the German people were being reeducated. Julius Streicher, a familiar figure on the streets of Vienna gave a speech in Germany proper to the Hitler Youth, on June 22, 1935: "Boys and girls, look back to a little more than ten years ago. A war—the World War—had whirled over the peoples of the earth and had left in the end a heap of ruins. Only one people remained victorious in this dreadful war, a people of whom Christ said its father is the devil. That people had ruined the German nation in body and soul…{ Hitler arose so that} the human race might be free again from this people which has wandered around the world for centuries and millennia, marked with the sign of Cain.

"Boys and girls, even if they say that the Jews were once the chosen people, do not believe it, but believe us when we say that the Jews are not a chosen people. Because it cannot be that a chosen people should act among the peoples as the Jews do today.

"A chosen people does not go into the world to make others work for them, to suck blood. It does not go among the peoples to chase the peasants from the land. It does not go among the peoples to make your fathers poor and to drive them to despair. A chosen people does not slay and torture animals to death. A chosen people does not live by the sweat of others. A chosen people joins the ranks of those who live because they work. Don't you ever forget that.

".....For you we had to accept mockery and insult, and became fighters against the Jewish people, against that organized body of world criminals, against whom already Christ had fought, the greatest anti-Semite of all times."[30]

The Jews had by 1935 been eliminated from all Civil Service positions in the arts, the universities, the government. Still Germany held on to a tattered remnant of legality. Emanuel Feuermann, fired from his position as Professor of Violoncello at the Berlin *Hochschule für Musik* in March of 1933, received a request in September, 1933, while living temporarily in Paris, from the *Judische Kulturfarband, Rhein-Ruhr*, asking if he could give several recitals in the synagogues of the area to bolster morale, there had been many suicides since Hitler's ascent to power. Feuermann had once lived in Cologne, as a teacher in the Gurzenich Conservatory. Since it was still not illegal for the Jews of the area to have musical concerts, the threat was only of brown-shirt disruptions, Feuermann agreed and played a series of concerts between October 14 and 19, 1933 in the synagogues of Cologne, Krefeld, Aachen, Essen, Bocham.[31]

In the spring of 1937, Feuermann, still carrying a German passport, traveled through Berlin by rail. On the train bound for Vienna, he met Hans Knappertsbush who implored understanding of the fact that he had accepted Nazi sponsorship of his conducting career, pleading for Feuermann to play under him in Vienna, as it was still free. Feuermann declined. Ironically a year earlier, 1936, Feuermann had turned down an invitation from William Steinberg, a Jewish conductor, who asked him to solo with an orchestra in Frankfurt, possibly a Jewish group.[32]

By 1935, there was concern within the government, especially by the head of *Reichsbank*, Hjalmar Schacht, that random attacks on the Jews and their property by the S.A., Brownshirt irregulars, and the SS, were proceeding in an unlawful and chaotic, manner, interfering with the financing of the re-armament program. His fear was the arousal of foreign Jewish economic opposition.[33]

On November 7, 1938, a 17-year-old Jewish immigrant to France entered the German Embassy in Paris and assassinated a minor German official of the Embassy. On November 9, Goebbels implied to a group of party leaders in Munich that riots had broken out against the Jews in several cities, and that Hitler suggested it might spread spontaneously throughout the Reich, now including Austria. The SS went to work, 20,000 Jews were arrested, this reported by Heydrich to Goering.

In reality, at least 35,000 were arrested and sent to a variety of concentration camps, 36 Jews were killed, amidst the vast destruction of *Kristallnacht*. Goebbels suggested a fine for the Jews of Germany of one billion Reichsmarks, the equivalent of four hundred million dollars. Interestingly, there was great consternation and opposition within the Nazi camp to the carnage of Nov. 9. Himmler tried to stop the looting that evening by ordering the SS out. Funk, the

Economics Minister and successor to Schacht, as well as Goering thought the riots were madness, as the international reaction was stern, and boycotts of German businesses and goods began to be put into effect all over the world.[34]

Because of the riots of *Kristallnacht*, the insurance and other damage incurred by Aryan businesses alone in Germany/Austria were estimated by Heydrich to be in the hundreds of millions of *Reichmarks*.[35] Of 30 men who had committed "excesses," meaning killing Jews, all of them party members, only four were expelled from the party and turned over to the courts. These, in February 1939, for moral crimes, *e.g.,* rape of Jewish women.[36]

Goering had very strong antipathy toward pogroms, because of the chaos, the unleashing of baser instincts, and their economic and political dangers. Even in September 1941, when remaining Jews in Germany and its territories were required to wear a yellow Star of David, Martin Bormann, chief of the Party Chancellery, announced that no molestation of individual Jews would be allowed…"it remains strictly prohibited," Jews would be dealt with in a rigorously "legal fashion."[37]

Note that on September 16, 1919, Hitler, in Munich as Private First Class in the German Army's intelligence and propaganda group wrote, at the request of his commander Captain Karl Meyer, a critique of anti-Semitism. He distinguished between "*geffuhlmaessigen*/emotional" anti-Semitism, leading to the chaos of a pogrom and an anti-Semitism of "reason/*vernunft*…which in the hands of a powerful government could lead to planned measures against the Jews and, in the end could bring about their complete elimination (*Entfernung*)."[38]

Austria

The dissolution of the Hapsburg Empire after the defeat in W.W.I, the creation of many new nations to the East, left Austria a small and weak player on the international scene. Here too, as in Germany proper, the economic situation was grave. The Jewish situation was likewise critical. There had been a diminution of Jewish immigration, as well as some Jewish emigration after the war. Here, the popular hatred of the Jews, their successes, power, the wealth and fame that they had brought to this nation and its capital, festered amongst the working classes.

Monsignor Ignaz Seipl, was elected Chancellor of Austria, in 1920. He saw the Jews as a people without a fixed territory, a people able to adapt to the environment of others. The Jews constituted an internal commercial society; they tended to make money without engaging in productive work. His fear was that they could use these skills to spread their own commercial spirit throughout remnant Austria. Austria therefore, must take steps to not becoming "culturally, economically, and politically dominated by Jewry."

Seipl, a subtle anti-Semite, used many individual Jews for his own political needs, but, in general wanted to keep them separated from Austrian life as "a decomposing element."[39] Yet, he could not suppress the fact that the Jews had served bravely in all the Austrian wars. In World War I, while Jews made up only 4.5 percent of the Empire's population, they made up eight percent of military officers.[40]

Engelbert Dollfuss became Austrian Chancellor in May 1932. He was a mild anti-Semite, allied with Mussolini in trying to keep the Nazis at bay. A tiny man, 4'11", and at 39, he was the youngest national leader in Europe. The Social Democratic Party which he had outlawed in 1934 revolted. Dollfuss put down the revolt with the army. The coming of the Nazis to the north had created a time of political chaos for Austria. Dollfuss, on the advice of Mussolini tried to outlaw all parties including the Austrian Nazis. A group of Nazis killed him in July 1934. Mussolini rushed divisions to the border, Hitler drew back, and Kurt von Schuschnigg, became Chancellor. After the Italian invasion of Ethiopia, Franco's fascist revolt in Spain, Hitler's invasion without opposition into the Rhineland, all in 1936, Mussolini switched allegiances and joined as a junior partner to Hitler.[41]

Vladimir Jabotinsky, came to Vienna amidst a growing Nazi movement, in December 1937. He spoke at the *Konzerthaus* with representatives of von Schuschnigg's government present on stage. After a four-hour speech, Jabotinsky, the fiery radical of the Zionist movement, raised before the audience a suitcase that he had kept hidden, and cried out, "Run, Jew, run."

Hitler had forced von Schuschnigg to appoint Arthur Seyss-Inquart, a devout supporter of the Nazis, as Interior Minister. Hitler then, before von Schuschnigg's planned and supported plebiscite over the question of Austrian independence from Germany, massed troops on the border demanding that von Schuschnigg allow Seyss-Inquart to form a government,. Schuschnigg resigned, and the Austrian Nazis, stormed into power, March 11-15, 1938, to take over Austria. Hitler would soon march in.[42]

Scenes, Vienna, March 1938: Orthodox women forced to remove their wigs, burn them and then dance in the Tabourstrasse of the Leopldstadt area of Vienna; a young Jewish girl outside her parents shop forced to bend down and rise up with a sign around her chest saying, "Please do not buy from me, I am a Jewish sow"; Austrian men urinating on the heads of Jewish women; Orthodox Jewish men forced to dance on torn-up Torah scrolls in the Wahring, outside their wrecked temples and prayer halls; Hitler youth gleefully cutting off a rabbi's beard; Chief Rabbi Taglich, aged 76, and former Vienna Surgeon General Pick, aged 77, on their knees scrubbing the street with caustic acid solutions; a blind Jew pushed from one Nazi to another inside a circle of young playful Nazis; cabaretist Felix Grunbaum clubbed to death; director of Scala Theatre,

Rudolf Beer, Solomon Frankfurter, 82, librarian for the University of Vienna, both jailed; Nobel Prize winner, Oscar Lowi and famed ear surgeon, Heinrich von Neuman, 79, jailed. Count Ciano, Mussolini's son-in-law, foreign minister protested to Germany about the inhumane treatment being given to the latter.[43]

Emanuel Feuermann, hearing that his concert violinist brother Sigmund was seen washing the streets bare-handed with brush and caustic acid appealed to Arturo Toscanini to help get Sigmund and the rest of the family out of Austria. Toscanini responded and with such outside influence, the family was able to leave, and emigrate to Palestine.

"What one saw in Vienna was unbelievable. The Viennese usually so soft and sentimental, were behaving worse than the Germans, especially toward the Jews. I have never seen quite such humiliating scenes in Berlin or Nuremberg. Or such Nazi sadism."[44] In Vienna, the sight of famous surgeons scrubbing the street with an acid solution, "the Viennese little man and his wife just grinned approval at the glorious fun."[45]

The German soldiers who marched into Austria took no part in these street scenes, while a few of their officers openly showed distaste. When a guide escorting two officers around Vienna pointed to a street-cleaning action, and remarked, "See how our Fuhrer has found work for the Jews," one of the officers replied, "That's not work, it's a *Schweinerei* {obscenity}." On another occasion two other officers went up to two elderly Jews scrubbing the pavement and, kicking over their buckets, told them they could go. The officers then cursed the Austrian storm troopers supervising them.

When Austrian Nazis crammed eighty Jews into a miserably small cell—their offense was that they had been reluctant to shine the shoes of gentile bystanders before a cafe—a German officer transferred twenty of them to another jail to relieve the insufferable overcrowding. When a sixty-five-year-old woman with heart disease broke down while street scrubbing, a car carrying German soldiers stopped and took her home.[46] This last incident is notable for another reason. Shortly before the car appeared, the woman's sixteen-year-old grandson had pleaded with the {Austrian} Nazis to let him take his grandmother's place. His plea had evoked the following response from a woman spectator: "Congratulations, Franky. That's interesting. That shows real class." The onlooker evidently knew the family and was observing the scene without too much concern.

Of course, cosmopolitan and left-wing Berlin had never been a Nazi stronghold, but the situation elsewhere in Germany proper was apparently not very different. Benno Weiser Varon, passing through the western part of Germany in September 1938 on his way to Holland, does not recall "a single derogatory remark or unfriendly gesture," though he was easily distinguishable as a Jew. "Even the Gestapo man whose advice I asked—for I had official permission for my transit—was friendly and helpful. It struck me that his anti-Semitism must have been impersonal. That of the Austrians was quite different."

In the eastern part of the country, some Jews in Stettin, sheltering a group of Austrian Jews trying to emigrate to Latvia, hardly a hospitable or even safe sanctuary for Jews in any case, could not understand the desperate desire of their Viennese co-religionists to emigrate at any price.

A few weeks later, the Nazis staged *Kristallnacht.* While *Kristallnacht* set a new low in anti-Semitic savagery throughout the Reich, Nazi fury in Austria surpassed the level reached in Germany. Innsbruck alone, with 130 Jews, accounted for over ten percent of all Jews killed outright during the eruption. (The official figure, reported by Gestapo chief Heydrich to Goering, listed thirty-five Jewish dead.). "Compared to Crystal Night in Vienna," says Simon Wiesenthal, "the one in Berlin was a pleasant Christmas festival."

The reactions of the German and Austrian publics were also different. A report of the American consul in Leipzig, Germany, for example, speaks of the Nazis throwing Jews into a small stream and then "*commanding* {italics. added} horrified and reluctant spectators to spit at them, defile them with mud, and jeer at their plight." In Baden-Baden, where all the Jewish men were rounded up and marched to the synagogue, one of the marchers later reported, "I saw people crying while watching from behind their curtains." Many non-Jews, he says, deeply resented the round-up. In Düsseldorf a German woman felt compelled to apologize to her Jewish fellow-passengers on a streetcar the following day.[47]

Note: Germans outnumbered Austrians in the SS by less than 6 to 1, while they outnumbered them in population in greater Germany by 11 to 1.[48]

Final Solution

Perhaps the most comprehensive and dispassionate, if deeply-angered analysis of the "final solution" is Raul Hilberg's *The Destruction of the European Jews*.[49] His analysis of the thinking that underlay the hysterical hatred and fury that Nazi rhetoric tried to drum up among all the Europeans, not merely the Germans, is succinct.

The Destruction Process: 1. 1933-1940—emigration; 2. 1940-1945—annihilation.

Steps in 2: A) Definition; B). Expropriation; C). Concentration; These were the stepping-stones to annihilation for the Jews who did not or could not get out. A). Definition: Required labeling the Jews in a systematic legal manner, so that they could be identified and regulated. B). Expropriation next led to the elimination of all Jewish wealth, personal, business, this taken over by the Nazi government. C). Required that the Jews be separated from the German or other peoples that had become part of the Third Reich so that their fate could be more easily organized and dispatched.

Annihilation by Nazi bureaucratic procedures: a) Laws; b) Implementation decrees; c) Ministerial or territorial ordinances or regulations; d) Announcements to the public in pursuance of laws and decrees; e) Announcements by local officials acting only in accordance with presumed necessities; f) Written directives not published; g) Broad authorizations to subordinates not published; h) Oral directives and authorizations; i) Basic understandings of officials resulting in decisions not requiring orders or explanations.[50]

To achieve the above goals, the Nazis had to reorganize the already highly polished German bureaucratic system and create an efficient operational structure. The bureaucracy easily fell into line.

Administrative Apparatus: A. Führer-Hitler; B. four hierarchical groups—1) ministerial bureaucracy; 2) armed forces; 3) industry; 4) party.[51]

The problem of "Definition" early on required a difficult set of decisions, prolegomenon to any further actions to be taken against the Jews. The Jews of Germany, especially, were well integrated into German life, intermarriage having been common for generations.

"Definition": The problem of assigning the label "Jew." Proposal, in early 1935—by race specialists of the party—suggested that all one-quarter-Jews be considered German, this by Dr. Kurt Blome, secretary of the medical association: "Among half Jews the Jewish genes are notoriously dominant" His proposal was rejected; perhaps it was not subtle enough. By November 14, 1935, the problem was decided, but the actual terminology not then adopted; later it was added by the Interior Ministry.[52]

Non-Aryans—

1. Jews: Persons descended from two Jewish grandparents belonging to the Jewish religion or married to a Jewish person on September 15, 1935, and persons descended from three or four Jewish grandparents.

2. *Mischlinge* of the 1st Degree: Persons descended from two Jewish grandparents but not belonging to the Jewish religion or not married to a Jewish person on September 15, 1935.

3. *Mischlinge* of the 2nd degree: Persons descended from one Jewish grandparent.

Both classes of *Mischlinge* could be "liberated" by special order of the Führer, from the Interior Ministry and the Reich Chancellery or the Army High Command and the Führer Chancellery.[53]

Behind all the careful bureaucratic decisions and the organization necessary to deal with the "Jewish question," as well as the planning out of the expansion and occupation of Europe by the Nazis and their foreign acquiescers, the Führer made his own thinking clear.

Speech by Hitler, January 30, 1939, German Press: "And one thing I wish to say on this day, which perhaps is memorable not only for us Germans: In my life I have often been a prophet, and most of the time I have been laughed at. During the period of my struggle for power, it was in the first instance the Jewish people that received with laughter my prophecies that some day I would take over the leadership of the state and thereby of the whole people, and that I would among other things solve also the Jewish problem. I believe that in the meantime that hyenas laughter of the Jews of Germany has been smothered in their throats. Today I want to be a prophet once more: If international-finance Jewry inside and outside Europe should succeed once more in plunging nations into another world war, the consequences will not be the Bolshevization of the earth and thereby the victory of Jewry, but the annihilation [*Vernichtung*] of the Jewish race in Europe."[54]

By November 1940, with Czechoslovakia and Poland already under his belt, Northern France, Scandinavia and the Low countries, being digested, England undergoing the Blitz, Hitler was confident, now a subtle rationalization.

Hitler, November 10-11, 1940: "It was a battle against satanical power, which had taken possession of our entire people, which had grasped in its hands all key positions of scientific, intellectual, as well as political and economic life, and which kept watch over the entire nation from the vantage point of these positions. It was a battle against a power which at the same time, had the influence to combat with the law every man who attempted to take up battle against them and every man who was ready to offer resistance to the spread of this power. At that time, all powerful Jewry declared war on us."[55]

Chief of Reichchancellery Lammers to Martin Bormann, June 7, 1941: "The *Führer* has not agreed to the regulation proposed by the Reich Minister of the Interior, {that the Reich Jews were stateless or protectees} primarily because he is of the opinion that after the war there would not be any left in Germany anyhow."[56]

On June 22, 1941, Nazi Germany invaded Russia, first through the Russian occupied Polish territories. They made rapid advances, massive numbers of Russian troops surrendering. Stalin, incompetently, was caught by surprise, believing in the integrity of the Non-Aggression Pact with Germany, signed in August 1939. This agreement allowed for the September 1940 dividing up of Poland. Stalin subsequently attacked Finland and the Baltic States. Earlier, 1939, Hitler did not believe that the French and British would make good on their guarantees to Poland on its political integrity. And thus W.W. II officially began.

One month after the invasion of the Soviet Union, "On July 22,1941, Hitler speaking to Croatian Marshal Kvaternik, said that if there were no more Jews in Europe, the unity of the European states would not be disturbed anymore."[57]

'Eichmann was called into Heydrich's office, toward the end of summer, 1941, where Heydrich said to him: I have just come from the *Reichsführer*: the *Führer* has now ordered the physical annihilation of the Jews.'[58]

{Correction by Hilberg}: Order of July 31, 1941. Three-sentence letter from Goering to Reinhardt Heydrich, giving him the authority to organize the Final Solution to the Jewish Question in Europe. Eichmann in his Memoirs stated that at Heydrich's request he {Eichmann} had drafted the order, so that Heydrich could submit it to Goering, who then signed it as an open-ended order awaiting Hilter's nod. Heydrich wanted it *his* to be done. Hitler did, as Eichmann states, sign on. Not long after that, Heydrich did come into Eichmann's office to tell him that Himmler had received the oral order from Hitler, then passed it down to Heydrich.[59]

"Ribbentrop himself assured the Bulgarian Foreign Minister, Popov, November 27, 1941 "...that at the end of the war all Jews would have to leave Europe. That was an unalterable decision of the *Führer.*"[60]

On November 29, 1941, Heydrich sent messages to the *Staatssekretarie* and chiefs of the SS main office for a "Final Solution" conference. In the invitation he said:

"Considering the extraordinary importance which has to be conceded to these questions, and in the interest of achieving the same viewpoint by all central agencies concerned with the remaining work in connection with the final solution, I suggest that these problems be discussed in a conference, especially since the Jews have been evacuated in continuous transports from the Reich territory, including the *Protektorat* of Bohemia and Moravia, to the East, ever since October 15, 1941."[61]

The conference was originally scheduled for December 9, 1941, postponed at the last minute, {*i.e.*, December 7, 1941—The Japanese attack on Pearl Harbor}. The conference was held at Am Grossen Wansee No 50/58 Headquarters of the RSHA (just north of Berlin) on Jan. 20, 1942 at`12 noon.[62]

Clearly this conference that settled the structure of the fulfilling of the "final solution" was planned while the Nazi war machine was still in the ascendancy. The failure to capture Moscow in December/January 1941/42 was merely an 'unfulfilled promise', the disaster at Stalingrad still a year off, February, 1943.

Goebbels: "Not much will remain of the Jews...A judgment is being visited upon the Jews [which is] barbaric...The prophesy which the *Führer* made about them for having brought on a new world war is beginning to come true in a most terrible manner."[63]

Hitler, September 30, 1942: "In my *Reichstag* speech of September 1, 1939 {really January 30,1939}, I have spoken of two things: first, that now that the war has been forced upon us, no array of weapons, and no passage of time will bring us to defeat, and second, that if Jewry should plot another world war in order to exterminate the Aryan peoples of Europe, it would not be the Aryan peoples which would be exterminated, but Jewry....At one time, the Jews of

Germany laughed at my prophecies. I do not know whether they are still laughing or whether they have already lost all desire to laugh. But right now I can only repeat; they will stop laughing everywhere, and I shall be right also in that prophecy."[64]

Special communication to Hitler on the progress of the second sweep of the SS *Einsatzgruppen "fighters"* a more systematic destruction of the Jews of Russia and the Ukraine than had occurred in the first killings by small groups of SS working behind the front lines in 1941, consequent on those advances into Eastern Poland, the Baltic States, the Ukraine, White Russia and Russia proper "The figure of Jews killed in Bialystock, South Russia, and the Ukraine from August through November 1942 was 363,211—Himmler to Hitler, December 29,1942, NO-1128.[65] Hilberg here notes that by the end of 1942, the Jews of the Ukraine had been wiped out, here with much help from Ukrainian volunteers, whose especially "desirable" assignment, sometimes intolerable for Germans, was the killing of Jewish women and children; also participating, Roumanian units, Latvian and Lithuanian auxiliaries, the latter, well paid in *Reichsmarks*.[66]

A year later: "Goering spoke of burned bridges and of a position 'from which there is no escape.'"[67] "Himmler and also Goebbels explained that the 'Final Solution' was a task that could not have been postponed, because in world history there was only one Adolf Hitler and because the war had presented to the German leadership a unique opportunity for 'solving the problem.'[68]

Clearly, at this late date, February 1943, after 500,000 German and other Axis casualties and many more hundreds of thousands captured at Stalingrad, the writing on the wall began to seem clearer. By July 1943, the Allied invasion of North Africa had been completed, 250,000 German and Italian troops killed and captured.

At the same moment the great failure of the Nazi tank armies against the Russians at Kursk, July-August, 1943, was occurring, and in August, the invasion by the British and Americans of Sicily, then Italy (September) 1943. It was becoming clear that the only offensive tack open to Nazis was against the unarmed Jews. On October 4, 1943, Himmler addressed a meeting of SS-*Gruppenfueherer* (lieutenant generals): "I also want to refer you here, in complete frankness, to a really grave matter. Amongst ourselves, this once, it shall be uttered quite frankly; but in public we shall never speak of it....

"I am referring to the evacuation of the Jews, the annihilation of the Jewish people. This is one of those things that are easily said. 'The Jewish people is going to be annihilated' says every party member. 'Sure it's in our program, elimination of the Jews, annihilation—we'll take care of it.' And then they all come trudging, eighty million worthy Germans, and each one has a decent Jew. Sure, the others are swine, but this one is an A-1 Jew. Of all those who talk this way, not one has seen it happen, not one has been through it. Most of you must know what it means to see a hundred corpses lie side by side, or five hundred, or a thousand. To have stuck this out and—excepting cases of human weakness—to have kept our integrity, this is what has made us hard. In our history, this is an unwritten and never to be written page of glory..."[69]

Again, Himmler, in a speech, June 21, 1944, two weeks after the successful Normandy, France landings by American and British troops, rationalized the now expeditious destruction of the Jews by noting that "Later generations would have neither the strength nor the opportunity to finish the Jews."[70]

Hilberg's research revealed to him that the hierarchy of Nazism, Hitler, Goering, Goebbels, Himmler, Heidrich, Eichmann, knew from the beginning both the plans and the factuality of what was going on in pursuit of the destruction of European Jewry. Hilberg: "Hitler himself may never have signed an order to kill the Jews. On the other hand, there are records of his utterances in the form of comments, questions, or 'wishes'. What he actually meant, or whether he really meant it, might have been a matter of tone as well as of language. When he spoke 'coldly' and in a 'low voice' about horrifying decisions 'also at the dinner table' then his audience knew that he was 'serious.'"[71]

Realities

On August 15, 1941, Himmler himself visited Minsk. The war in the East was going very well. He asked *Einsatzgruppe* B Commander Nebe to shoot a batch of a hundred people, so that he could see what one of these "liquidations" really looked like. Nebe obliged. All except two of the victims were men. Himmler spotted in the group a youth of about twenty who had blue eyes and blond hair. Just before the firing was to begin, Himmler walked up to the doomed man and put a few questions to him.

> Are you a Jew?
> Yes.
> Are both of your parents Jews?
> Yes.
> Do you have any ancestors who were not Jews?
> No.
> Then I can't help you!

As the firing started, Himmler was even more nervous. During every volley he looked to the ground. When two women could not die, Himmler yelled to the police sergeant not to torture them.

When the shooting was over, Himmler and a fellow spectator engaged in conversation. The other spectator-witness was *Obergruppenführer* von dem Bach-Zelewski, an extremely high ranked SS officer, who was later delivered to a hospital.{nervous breakdown} Von .dem Bach addressed Himmler:

Reichsführer, those were only a hundred.

What do you mean by that?

Look at the eyes of the men in this *Kommando*, how deeply shaken they are! These men are finished *(fertig)* for the rest of their lives. What kind of followers are we training here? Either neurotics or savages!

Himmler was visibly moved and decided to make a speech to all who were assembled there. He pointed out that the *Einsatzgruppe* was called upon to fulfill a repulsive *(widerliche)* duty. He would not like it if Germans did such a thing gladly. But their conscience was in no way impaired, for they were soldiers who had to carry out every order unconditionally. He alone had responsibility before God and Hitler for everything that was happening. They had undoubtedly noticed that he hated this bloody business *(dass ihm das blutige Handwerk zuwider ware)* and that he had been aroused to the depth of his soul. But he, too, was obeying the highest law by doing his duty, and he was acting from a deep understanding of the necessity for this operation.

Himmler told the men to look at nature. There was combat everywhere, not only among men but also in the world of animals and plants. Whoever was too tired to fight must go under *(zugrunde gehen)*. The most primitive man says that the horse is good and the bedbug is bad, or wheat is good and the thistle is bad. The human being consequently designates what is useful to him as good and what is harmful as bad. Didn't bedbugs-and rats have a life purpose also? Yes, but this has never meant that man could not defend himself against vermin.

After the speech Himmler, Nebe, von dem Bach, and the chief of Himmler's Personal Staff, Wolff, inspected an insane asylum. Himmler ordered Nebe to end the suffering of these people as soon as possible. At the same time, Himmler asked Nebe "to turn over in his mind" various other killing methods more humane than shooting. Nebe asked for permission to try out dynamite on the mentally ill people. Von dem Bach and Wolff protested that the sick people were not guinea pigs, but Himmler decided in favor of the attempt. Much later, Nebe confided to von dem Bach that the dynamite had been tried on the inmates with woeful results.[210]

The shooting scheduled for the morning, was to be followed by an inspection of a prisoner transit camp, lunch, a drive through the ghetto, the inspection of the mental asylum, and a visit to a farm.[72]

In November 1943 in Westerbork, a Nazi transit camp in Netherlands a premature baby born of a Jewish woman was brought to the officials of the camp. "There it received medical attention on order of the commandant, was placed in an incubator, and, once viable, deported to Auschwitz."[73]

Hitler's final political testament, April 29, 1945:

"It is untrue that I or anyone else in Germany wanted the war in 1939. It was desired and instigated exclusively by those international statesmen who were either of Jewish descent or worked for Jewish interests.......Centuries will pass away, but out of the ruins of our towns and monuments the hatred against those finally responsible, whom we have to thank for everything, international Jewry and its helpers, will grow....

"I also made it quite plain that if the nations of Europe were once more to be regarded as mere chattel to be bought and sold by these international conspirators in money and finance, then that race, Jewry, which is the real criminal of this murderous struggle will be saddled with the responsibility. Furthermore, I left no one in doubt that this time not only would millions of children of Europe's Aryan people die of hunger, not only would millions of grown men suffer death, and not only would hundreds of thousands of women and children be burned and bombed to death in the cities, but that the real criminal {the Jew} would also have atoned for his guilt, even if by more humane means {gas chambers}.

"...I do not wish to fall into the hands of an enemy who would require a new spectacle organized by the Jews for the amusement of their hysterical masses...."[74]

Hans Frank, General Gouverneur of Poland, 1939-1945, speech, December 19, 1940: "...relatives of military personnel surely were sympathizing with men stationed in Poland, a country 'which is so full of lice and Jews.....he {Frank} could not rid the country {Poland} of lice and Jews in a year."[75]

Testimony by Hans Frank, General Gouverneur of Poland, 1939-1945 April 18,1946[76]

German Defense Counsel, Dr. Seidel: "Did you ever participate in the annihilation of the Jews?"

Hans Frank: " I say 'yes'; and the reason why I say 'yes' is because, having lived through five months of this trial, and particularly after having heard the testimony of the witness Hoess, my conscience does not allow me to throw the responsibility solely on these minor people. I myself have never installed an extermination camp for Jews or promoted the existence of such camps; but if Adolf Hitler personally laid that dreadful responsibility on his people , then it is mine too, for we have fought Jewry for years; and we have indulged in the most horrible utterances—my own diary bears witness against me. Therefore, it is no more than my duty to answer your question with 'yes'. A thousand years will pass and still this guilt of Germany will not have been erased."[77]

Affidavit by Hermann Friedrich Graebe, November 10, 1945, post-World War II questioning of German eye witnesses, by allies.[78]

"The father was holding the hand of a boy about ten years old and was speaking to him softly; the boy was fighting his tears. The father pointed to the sky, stroked his head, and seemed to explain something to him…I remembered a girl, slim with black hair who passed close to me, pointed to herself, and said 'Twenty-three.'….The people, completely naked, went down some steps which were cut in the clay wall of the pit and clambered over the heads of the people lying there, to the place where the SS men directed them. Then they lay down in front of the dead or injured people; some caressed those who were still alive and spoke to them in a low voice. Then I heard a series of shots."[79]

Endnotes, Chapter 9

[1] Quoted in Gilman, S. 1996. *Smart Jews: the construction of the image of Jewish superior* intelligence, Lincoln, NB: Univ. of Nebraska Press, p. 45.

[2] Galton, F. 1885. "Photographic Composites," in *The Photographic News* 29, April 17:243-246; Galton, F. (1852). *Narrative of an Explorer in Tropical South Africa*, London: Ward, Locke and Co., 1890, pp. 53-54.

[3] Galton, F. 1869. *Hereditary Genius: An Inquiry into its Laws and Consequences*, London: Macmillan, Ch. 23 on Race, Ch. 4 on Jews and Italians; Gilman, *op. cit.*, quotes, pp. 33-34; C. Russell writing in 1900 states of the Jewish East End school children: "The foreign children in the East End are universally allowed to be sharper and more intelligent than the English and they carry off a large percentage of the prizes and scholarships." In Weyl, N., and Possony, S. T. 1963. *The Geography of Intellect*, Chicago: Regnery, p. 162.

[4] Jacobs, J. 1886. "Are Jews, Jews?"; in "The Comparative Distribution of Jewish Ability," *Journal of the Anthropological Institute of Great Britain and Ireland*, 15:365, xxxiii, in Patai, R. 1977. *The Jewish Mind*, N.Y.: Scribner, pp. 325-327; Gilman, *op. cit.*, pp. 36-38.; see also, Hughes, A .G 1928. "Jews and Gentiles, Their Intellectual and Temperamental Differences," *The Eugenics Review*, London, July.

[5] Jacobs, J. 1891. *Studies in Jewish Statistics*, London: D. Nutt; Jacobs, J. 1886. "The Comparative Distribution of Jewish Ability," *Journal of the Anthropological Institute of Great Britain and Ireland*, 15:365, in Patai, *op. cit.*, pp. 325-327; Gilman, *op. cit.*, pp. 36-38; Darlington, C .D. 1969. *The Evolution of Man and Society*, N.Y.: Simon and Schuster, pp. 187-189.

[6] Marsh, M. 1874. "Jews and Christians," in *The Medical and Surgical Reporter*, 30: 343-344; in Gilman, p 53.

[7] Leroy-Beaulieu, A. 1893. *Israel among the Nations: A Study of Jews and Anti-Semitism*, Paris: Levy, p. 226.

[8] Leroy-Beaulieu, *op. cit.*, p. 236; Gilman, p. 51; Leroy-Beaulieu, pp. 171-172.

[9] Gilman, p. 4*ff.*

[10] Twain, M. 1985 (1898). "Concerning the Jews", Philadelphia: Running Press; in Foner, P. S. 1958. *Mark Twain, Social Critic*, N.Y.: International Publishers; quoted in Gilman, pp. 19-20.

[11] Veblen, T. (1857-1929). 1919. "The Intellectual Preeminence of Jews in Modern Europe," *Political Science Quarterly,* 33-42.; Patai, pp. 331-332; Gilman, p. 42.

[12] Gilman, p .41, quotes Rice, T. B. 1929. *Racial Hygiene: A Practical Discussion of Eugenics and Race Culture,* N.Y.: Macmillan, pp. 13-14.

[13] Kretschmer, E. 1919. *Geniale Menschen,* Berlin: Julius Springer, 1929, p. 79; Gilman, pp. 53-54.

[14] See also a contemporary Jewish analysis: Fishberg, M. 1918. "Rassenlichtung der Juden," in *Statistik der Juden,* Berlin: Judischer Verlag, pp. 70-86.

[15] Guenther, H. F. K. 1930. *Rassenkunde des judischen Volke,.* Munich: J. F. Lehmann, pp. 202-203, cited in Patai, pp. 304-305.

[16] Lenz, F., Bauer, E., Fischer, E. 1931. *Human Heredity,* Ch. by Fritz Lenz, "The Inheritance of Intellectual Gifts," N.Y.: Macmillan, pp. 674-677; Patai, p. 327*ff;* Gilman, pp. 53-54.

[17] Quoted in Sachar, H. 2005. *A History of the Jews in the Modern World,* N.Y.: Knopf.

[18] Feuer, L. 1983. "The Sociobiological Theory of Jewish Intellcctual Achievement: A Sociological Critique," in J. Meier *et al.,* eds. *Ethnicity, Identity, History…* New Brunswick, N.J.: Transaction, pp. 93-125.

[19] Medawer, J., and Pyke, D. 2001. *Hitler's Gift,* N.Y.: Arcade.

[20] Gilman asserts that most listings of Jewish Nobel Laureates in Storfer, M. D. 1990. *Intelligence and Giftedness,* San Fransisco: Jossey-Bass, especially, pp. .322, 273, 379, underrate the number of Jewish/German winners;. Herman, A., ed. 1978. *Deutsche Nobelpreiztrager,* Munich: Moos; also, Stenzel, D., and G. 1992. *Das grosse Lexikon der Nobelpreistrager,* Hamburg: Verlag Dr. Kovac; Bagchi, A. K. 1988. *Hinduja Foundation Encyclopedia of Nobel Laureates, 1901-1987.* Delhi: Konark; Breit, W., and Spencer, R. W. 1990. *Lives of the Laureates: Ten Nobel Economists,* Cambridge: MIT Press; Crawford, T. 1992. *Nationalism and Internationalism in Science, 1880-1939,* Cambridge: Cambridge Univ. Press; Feuer, L. 1983. "The Sociobiological Theory of Jewish Intellectual Achievement: A Sociological Critique," in *Ethnicity, Identity, History: Essays in Memory of Werner J. Calman,* ed. by J. B. Maier and C. I. Waxman, New Brunswick, N.J.: Transaction; Gilman, p. 18, note 28; Patai, R., and Patai, J. *The Myth of the Jewish Race,* pp. 158-159.

[21] Dawidowicz, L .C. 1975. *The War against the Jews, 1933-1945.* N.Y.: Holt Rinehart and Winston, p. 3; Adolf Hitler, *Mein Kampf,"* the final chapter.

[22] Dawidowicz, *op. cit.,* p. 47.

[23] Dawidowicz, *op. cit.,* p. 46. Rathenau, a Jewish Chancellor of Germany, was to be assassinated in 1922.

[24] Cowen, Tyler. 1997. "The Socialist Roots of Modern Anti-Semitism," *The Independent Institute*; Rivkin, Ellis. 1971. *The Shaping of Jewish History,* N.Y.: *On-Line;* Rivkin, cited in *On-Line,* argues that Jews have always prevailed, benefited under capitalism, suffered under socialism.

[25] Adam, Uwe, 1972, *Judenpolitik in Dritten Reich,* Düsseldorf, cited in Hilberg, R., ed. 1985. *The Destruction of the European Jews,* 2nd ed., Vol. I, New Haven: Yale Univ. Press, p. 33.

[26] Cited in Dawidowicz, p. 52.

[27] Berkley, G. E. 1988 *Vienna and Its Jews, the tragedy of success* Cambridge, Mass: Abt Books, p. 306; see also Evans, R. 2005. *The Third Reich in Power, 1933-39,* N.Y.: Penguin Press.

[28] Zweig, A. 1983 "Ruckblick auf Barberei und Buchverbrennung," in *Das Vorspiel: Die Bucherverbrennung am 10 Mai 1933,* ed. by Thomas Friedrich, Berlin: LitPol, 1983, pp. 43-45; Gilman, p. 84.

[29] Berkley, *op. cit.,* p. 360*ff.*

[30] In Hilberg, Vol. I, 2nd ed., p. 20.

---

[31] Itzkoff, S. W. 1995. *Emanuel Feuermann, Virtuoso*, 2nd ed., Kronberg/Frankfurt, Germany, pp 128-129.

[32] Itzkoff, *op cit.*, p. 180.

[33] Hilberg, R., 2003. *The Destruction of the European* Jews, Vol. I, 3rd ed., New Haven: Yale Univ. Press, pp. 34-35.

[34] Hilberg, Vol. I, 3rd ed., *op. cit.*, pp. 36-41.

[35] Hilberg, Vol. I, 3rd ed., pp. 42-43.

[36] Hilberg, Vol. I, 3rd ed., pp. 44-45.

[37] Hilberg, Vol. I, 3rd ed., pp. 45-46.

[38] Deuerling, Ernst, ed. *Der Aufstieg der NSDAP in Augenzeugenberichten* Munich, 1974, in Hilberg, Vol. 1, 3rd ed., pp. 46-47.

[39] Berkley, p. 146.

[40] Berkley, p. 37*ff.*

[41] Berkley, p .209 *ff.*

[42] Berkley, p. 247.

[43] Berkley, p. 260*ff.*

[44] Shirer, William. 1947. *The Nightmare Years 1930-1940*, N.Y.: Knopf.

[45] Berkley, Ch. 25 "The Righteous Are Too Few," pp. 307-308

[46] Berkley, p. 308.

[47] Berkley, p. 310.

[48] Berkley, p. 315.

[49] Hilberg, Vol. I, 3rd ed.

[50] Hilberg, Vol. I, 3rd ed., p. 50 *ff.*

[51] Hilberg, p. *52ff, op cit.*; Neumann, F. 1944. *Behemoth*, 2nd ed., N.Y.: Harper and Row. pp. 365-399, 468-470.

[52] Hilberg, Vol. I, 3rd ed., pp. 61-77.

[53] Hilberg, Vol. I, 3rd ed., pp. 75-77.

[54] Hilberg, Vol. II, 3rd ed., p. 410.

[55] Quoted in Hilberg, Vol. I, 2nd ed., p. 19.

[56] Hilberg, Vol. II, 3rd ed., p. 417, note 26.

[57] Hilberg, Vol. II, 3rd ed., p. 417, note 28.

[58] Hilberg, Vol. II, 3rd ed., p. 418 (copied from earlier editions).

[59] Hilberg credits Uwe Adam for uncovering the method of Nazi bureaucratization of the death structure; Hilberg, R. 1996. *The Politics of Memory* Chicago: Ivan Dee, pp 78-80.

[60] Hilberg, Vol. II, 3rd ed., p. 800, note 32, November 27, 1941.

[61] Hilberg, Vol. II, 3rd ed., pp. 420-421, note 37.

[62] Hilberg, Vol. II, 3rd ed., p. 421.

[63] Hilberg, Vol II, 3rd ed., pp. 423-424, note 44; Lochner, L., ed. 1948. *The Goebbels Diaries*, Garden City, N.Y.: Doubleday, entry for March 27, 1942, pp.147-148.

[64] Hilberg, Vol. II, 3rd ed., p. 424, note 47—in German Press.

[65] Hilberg, Vol. II, 3rd ed., p. 406, note 107.

[66] Hilberg, Vol. III, 3rd ed., pp. 1068, 1083.

[67] Lochner, L., ed., *op. cit.*, Goebbels entry for March 2, 1943, p. 266.

[68] Hilberg, VolII, 3rd ed., pp. 423-424.

[69] Dawidowicz, L. *op. cit.*, *Trial of Major War Criminals*, 29 Doc. 1919-PS, pp. 110-173; in Dawidowicz, *op. cit.*, p. 149.

[70] Hilberg quote, Vol. II, 3rd. ed., p. 424, note 46.

[71] In Hilberg, Vol. III, 3rd ed., fn. 8, p. 1062. Affidavit by Albert Speer, June 15, 1977, facsimile in A. Suzman and D. Diamond. 1977. *Six Million Did Die*, Johannesburg, pp.109 -112.

[72] Hilberg, Vol. I, 3rd ed., pp. 343-344. The story of the Himmler visit, as told by von dem Bach, was printed in *Aufbau* (New York), August 23, 1946, pp. 1-2. See also statements by other witnesses in Case Wolff, l0a Js 39/60, particularly Z-Prot II/ vol. 2. The date is noted in Himmler's appointment calendar, Center for the Preservation of Historical Collections, Moscow, Fond 1372, Opus 5, Folder 23.

[73] Eberhardt Jaeckel in Beck, W., ed. *The Jews in European History*, p. 13; from Rosh, L. Jaeckel, E. 1990. *Der Todt ist ein Meister aus Deutchland,* Hamburg, p. 112.

[74] Quoted in Hilberg, Vol. III, 3rd ed., pp. 1057-8.

[75] Speech by Frank to the men of guard battalion, Frank Diary, PS-2233, cited in Hilberg, Vol. III, p. 1097.

[76] *Trial of Major War Criminals*, XII, 13.

[77] In Hilberg, Vol. III, 3rd ed., p. 1136.

[78] Nuremberg trial document, PS-2992.

[79] In Hilberg, Vol. III, 3rd ed., p .1118.

10

The Meaning of the *Holocaust*

History

In 1943, the Nazis set out upon an *ex post facto* program of demonization of the Jews, to attempt to rationalize to all who would listen why their "final solution" was justified. One of these works of research, published in Vienna, 1944, was an analysis of Jewish financial control of German society. The researcher concluded that Jewish influence in the German-speaking nations reached its zenith in 1913. This research was hurriedly hushed up.[1]

Clearly, the start of World War I directed much Austrian and German investment, and thus profits, to the war and armament industries, such as Siemens Krupp, and I. G. Farben, not under Jewish control. After the war, Jewish investment tended to go into the new nations of Eastern Europe and abroad, as the Germanies themselves were in decline, more opportunity in the Americas and elsewhere.

As this decline set in, in both Austria and Weimar Germany the pace of political extremism from the left and right picked up, with the Nazis gaining the most leverage because they had found a more tangible scapegoat in the Jews, far more emotional (limbic system thinking) than the more abstract Marxist themes of economic exploitation of the industrial proletariats by international capitalism, Jewish and other. The Nazis dug into the ethnic pride of Germans, taking their cue from a great and expansive cultural and economic heritage, now being held under water by the victorious allies, and behind it all, the supposedly internally traitorous Jewish minority.

It is important to recall this rich German cultural, scientific tradition that argued for German superiority over other ethnic groups, including the Jews. The German elite: Goethe, Schiller, Lessing, Dürer, Kepler, Leibniz, Buxtehude, Bach, Handel, Telemann, Mozart, Beethoven, Schubert, Mozart, Schumann, Brahms, Wagner, Bruckner, Richard Strauss, Kant, Wolfe, Fichte, Schelling, Hegel, Schopenhauer, Nietzsche, von Humboldt, Mendel, Riemann, Kepler, Planck, Mach, Helmholtz....

What had the Jews contributed, at the time of their emancipation, only Moses Mendelssohn, barely out of the Yiddish ghetto? Then, his grandson Felix, and of course the "slimy" Jews of the mid- to late-19th century when they and their Jewish capitalist brethren were supposedly attempting to place Germany under the Jewish heel. To the small town and urban lower middle classes who flocked to Nazism, the Jews should have been abject servants of the German people. Note that while the Nazis killed many Gypsies and Slavs as part of their often wholesale netting of the vulnerable, including the infirm, they never accused these people of attempting to take the German nation down, to control its fate. These latter were natural *Untermenschen*.[2]

The Jews, however, had to be characterized and specially labeled as a unique breed of vermin and filth. You could not rationalize merely destroying a higher intelligent minority, could you? It is interesting to note that the Germans would allow, during the war, sexual relations between Germans and Norwegians, Danes, Dutch, and Flemings, never between east Slavs rarely between Czechs.[3]

You cannot propagandize to destroy a people of high achievement, merely because they are able. The first task then, is to tar and cloak them in immoral vestments, no matter how fantastic the reality. And that is the point, the mind cleaning ideology necessary to overcome the sense of a failed Germany had to be explained. This could only be done by building on the now-century-old poison of cultural or racial anti-Semitism, this having now been transmuted far beyond the medieval anti-Jewish religious *clichés*.

Dawidowicz saw the roots of the *Final Solution* in the paranoid delusions arising from military defeat, political instability, economic distress, the humiliation of Versailles, the by now screaming anti-Semitism of both the Austrian and German cultural traditions. Who could have predicted in the Germanies that the emancipation of the Jews would yield a people that contributed to, perhaps even dominated a Germany that was rising up to international greatness? Perhaps Martin Luther's 16th-century diatribe against Jewish power had been prescient.[4]

Dawidowicz further describes the publication of a popular children's book of the time, 1938: "Without solution of the Jewish question, No salvation of mankind."[5] "Belief in National Socialism was like belief in magic and witchcraft during the Middle Ages, similarly ruling and inflaming the minds of men."[6]

But we must consider the historic realities, those discussed in preceding chapters. The Jews did not come meekly into emancipation. They came storming in, to become part of that symbolic system of ideas and institutions that the intelligent, creative German elite had established as a cognitive ground. This industrial/technological and military prowess, the Germans were able to project from the mid-18th century on. The Jews surrendered the encapsulated Talmudic chess game of holy belief and behavior for this new open ended structure of knowledge and power, now supposedly available to them equally with Germans of Protestant and Catholic heritage.

The power and influence of the one percent of Jews in Germany, north, and 4.5 percent of Jews in Germany south (Austrian Empire), especially when one considers the fact that most of the Jews in the Austrian Empire were still enclosed in their *shtetl* or ghetto urban life, was significant. What scared the ordinary German, himself seemingly shut out of this urban eruption, was that the Jews seemed never ending in their surging influence on the shape of the modern western German world. A survival birth rate twice that of the Gentile, created 16 million Jews worldwide, as we entered that dark decade plus of Nazi rule and freedom for evil.

In short, we cannot back away from the fact of relative Jewish dominance in both Germanies, economic and cultural. The Jews indeed were re-shaping the nature of German and European culture. Their influence in France and Britain was perhaps somewhat less, and the very different conditions of political life in these nations as well as in the U.S.A. across the ocean, acted as a protective coating around this smaller percentage of Jews in each of these nations. Austria and Germany were different; these political entities had reached for dominance, but had suddenly become the tangible losers in the competitive struggle for western national political and military suzerainty.

We must understand the situation of the ordinary German, not necessarily the elite here intermarrying with the successful Jews. For these lower middle classes, Hitler's magnetic and irrational influence was irresistible. He assuaged the emotional needs of those whose identities and self-respect had been undermined by fast moving events, those who searched for some kind of understanding and hoped for improvement in their material condition. Sadly, the most raucous, bile-filled rationalizations were shoveled out. The shrill Nazi simplicities of hate resonated.

The Ethnic Membrane

Even today the reality of ethnicity is hardly understood. In the main, as we enter the 21st century, ethnicity is seen as a bar to the progress of globalization, the creating of an international world of free enterprise and democratic polity.

Those nations that are most fixed on preserving their ethnic heritage are seen as recidivistic, nationalist, intolerant of diversity, here cultural as well as racial.

The membrane of ethnicity, as the Western nations of Europe and North America have demonstrated can be flexible. The waves of immigration into the New World, throughout the 19th century certainly diluted the founding Anglo-Saxon ethnicity of the United States. Canada has remained a nation in spite of its dual French and British heritage. Today, Canada is far more diverse, with its new immigrants from the Arab world and elsewhere. Of course, the United States today, even after absorbing a hundred million immigrants from various European ethnicities and religions, now struggles to absorb and deal with many millions of Hispanic immigrants legal and illegal, even at a time when the wide open spaces of assimilation are choked. Further, the possible expansive economic opportunities which these spacious lands and their enormous natural resource once availed, are now scarce. There is no longer unlimited plenitude.

From the perspective of the modern world, we can see more clearly that this membrane of ethnic integrity or exclusivity is bendable. In times of cultural expansion, for that is what the economic, industrial, and technological explosion of change really is, a change of symbolic meaning, ethnic and national centripetality can be weakened.

In times of slower cultural change, where geography and close association of peoples become the cultural/historical norm, the ethnic membrane can seem to solidify, people holding language, religion, historical association as critical values. However, the rules are slippery, and the issue of ethnicity is not subject to mathematical, material/physical predictability.

One example involves the Greeks. From the days of the Mycenaean era, c.1200 BCE, they wandered the seas, invading, raiding, trading, migrating, any sense of Hellenic nationalism hardly pertinent. They were sea peoples absorbed by Egypt, becoming Philistines, eventually an element in the larger Semitic cultural realm. Even the so-called Phoenicians were largely Greek invaders, traders who stayed on along the Asiatic coast and settled in. Young David and the Israelites in that era, welcomed Cherethites, Hittites, Hurrians, Shasu nomads, and a variety of others to join them in political association and war.

Go forward some centuries. The Greeks, now with Dorian ethnic additions, c.600 BCE, developed modern city states, stable, ethnically homogeneous. They were full of moxie, able to defeat the invading Persians, fellow Indo-Europeans, but still "barbarians" not speaking the pure, literate, Hellenic tongue. The Hellenes now were nationalistic, yet not hesitating to kill each other. Proud of their military and cultural accomplishments they strongly resisted becoming part of a degenerate international world, even while welcoming foreign mercenary armies to help them in a war, as did the Thebans, c.490-479 BCE, when allied with the Persians. The Greeks too became mercenaries for foreign rulers, Xenephon, a loyal Athenian student of Socrates, describes his Greek adventures on foreign Persian controlled soil, the *Anabasis,* c.370 BCE.

A half-century down the road we had Alexander, the Macedonian, at the periphery of the Greek world, conquering the Persian domains that extended from Afghanistan to Egypt. Hellenism was transformed into the international Greek Hellenistic. Alexander's generals were ordered to marry locally, to create a new ethnicity, trans-national in character, even if dominated by the Greek language, culture, and military program. The Hellenic ethnic membrane was now stretched and diluted, not unlike twentieth-century European civilization.

The Romans followed the Greek pattern; in their early Republican days, c.400-200 BCE, ethnically hostile to a sophisticated, and in their minds corrupt Hellenic civilization. First the Romans had to defeat their other Latin contenders for Italic dominance. Then came the struggle with the dominating Etruscans of the north, Tuscany/Etruria, the Greeks of south Italy and Sicily, finally struggling with Hannibal leading the Carthaginians of North Africa, these, Phoenician colonists, fighting them in Spain, Sicily, Italy and finally obliterating them in their domicile of Carthage.

When the bloodletting was over, the Roman ethnicity was international, now united in begrudging sophistication with the defeated Greeks, a new civilized world order. Both ethnicities had lost their unique sense of blood unity, flourishing in international prosperity and relative peace, Latin in the West, Greek spoken in the East.

We must recall that the ethnicity of the Jews was diluted during the entire Hellenistic/Roman period prior to the revolts of 67-135 CE. Then, millions of people of a variety of heritages claimed to be religious associates of the "god fearers," at the least, nominal adherents to the Biblical faith. Only after the above military defeats, and the gradually expanding Christian universalism and then persecution, did Jewish ethnicity recoil upon itself in defensive protection of their cultural life, now to be centered on their sacred books.

Finally, recall the first ethnically centripetal people, the Sumerians. They were newcomers to southern Mesopotamia, c.5000 BCE, amidst the sparse indigenous post-Ice-Age Semitic inhabitants. During and after their first explosion of discovery and urban development, 4000-3000 BCE, their expansive trade with surrounding peoples, including Egypt, they without hesitation claimed for themselves, "the black haired people—salt of the earth." Simply, their accomplishments, unique to the known world, a written language, systems of laws, the expansive industrial agriculture, technological innovations, the consequent material prosperity, their richness of cultural forms of pleasure, religious/civic monuments that soared to the heavens, teachers not only of the Egyptians, but the entire world.

Only later, first conquered by the Semite Sargon, c.2350 BCE, did they accept the reality of demographic absorption by the pervasive external Semitic populations, the latter drawn as by a magnet to the Sumerian produced riches of the two valleys. This wealth and security, gradually became the core of an expansive international civilization. Successor conquerors themselves adopted the general Sumerian/Semitic syncretic way of life, here drawing renewed inspiration from the ancient religious forms. Ethnicity had been expanded in its allegiances, the Sumerian heritage the core sense of identity and meaning, respected if not spoken or worshipped to the very end of Semitic control, Babylon/Chaldea, c.540 BCE.

Generally speaking, ethnicity within a geographical/historical grouping usually becomes a strong locus for religion, language, material techniques and esthetics, the arts, military success. These all lead toward a propinquitous bonding. This glue is reinforced as an outcome of struggle and success, necessarily, now an interbreeding people obtaining a sense of historicity and permanence.

The ethnic membrane can be attenuated by overwhelming success, military, technological, religious, or economic, such that many new peoples are thus attracted to the national or international presence. Expansion leads the sensory perceptions of the citizenry away from the center toward ever more distant centrifugally expansionary horizons.

The power of the new, economics, religion, militarism, the exciting dynamics of this creative expansion of the menu of symbolic/meaning allegiances, allows for the ethnic center to move toward a new equilibrium level. As old ethnicity loses relevant meaning, new values become central. These too await the slowing down of this expansionary centrifugal dynamic. The germination of a new and tighter ethnic center of commitment only needs time.

Why Ethnicity?

We humans are naked instinctually. This, the existentialists have taught us, alone in the universe. We lack automatic responses to the challenges of nature and man. Evolution has substituted for instinct, the human symbol system of meanings, perceptions, mental urges. The entire repertoire of sensory inputs that pour in upon the human brain, the data needed to express meaning comprises the essence of our human nature. These symbolic meanings are guided outward by a system of psychological vectors that attain tangibility in the institutions that we create, synagogues, churches, opera houses, jewelry, sports competitions, cuisine, war and killing.

Part of this response network of symbols, the languages, religions, art forms, the urge to mold the material world to the will of our minds, is built out of the need to understand what this blooming buzzing life is all about. Ethnicity gains its reality in this rainbow of human symbolic expression, in that it becomes the locus of all these expressive symbolic forms. This is the core meaning of culture. Pure universal meaning does not exist in the human species or in human experience. Plurality, of meanings and symbols systems is what has been dominant in the historic course of humankind. Observe the diversity of human cultures as Europe and North America found them in the 19th century. Many languages, religions, arts. But interestingly, within each culture, a coherence, a locus of meaning. Herein, all these vectors of symbolic expression create a way of life. Within this unified existence people can share a wholeness of meaning in their short lives. Thus, ethnicities are created out of deep intentionalities that emerge from the human brain.

The idea that the peoples of the world can exist under one universal meaning structure is a chimera. As long as humans live close to one another as neighbors, not address ciphers, they will want to share their conjoint experiences in symbolic cultural/ethnic terms. The European Union is an exemplar of a misguided program that assumes that long-existing separate nationalities can even come together on supposed shared economic issues, thus to dissolve boundaries and all float together in a mass, regulated by an external system of rules conjured up by bureaucrats in Brussels.

The United States in the struggle to create a level socio-economic playing field also suffers through the dilemma of indigestible diversities of tradition. People attend different institutions of worship; they tend to congregate in various fields of economic or intellectual endeavor. They also therefore, want to live close to each other to share each others' deeper personal human values. Under a different national political setting, New Mexico and Vermont would develop, over time, very different cultural ambience, *in nutrio*, a different ethnicity. They would marry within their state, when pushed, would argue for secessionist values, if other states, here New Mexico or Vermont would attempt to nationalize (universalize) its own state's sense of value.

This is what happened to the Jews under the Roman Empire. Two hundred fifty years before their final revolts, in c.166 BCE, they had been able by force of arms to assert their ethnic uniqueness against the Seleucid Macedonians. Under Rome, the various communities of the *Diaspora* as well as in Judea were enveloped in Roman political/military hegemony. The possibility of the Roman subjugation of Judaic religious values, including the new international if yet nascent Judaic ethnicity, became an intolerable mental/cultural burden for contemporary Judaism.

The Jewish attempt to enforce this desire for freedom failed, in a series of international revolts, c.67-135 CE. Two hundred years later as Rome weakened militarily as well as culturally, Christian values seeping into its inner pores, the earlier struggle of the Jews might have carried. The universal claims for a Roman ethnicity were dissolving, c.350 CE, and Rome began to break up politically, geographically, and culturally.

Ethnicity, then, is the lens through which humans see themselves. It is a human-made circle of symbolic meanings that runs through the entire gamut of forms and institutions of life, from cuisine to technological styles of architecture and military armament and tactics. In times of great advance from one vector of the rainbow of symbol systems, religion or technology, it can carry people away from older ethnic unities, toward a new, often universal configuration of meaning. But ethnicity cannot for long be attenuated. It is the underlying cement that molds our relationship to our fellow humans, close up and intimate.

German and German-Jewish Ethnicity

There was a loose ethnic confederation of small Christian states at the end of the fifteenth century. Already the Renaissance was adding much experimentation to the arts, mechanics, gun powder warfare, and trade. The world was opening up to exploration and the discovery of a new and undeveloped world of peoples, to now convert, subjugate and exploit. In two to three centuries, this alteration in the medieval conceptual view of the universe and the dominant religious institutions that previously guided the people would change the character of human life.

The English and American revolutions followed by the German *Aufklärung* and the French Revolution would culminate the revolution. In substitution for the universality of the Church, an almost inchoate ethnic identification of the citizenry had been shaped into large, new, powerful nation states.

The exhilaration with modernity extended down into subjugated Ashkenazic Judaism. The new democratic, secular political forces paralleled by the waning power of organized religion opened the doors for the Jews to reexamine their place in the universe. The German Jews were perhaps the first to take the opportunity for "Enlightenment, Emancipation, and Assimilation," despite grudging elimination of legal barriers that the national monarchical authorities still attempted to maintain.

Under the leadership of Moses Mendelssohn on one side of the coin, and Napoleon Bonaparte on the other, they accepted the trade-off, gradually pushing their tight Judaic, Talmudic, Yiddish ethnic bonding into the background, this for their hoped-for acceptance of citizenship alongside their Christian neighbors. Now, they were to be citizens of the nations first, Jews, second.

Germans, both the Catholics in the south and the Lutheran Protestants in the north were gradually reforming their ethnicity into a larger political sense of identity. The wars of internal Germanic unification, and then against Slavs on the East, Scandinavians in the North, the French on the West, cemented this identity, especially as the great cultural and political/military achievements of the German speaking Christian people began to place them ever higher on the international ladder of ethnic power.

The Jews were allowed into this expanding universe of opportunity and progress. Almost from the beginning, as we have shown, the suspicion was that the Jews could not shed the old ethnic identities and values for the new allegiances that had suddenly opened up for them during this modernizing trend. Then quickly, this suspicion turned to resentment. The Jews had done too well in matching German achievement, wealth, fame and power. The Jews themselves did not understand this stark revolutionary set of accomplishments. Conflicted with doubts about the past, their *Yiddishkeit*, concerned with acceptance and assimilation in the present and future, all became part of the cloud of self-abnegation. Karl Marx' exuded vituperation about his own people was only emblematic of his almost naïve openness to these deeper feelings among the Jews. It was understandable in that this 19th-century environment was heady and chaotic with social and technological change. The very nature of ethnicity among the nations of the West was being transformed. And in many ways, the Jews were the test case in this challenge.

For many of the still rural and lower-to-middle artisan class Germans, Jewish accomplishment and wealth, even if representative of a small a minority of "Germans," constituted a repugnant invasion of their home ethnicity. Even in conversion, Jews were still Jews. 'You can change your clothes, but you cannot change your nose.' Social class is competition for the rewards and responsibilities of wealth and power. It has never been eliminated, whether sponsored by royalists or democratic capitalists, even communists. And thus, over any relatively short period of time, these frictions within a dynamic ethnic environment, rubbed. Especially, in terms of relative social status, non-accomplished traditional Germans gazed in resentment at highly accomplished and rising parvenu, Jewish Germans.

It is one thing to be part of an expanding successful German nation, of which the Jews were a small element. It is another, when in the 20th century this German expansionism, rising tide of optimism and ethnic snobbery was brought to a sharp halt by defeat in World War I. As noted above, when ethnicities begin to contract, the ethnic membrane tends toward impermeability.

Solutions to soften the bitter abnegations of national defeat came from two ends of the ideological spectrum. One, the universalist appeals of Marxist socialism and communism. These denigrated ethnicity in favor of a world-wide revolution of proletarian industrial workers foregoing any nationalistic, religious, ethnic identification. Here the enemy was international capitalism, the Jew yes, but many others also. Two, the Nazi exploitation of nationalistic German ethnicity, their spleen focused on the Jew. The Nazis touched a deeper vein of frustration and resentment in Germany and Austria than the Bolsheviks. Capitalists were abstract figures. Jews were tangible, identifiable, 'nose on nose'..

Ethnicity essentially is a product of a perception about who we are, who they are. It is not grafted onto the clouds. The Jews perceived themselves as loyal, patriotic Germans, but forced by the anti-Semitic rhetoric to be mostly Jews, alongside their Protestant and Catholic colleagues, whose religion was integral to their German ethnic identity. But the indigenous German Jews, not the recent in-migrating East European Jews of the Austrian Empire were preponderantly middle class and higher. The ordinary non-Jewish ethnic German had taken the brunt of the failures in war and living standards. Relatively uneducated and susceptible, they, with Hitler's magnetic cajoling, eagerly bought into this irrational hate filled scenario. Just think, the growing Nazi voting constituency really believed that a utopia of a Jew-less Germany could triumph with renewed power. The dream, because of the implicit power of all Jews, a Europe cleansed of this 'Jew plague.'

The ordinary German, giving the salute, *sieg Heil*, could not foresee or even digest the ultimate programmatics contained in Hitler's and his cronies' demonical plans. Nor could they anticipate the possibilities for complete totalitarian controls over this ever more economically integrated nation, its modern industrial potential for new forms of mechanized warfare. This was now a nation where one could no longer hide, all citizens interconnected in communications and transportation. What they were taught to want were the simple bucolic joys of an ethnic Germany, without Emperors, but now unified in the symbolics of renewed power and thus individual dignity. Understandably the goose-step, the swastika, the brown shirts, the raised arm of *Heil Hitler*, the adolescent longings for the leader, *unser Führer*, the perverted language of Nazidom, all resonated, an optimistic Grimm fairy tale.

Indeed, the Soviets were on their way, in emulating such symbols of ethnic/political allegiance, 'red flags, hammer and sickle, the *Internationale*, the raised fist.' A new ideological world of mythological meanings had descended on Europe. People delved deep into their protean human nature to find significance amidst the chaos of cultural change.

These deeply rooted issues of ethnic allegiance were never brought into an open airing for their intellectual meaning. People felt deep tugs, but did not understand these ethnic loyalties. It all stayed below the surface of thought. One could call this a political revolution for the times. It also could be seen as a primal exploitation of the inchoate industrial masses, they who had lost their sense of historic identity, their capacity for reasoning to order and balance out the dismaying events of this historical change.

Ironically, Karl Marx foresaw this alienation of the proletarian masses, under the surge of industrialization and population explosion from the bottom. His utopian solution was a chimera, as more diabolical actors, not thinkers, gained political control. This socialist vision turned into an exploitative ideological totalitarianism which now imprisoned the masses and foretold massive 20th-century genocide, culminating in the *Holocaust* of the Jews

The Intelligence Factor

Here, too, a critical element of human nature, that still lies below the surface of intellectual understanding, and thus rational discussion and policy-making. With regard to the Jews, we have alluded to their social, financial successes in the modern world, the ancient tenacity of their devotion to Biblical and Talmudic study of the most important laws of human relationships, their moral obedience to a higher set of principles than is given by mortals to each other.

The claim here is that it was this development of Jewish intelligence to a position equal to the highest levels of western achievement that precipitated the loathing that the Jews experienced as they entered the 20th century in Europe. This ambivalence of admiration for, and then envy of the Jew, was in the opinion of the controversial American psychologist, Henry Goddard, the reason for the anti-Semitic travail of the Jews over the ages.[7] And, sadly, it was that intelligence that separated the Jewish/German ethnicity from the ethnicity that the ordinary German perceived to be his own. That is why Goebbels at a book burning of Jewish writers in 1933, heralded this act as the beginning of a new age, now 'to be rid of Jewish intellectualism.' (See Chapter 9.)

We need to discuss the issue of human intelligence variability to understand its significance in the events of the *Holocaust*. As noted in Chapter 2, high intelligence in humans came with the development of the Cro-Magnon sub-species of *Homo sapiens* in Eur-Asia, c.200,000-100,000 years ago. This form of humans came into the world with a huge and bulging skull, a great cortical brain overlain by an egg-shell-thin covering of bone. Eur-Asian Cro-Magnon pulsated with creative symbolic energy; they created the first proto-civilization in Europe some 45,000 years ago. We have residual evidence of the rich cultural environment that these people spontaneously created for themselves in their art and technology.

It is important to underline the fact that these Cro-Magnons (*Homo sapiens sapiens*) were not alone in the contemporary world of humanity at that time. Throughout the continents, with the exception of Antarctica and North and South America, there were other human groups, *e.g.*, borderline sapiens; then the Neanderthals of Europe and West Asia with whom the Cro-Magnons intermingled and competed with. The Neanderthals were eventually displaced and disappeared, c.27,000 years ago.

Intelligence, and the large brain that made it possible, as we noted, was always a powerfully adaptive technique, developed within the class of mammals.

It was useful in a dynamic environment in which intra-generational adaptation to change was useful for survival, the raising of the young to reproductive maturity. In humans, high intelligence has become the preeminent pathway of adaptation and survival. The ability to anticipate intellectually, future events, and to pre-adapt to these events required "time-binding" brain power.

Awareness of the significance of intelligence, and its variability, as with ethnicity, has always lain below the surface of comprehension. As with so many deeper elements in human expression, we have developed euphemisms to deal with the reality, metaphors that explain to us how this subtly perceived reality works.

The ordinary day to day decisions of families with regard to the marriage of their children, judging family backgrounds, the behavior of siblings of the family in question, the character and accomplishments of grandparents, are universal. Even within nations, the ensuring that marriage is endogamous is a continuing recognition of the need to conform to and preserve the norms of the ethnicity.

Underlying this often unstated rule of life, is the equally recognized need to insure and protect the ethnic defensive line, group survival, this by ensuring that few weak human links enter the community. The young, passionate and hot-blooded, do not yet perceive these long term survivalistic elements. Thus, the decisions of elders often prevail, ostensibly to protect the family's and then the group's existence.

Up until the early 20th century, the understanding of intelligence was thus largely anecdotal. In its larger national or ethnic expression it revealed itself in the assertions of inherent power residing in the nation or ethnicity. Here this success and perdurance over time and travail gave evidence of the ability of a people, a nation.

The egotism of the Sumerians, often anecdotally expressed against those primitive nomadic peoples "who did not know how to stoop," meaning plant crops; else the Athenian gloating about their *paideia,* educational ideals that led to the building of the Acropolis, their subsidization of playwrights, architects, sculptors, which added to the cultural ennoblement of the people, not to say the leadership in war against the foreign enemy, Persia. Else, the smug satisfactions of the Romans, their hard gained military solutions, their system of laws, engineering know how, the roads that would endure for a thousand years. These accomplishments certainly redounded to the fecund power of the Roman matron.

Certainly the Jews were not hesitant in proclaiming their intellectual gifts at all times in the Talmudic period and beyond, within the Kahals in Mesopotamia, where they exercised their dialectical skills in creating this evolving moral document, nor in debates with Christian theologians, throughout the Middle Ages. Because they were a vulnerable minority, they usually spoke about such matters in quiet discussions amongst themselves, fearful to bring the sword of the majority down upon themselves.

Even today, as the civilizational weight begins to shift toward northeast Asia, one hears an occasional and indiscreet Chinese, Korean or Japanese official or scholar mention the educational or entrepreneurial superiorities of their own ethnic group over the decadent and descending Caucasians. As we write, the issue of intelligence is whispered, open discussions under interdict, for fear of inciting prejudice against the growing majority of the socially vulnerable.

By the mid-1930s, when Hitler was amassing his power, the issue of human intelligence variability had been raised to a scientific and theoretical level of study, with I.Q. being the standard of cognitive/relational intelligence. Any comparative discussion of mean I.Q. differences between intra-breeding communities, racial or ethnic, was even then viewed with suspicion.

The concept of "g", as we described it in Chapter 9, was still the integrating standard of massive testing programs going on all over the civilized world, in education, the armed services, in professional aptitude testing. It proved predictive in evaluating individuals for their potential in high-level education or professional employment.

I.Q. or achievement testing transcended those anecdotal and thus necessarily prejudicial inter-personal evaluative measures. Here was a way of looking at human ability that allowed at the least, a partial examination of cultural attainments of value, a way of seeing the human species in the cool light of reason rather than in the heat of deeply rooted psychological or social passions. Discriminations of race, nationality, religion, ethnicity could potentially be left behind.

The traditional politically and ideologically correct view of Jewish intelligence, sees this phenomenon as one cultivated as a product of family influence and devotion. Here, Zoborowski and Herzog:

The Jewish baby: "…is treasured as a potential adult, and the admiration of his audience is most evident when he shows signs of precocity. Early sitting…standing, walking, above all early talking give tremendous satisfaction to parents and family. A smile, an unexpected gesture, an imitation of an adult's expression will be taken as a sign of exceptional intelligence. Everything the child says is a bright saying, and everyone likes to hear the baby say and do things."[8]

"In Orthodox Judaism, the ultimate degree of prestige, respect, authority, and status is shown to any one (even a pre-pubescent boy) who has mastered the Talmud and has 'the gift of Talmudic reasoning.' But in every branch of Judaism, 'intellectual achievement is the universal goal. Lifelong study is considered to be commanded directly by God and highest social status goes to him who can give evidence of prolonged and fruitful study."[9]

It is this family and community environment that supposedly creates and shapes the high intelligence of the Jews. And of course, Miles Storfer, echoing the established environmentalist view, states that such an application of family and community nurturing can be universalized as efficient cause in the raising up of all of humanity.[10]

As we were learning during the 1930s and increasingly throughout the 20th century, the scientific and universal reasons (causation=consequence) for high Jewish accomplishment, first, was *not* the womb of family nurturing, although that was truly an outgrowth, a consequence of high human intelligence and the defensive cultural system that flowed out of such high literacy and intellect. The Jewish concentration on the value of education, literacy, and learning was both the necessary product of high inborn biological intelligence, and of course the sufficient pathway of nurturing, so that promise could be translated into fulfillment. The Jews made sure that the next generation would be of at least equal intelligence to the former. That meant that the Talmudic scholar was required to bring more children into this world and then to reproductive maturity, than the *chochem-etz.*

Ashkenazi Jews score at a full standard deviation above the European Caucasian mean of I.Q. 100. This translated into a median I.Q. among Jews of about 115, some authorities even arguing that it ranged as high as an I.Q. 117-118, perhaps higher.[11] Statistical evidence shows that human biological attributes reveal themselves to range over a probability curve. Thus average size, weight, I.Q. are distributed such that the majority of individuals so analyzed are concentrated in proportion at the mean, more rare manifestations of an attribute, higher or lower, at the tails of the probability (bell) curve. This concept was crucial in understanding why a higher Jewish mean, *e.g.*, 115-118 I.Q., would naturally precipitate Jewish intellectual/creative predominance at the higher ends of this curve of probability.

This higher average in intellectual potential had the result of throwing off a much larger proportion of "geniuses." One scientist, in recent years argued that the majority European origin Caucasians in the United States, then, c.176 million would produce as many 160 I.Q. individuals as would the 4+ million Jews. This, because the Jews already had a one plus standard deviation advantage (15-18 points) over the established Caucasoid mean I.Q., 100.[12]

An important dimension of the biological understanding of such high intelligence in Ashkenazi Jews involves the existence of genetically-rooted auto-immune diseases, *Sphingolid* diseases, heavily placed within this population: Tay-Sachs, Goucher, Niemann-Pick, Tortion dystonia, Canavan, Cystic Fibrosis, and others. These conditions are now being identified in the fetus, and through genetic counseling and therapeutic abortions, are being gradually eliminated from the Jewish populations.[13] Because of the measured high intelligence of individuals with these conditions, it has been hypothesized that these genetic factors reveal high I.Q. linkages.[14]

This auto-immune condition that seems concentrated in Ashkenazi Jewish populations, and seemingly has linkages with high intelligence genetic factors, is not unique to Ashkenazi Jews. It has been noted theoretically as part of a larger phenomenon of auto-immune deficits in males associated with high hormonal production of testosterone in neo-natal development.[15] In follow-up I.Q. studies involving the college qualifying (usually of 17-18-year-olds), SAT test, a reasonable facsimile of traditional I.Q. tests, 10,000 male and female mathematically precocious youth at the seventh grade level, 13 years of age, were tested.

For those rare over 700, out of a possible perfect score of 800, on such SAT tests, 13 year old males dominated 13 year old females by a proportion of 13 to 1. At this score of above 700 out of a possible perfect 800 SAT level, twice the normal rate of left-handers were observed; five times the normal rate of auto-immune and allergy disorders were noted, it also included nearsightedness. As the researchers checked the scores of lesser achievers down from these unusual 13-year-old high scorers, some of them having achieved perfect scores (800), they found that the incidence of the above disabilities fell toward the normal range.[16]

The conclusions reached on the basis of the above Jewish exemplars of genetically-rooted auto-immune disabilities and the more generically disabled population, Jewish and Gentile, of extremely high math achieving, mostly male youngsters, seemed to argue that the genetics of high intelligence carries with it linkages for certain disabilities. These disabilities, because they are usually non-fatal, seem to have been overridden in societal history by the great contribution that high intelligence, even burdened with such disabilities, makes to the civilizational life and survival of any endogamous community.

These newly recognized relationships of high intelligence and auto-immune reactions can also explain the generally accepted psychiatric view that bi-polar mental disease often carries with it the potential for extremely high intellectual and creative achievement. The question that devolves is a heuristic one. Which element will come to dominate both the personal and social reality, the mental fragility or the contributing talent?

The hypothesis that highly inbred Ashkenazi Jewish communities passed on the *Sphingolid* genetic conditions and their linkages with the genes for high "g" general intelligence development and its consequent social defensive preciousness is highly suggestive. It is in addition buttressed by the above high incidence of auto-immune conditions found amongst all European origin youngsters of extreme precociousness in mathematics.

Conclusion: Hitler, aided by his eager genocidal cohorts, madmen all, led his gullible, intimidated European flock to their appointment with the devil, and then onto their own bloody *Götterdämmerung*. When one examines in even a cursory way the number of renowned scientists who fled Fascism and Nazism, it is clear that this psychosis of hate against the Jews, closed the trap door on any hopes for victory by the albeit tenacious, often brilliantly efficient work of the military machine that he seduced to follow him.

Refugees: A. Einstein; H. Bethe; N. Bohr; L. Szilard; F. Haber; M. von Laue; B. Pontecorvo;H. Bondi; L. Meitner; M. Born;V. Weiskopf; R. Courant; M. Delbruck; W. Pauli; W. Feldberg; H. Krebs; E. Wigner; O. Frisch; R. Peirels; E. Teller; J. von Neumann.

Most of the above were Jews, others *conversos*, half-Jews, often married to Jews. They were able to get out between 1933 and 1939, before the jaws of Fascism firmly closed. Many subsequently worked on the atomic bomb; all added to the weight of allied intellectual predominance that made inevitable the obliteration of Hitler, Mussolini, and their Japanese allies.[17]

The Genocide of the Intelligent

"...the mythic quality...attributed to the memory of the victims is inherent in the event itself....and no historical analysis will be able to solve this. All historical work on the events of this period will have to be pursued or considered in relation to the events of Auschwitz...Here, all historicization reaches its limits."[18]

The issue is historicization, meaning the setting into historical context of the events of the *Shoah*, not to see them as unique in human affairs, of such moral singularity that placing them down on the pages of passing history could only denigrate and obliterate the special memories and as a consequence, further insight into the horror and tragedy.

And yet these events were part of human history. The facts, evidence, memories, testimony, will never cease to arouse the passion to learn, to probe the meaning of our conjoint civilizational failure. Indeed, it must carve out an important niche in human memory. For, what happened to the Jews in such a singularly horrific manner, and at the hands of supposedly civilized people, indeed, a supposedly civilized continent, does not erase the fact that horrific events occurred elsewhere. Genocide has been pervasive in the 20th century, and indeed into the 21st.

We do not and cannot recite the facts that describe the events that overtook the million or so Armenian Christians, in 1915, at the hands of Muslim Turks and Kurds. Then there were the c.20 million that died in Russia and the Ukraine between 1932-1939, when Stalin undertook his massive collectivization of the land, ostensibly to uproot the *Kulaks* from their private farms. These farms were partially obtained in the time of the initiation of Lenin's New Economic Policy, c.1922-25. At the same time of this massive starvation, Stalin was engaging in his maniacal purges of possibly dissident intellectuals, many tens of thousands were executed, vast armies of prisoners rotted in the *gulags*.

In the post-World War II period, China, now a communist nation, under Mao, undertook his vengeance against the so-called "landlords," and then precipitated successive social upheavals to weed out any possible opposition. Estimates range from 30-40 million victims up to 70 million! In Red China, mass starvation as well as killings on a scale never known before.[19]

Then there were the Christian Igbo of Nigeria (1970s) at the hands of a Muslim government supported by the European powers. The Cambodian middle classes were eradicated by communist Pol Pot, also in the millions. Recall the genocide in Burundi/Rwanda, the Amharic speaking Tutsi minority by the majority Hutu. Consider the slaughter of European Muslim urbanites by their Serbian Christians neighbors in Bosnia. Today we are experiencing the destruction of Black Christians and animists in the Sudan by the governing Islamic regime in Khartoum.

The now well-chronicled, but least understood events were unleashed in their own right, simply for genocidal purposes of innocent populations. In this, they were similar to the underlying rational that precipitated the destruction of the European Jews. The victims were either highly intelligent, successful ethnic minorities of a nation or culture where the majority were of a different religious or language group. Else, as in the communist societies, the slaughters and starvations were initiated to rid the ruling classes of any potential social class, political or military opposition. In the ancient world, for losers, it was usually deportation and/or slavery. In the 20th century and into our own time, the pain for the morally tainted is ultimate, genocidal obliteration. No people, no opposition.

Consider the Armenians. During the hey-day of the Ottoman Empire they constituted the middle class glue, traders, craftsmen, farmers. Mostly dispersed from their homeland, divided up between Russia and the Ottoman Empire, this ancient Christian people was in 1915, essentially a memory of its ancient political import on history. In the Ottoman world the Armenians were in the main dispersed into the cities of Turkey, vulnerable. When the Turks went through the crisis of World War I, in danger of losing their empire, revolutionary Ottoman usurpers saw these middle-class foreigners (Christians) as prey, as means for their political survival. Thus, the Armenians were dispersed, slaughtered, and savaged by Turk and Kurd alike, and in the millions. The Armenian Diaspora was vulnerable, they being more advanced educationally, economically successful, in contrast to the average Ottoman. Given the reigning ideology of the demonization of the intelligent educated classes, they received their 20th-century reward for being productive and essential for modern intellectual life.

This was true of the Igbos of Nigeria, the latest and most successful of the indigenous African tribes to receive an English education. The Igbos flocked into the major cities of Nigeria, comprised a large proportion of the civil service, were successful in business, and perhaps because of their Christianity, were the focus of increased discrimination in a post-colonial Nigeria. Nigeria, then and now was a political concoction, a product of colonial occupation. The Igbos, fairly, opted for secession and independence, as the nation state, Biafra. The Europeans turned against them, and as an independent ethnic strand, they stood alone in the war. In defeat, the civilian populations suffered horrendously. Revenge was sweet for those in control.

A similar tale can be told about the genocide of the Tutsis of Rwanda/Burundi, mid-1990s. They, a people of mixed racial heritage, immigrants, speaking an Amharic, Ethiopic language, tall in stature, cattle raisers (related to the Watusi of Kenya), in Rwanda/Burundi, a small minority in number in these two post-Colonial entities. Through their higher abilities, they dominated the economy and politics of the two small nations, both during and after Belgian colonial rule. The Hutu, dominant in numbers, suddenly overwhelmed the Tutsi civilians and slaughtered them in most brutal massacres. Then, the few male Tutsi who were able to escape to the Congo, returned as an armed force and in face-to-face battle, easily defeated the bloated killers.

Intelligence creates humans who are potentially productive, independent, not servile wards of the state. Such a condition of independence and self-maintenance has been intolerable to the reigning 20th century ideology. In this ideology first stemming from the Marxists, independent, wealth producing, free thinking people have been demonized, to be considered, *a priori*, enemies of the proletariat. This theme has been enunciated repeatedly, often as prolegomenon to the darkening cloud of planned genocide. It did not matter whether the victims were Christian Igbos, Bosnian Muslims, Christian Armenians, not to omit the Jews of Europe.

This 20th-century ideology still casts its malign cloud into the 21st century. The Jews of Israel again face such a shadow, as Palestinian and Arab poverty, ignorance, chaos, self-inflicted violence are thrown in their face by world-wide anti- Semitism. The Jews, not the Arabs themselves, supposedly are the cause and the consequence of this pervasive internal religio/ethnic horror.

So, we must ask the question, why? Why has the world seen so much innocent blood shed, so casually, and over and over again? What is there about the human species, and at such a late stage in the progress of civilization's self-consciousness, that allows this frightfulness?

Finally, how should we understand the *Holocaust* in the context of these other terrible events; so many millions of the best minds of our species destroyed in the name of an ideology that makes a claim upon our moral sensibilities for justice and human dignity? The ideological 'egalitarians' still argue that the betterment of the human race, the striving towards the goal of equality, the withering away of institutions of repression and exploitation, requires forcible redistribution and retribution, too often at the cost of millions of lives.

The clue lies in our paradoxical human nature. We are a creature alone in this world with only a cortically advanced brain and its effusions to guide us. There are no instinctual barriers to allow us to freeze our behavior into automaticity, to say "*no*, beyond here you cannot go." Animal instinct has been honed over the millions of years to guide an animal's adaptive behavior and thus its possibilities for survival. Instinctual patterns of behavior depend upon the stability of the external environment. Nature slows down the mutational/genetic dynamic so that a species will not cross a behavioral line that would then put the species and its close *confrères* into jeopardy.

With humans this is not the case. The explosive growth of our brain and its consequent masterful adaptive power has allowed our species to change behaviors within a reproductive lifetime. Natural selection has thus eliminated this ancient repertoire of safeguards. We are thus alone with ourselves, our brain and its symbolic representations, searching for meaning, a basis of life within which to raise our children to their maturity. We are thus creatures dependent on our day to day mental reifications, understandings.

Adaptive life decisions should be based on knowledge, on the evidence of nature, of human history. In our minds there should ever lurk a sense of the possible, a futurity of richness of thought, peace and prosperity. The rapid changes in science, and technology, the demographic explosion of humans saved from extinction by scientific medicine, have suddenly placed before the human species enormous challenges and tensions.

War and killing have long been part of the human repertoire. This tendency is empowered by ignorance, a lack of understanding of our place in nature. War and killing recur because of this lack of awareness, self-consciousness of our own limbic/emotional response system. Ideology, the secular symbolic embodiment of these inchoate emotional trends, along with mythological pseudo thinking inherent in theology, cause to break the bonds of sober rationality, our ability to think clearly in terms of consequences, the factuality of events.

These irrationalities create a world of causes and consequences rooted in the deep pre-cognitive emotional recesses of our brain, envy, fear, nationalism, aggression. When things seem to go bad, these passions will explode, always accompanied by pseudo-explanations that can only dissolve the membrane of fact, all moral restraint, and catapult us into the ejaculatory enthusiasm of war and killing.

In the case of the 20th century, the technology for killing, an enormous dynamic of 'progress' in our time, has far outrun human ability for careful public consideration, slow and deeper analysis. The easy way is to summon the young men, the way of blood; humans, now without traditional instinctual restraints on the ancient animal within. Give humans an ideological cause, no matter how irrational in terms of the facts and out will come the 'sword' and the enthusiasm to kill. The infrastructure of modernity, science and technology, as we witness today with Islamic terrorism, is now at the whim of the maddened. The consequence, an ongoing and unlimited toll of innocents. Long ago in the 20th century we lost the old hierarchical, if modest disciplines of tradition. No substitute democratic self-restraint has emerged.

The uniqueness of the *Holocaust* lies in the reality that it took place in one of the most advanced nations of the world. The infrastructure of modernity, bureaucracy, transportation, communications, armaments, were thus easily co-opted. The "good German" bureaucrats tacitly obeying under the aegis of the Nazi overlords recorded the horror in almost unbelievable detail.

Jewish intellectuality had been branded with the taint of social conspiracy, a plan to dominate the less able Germans. This rhetoric of demonization is not too distant from the bourgeoisie targets reified by red socialism and the self-flagellating re-distributional ethos of our own time. The Germans, and then their European cohorts, once they felt themselves protected by this ideological rationalization for the total annihilation of the Jews, could enthusiastically get on with the job.

The other genocides of our time, those of Stalin, Pol Pot, Mao, for example were directed against the intelligent social classes. The methods, which combined terrible brutality, along with casual neglect, precipitated natural disasters, starvation, etc., that allowed tens of millions to die. To facilitate this barbarism, terrible emotional passions, ideological rationalizations, were conjured up leading to pogroms, brutal and bloody expressions of hate and fear.

The Germans, in contrast to their own Austrian southerners, would be clinically efficient. No passion would here enter into the planned killing of the entirety of European Jewry, six million. Hitler so warned his hit men. Modern political/military power, ideological irrationality, had given reality to inconceivable totalitarian madness.

Endnotes, Chapter 10

[1] Hoefler, Wolfgang. 1944. *Untersuchungen über die Machstellung der Juden in der Weltwirtschaft,* Vol. I, *England und das Vornationalsozialistische Deutschland,* Vienna, in Hilberg, Vol. III, p. 1092.

[2] Lewy, G. 2000. *The Nazi Persecution of the* Gypsies, N.Y.: Oxford Univ. Press.

[3] Hilberg, Vol. III, p. 1068.

[4] Dawidowicz, L. C. 1975. *The War against the Jews, 1933-1945.* N.Y.: Holt Rinehart and Winston, pp. 163-164.

[5] Quoted in Dawidowicz, *op. cit.,* p. 165.

[6] Leschnitzer, 1961. *The Magic Background of Anti-Semitism,* Cleveland; Trachtenberg, J. 1961. *The Devil and the Jews,* N.Y.; Dawidowicz, *op. cit.,* p. 164.

[7] Goddard, H. 1927. "Introduction" to Cohen, I. *Intelligence of Jews Compared with Non-Jews,* Columbus: Ohio Univ. Press, p. vi.

[8] Zoborowski, M., and Herzog, E. 1952. *Life Is with People,* N.Y: International Universities Press. p. 328.

[9] Zoborowski, M. 1949, "The Place of Book Learning in Traditional Jewish Culture," *Harvard Educational Review,* 19:87; in Storfer, M. 1990. *Intelligence and Giftedness,* San Francisco: Jossey-Bass, pp. 324-329.

[10] Storfer, *op. cit.,* pp. 329-330.

[11] Vincent, P. 1966 "The Measured Intelligence of Glasgow Jewish School Children," *Jewish Journal of Sociology,* 8:92-108; Eysenck, H. and Kamin, L. 1981. *The Intelligence Controversy,* N.Y.: J. Wiley.

[12] Page, E. 1976. "A Historical Step beyond Terman," in Keating, D. ed., *Intellectual Talent,* Baltimore: Johns Hopkins Press, pp. 305-306; Itzkoff, S. 2005. *Rebuilding Western Civilization,* Ch. 4, "Civilizational Intelligence," pp. 59-84, Ashfield, MA: Paideia.

[13] Kolata, G. 2003. "Using Genetic Tests, Ashkenazi Jews Vanquish a Disease," *The New York Times,* 2/18/03; Goddard, L. 2003. "Genetic Tests Offered," *Florida Sun-Sentinel,* 2/21/03.

[14] Cochran, G., Harpending, H., Hardy, J. 2005. "Natural History of Ashkenazi Intelligence," *The Journal of Bio-Social Sciences*"; Senior, J. 2005. "Are Jews Smarter?" *New York Magazine-On Line,* October.

[15] Geschwind, N., and Bekar, P. 1982. "Left-Handedness: Association with Auto-Immune Disease, Migraine and Developmental Learning Disorder," *Proceedings of the National Academy of Sciences,* August; Marx, J. 1982. "Auto-Immunity in Left-Handers," *Science,* 217:144; Money, J., and Eckhardt, A. 1972. *Man and Woman, Boy and Girl,* Baltimore: Johns Hopkins.

[16] Kolata, G. 1983. "Math Genius May Have a Hormonal Basis," *Science,* 222:1312; Benbow, C., and Stanley, J. 1983. "Sex Differences in Mathematical Reasoning Ability," *Science* 222:1029-1031.

[17] Werner Heisenberg, a noted Gentile physicist who could have led the Nazi atomic program, stayed behind in Germany, an ambivalent recruit to the Nazi war machine. Werner von Braun, an enthusiastic rocket scientist for Hitler's B-2 war against England, became an eager turncoat working for the American program after 1945.

[18] Christian Meier, Obituary to Martin Broszat, *Vierteljahrhefte für Zeitgeschichte,* 38:1 (January 1990):37.

[19] Chang, J., and Halliday, J. 2005. *Mao: The Unknown Story,* N.Y.: Knopf.

11

The Jews in Western Civilization

Understanding the Fate of the European Jews

We in the West have not yet learned or appreciated the unique intellectual contribution to human history represented by Western Civilization. The heritage of Cro-Magnon, our universal Eur-Asian progenitor made possible both the evil that has scarred great civilizations, but also the achievements of humankind that have precipitated the 20th- and 21st-century crisis, our enormous power over nature. At the core of this capacity was the discovery by Cro-Magnon of abstract symbolic thought and creativity that defines *civilization*.

Sadly, the majority of humankind, now festering in the *favellas* of the world, and ever-expanding demographically in both scope and tragedy, has no better record of human bestiality between peoples than the so-called civilizations of the West. What the Third World today lacks in terms of self-sustainability and intellectual clout gives evidence that the civilization of the West is not a sacrosanct inevitability. There is no immutable law that enunciates that the best values of high literate, intellectual civilization can live forever. The present morass may auger humankind's future.

If the intellectuals of the West, and here we include the Jewish minority, could fathom the real nature of the *Holocaust*, the attempt by the scum of European society to destroy the Jews, with the passive assistance of their most "beautiful and brightest," they would value more the nature and possibilities of high intelligence. The tearful attempt to redistribute the wealth of the middle classes of the developed world has been, is, becoming a chimera. And all know this. As the poor increase in extent within the developed nations, they themselves will run out of the re-distributionary resources.

Today, we play "make believe", that the downward slope can be redirected. But we are frozen into inaction by the same ideology that destroyed the Jews, the belief that high intelligence, civilized lawful behaviors, the desire for non-violence in our communities are elitist impositions. The idea that enterprise, creativity, abstract intellectual ability, indeed, that the high "g" of general intelligence serves to subvert the condition of the helpless, leads us inexorably to destroy the very foundations of civilization.

Remember, the Jews helped to create the civilization of Eur-Asia. Then, they were marginalized, forcibly shunted to the sidelines. In the shadows, they developed a planetary exemplification of high culture (Talmudism), of both great potential and realized depth. Then, in the eighteenth 18th century, the Jews-rejoined the secularizing Christian world, now to assist in the flourishing of and worldwide dominance of our scientific civilization.

Ironically, if Europe continues to decline, and innovation moves to Northeast Asia, considering the latter's high intelligence levels and educational drive to create modern societies, not a small attribution of Western European failure will justly be attributed to the horrible wars, and the universal destruction of young men of ability by these many sided Armageddons. The tens of millions destroyed in the 20th century, in addition to the Jews, cannot but have had an effect on the general levels of intelligence ability even political rationality. As West Europeans and North Americans today strive to push back the tide of historic degeneration, the shifting of power and leadership may be inevitable.

The destruction of the European Jews in the *Holocaust*, the earlier century and a half of vicious anti-Jewish agitation, has been explained as: Anti-Semitism. A kernel of this explanation rings true. The anti-Jewish prejudice made the transition from religious hostility to blatant racial antipathy, hatred of the Jews as a people, no matter their existing religious beliefs.

The irrationality of anti-Semitic rhetoric as it emanated from Christendom was perverse. For, Christianity as with Islam and Judaism derive from the same ostensible Semitic soil, Jesus, Paul, the Apostles all, were "Semites." Christianity is not only laden with the heritage of Judaism, but much of its ritual and mystery derive from the same eastern sources, during that fermenting era within the West Asiatic quadrant of the Roman Empire.

That these beliefs enfiladed Rome and created for itself a European home was due to the gradual decline of Roman institutions, plus the inherent historical power of one of these Eastern mystery religions, in this case Christianity, over the others. But before this the military failures of Judaism in the 1st and 2nd century CE must be accounted for. This process of petrification, the seeping into the pores of the Roman institutionalism by new religious and intellectual juices, allowed for Christianity to become a "Western" religion.

Thus, no critical analysis will allow for the justification of the genteel calumny of many French thinkers such as Ernest Renan, who, in attempting to explain anti-Semitism, argued that a great chasm stood between the Israelite "Semitic" mind and the "Indo-European" mind. "Nature does not play any role in the Semitic religions, they are all of the head, all metaphysical and psychological." Here Renan includes Christianity as part of this Semitic triumvirate, in contrast with the Indo-Europeans.[1]

In reply to Renan, Leroy-Beaulieu, a non-Jewish opponent of the reigning anti-Semitism of his day, critiqued his French colleague by emphasizing the Jewish talent for assimilating mathematical skills, an ability to mimic, to be open to outside stimulation, to soar far beyond the "sluggish intellects" of the Germans, but not the French. Here too, the key to the integrity of the Jewish mind, was to remain apart. By copying the French the Jews would thereby remain inauthentic. "I am inclined to find fault with these sons of Shem—as I find fault with the Orientals who adopt our customs—for resembling and copying us too closely."[2]

The patent fallaciousness of these "racial" claims is that even as these themes were being debated in the latter half of the 19th century, the Jews were proving themselves more than competent in matching Western mentality in the advancement of so-called Indo-European thinking and institutions. (See Chapters 9 and 10 for Nobel Laureates and other luminaries in a wide variety of creative disciplines.). These achievements, as we see today the advancements coming out of Northeast Asia, are universal achievements of Cro-Magnon intellect, now dispersed over a wider geographic span.

No, the explanation through the use of the term anti-Semitism obscures more than it explains. The hatred against the Jew reared itself up ever more virulently as the Jews accomplished their absorption into and leadership of so-called Aryan civilizational institutions. And it was Jewish competency and creativity, then dominance considering their paltry numbers that rubbed the so-called anti-Semites the wrong way.

It was and is still under 'interdict' to argue that it was high Jewish intelligence that was the burr in the gentile minds, giving expression to the envy, then the hate. Using a concept such as cognition or "g" would have given a universalist explanation to the position of the Jews. They then could not have been marked as a specially contaminated minority. One would have to secularly compare them with Chinese, Swedes, Nigerians, Cambodians in the calculus of abilities. The forbidden outcome, for the anti-Semites of our time would be that they would have to argue that the taint of "Jewishness" was rather, a 'taint' created by the significant intellectual contributions of the Jews to high Western Civilization.

And then, rational human beings could ask, as they are still fear to ask, if the Jews, why not others? If we would ask this question, as part of the debate and dialogue about our universal civilizational destiny, including the West, should we not then ask, why not such achievement of intellect and pacifism, for the rest of humankind? But such questions are avoided, especially by self-hating Jews. If facts do not surface to the consciousness of rational discussion, then they go underground and fester. The consequence is that we must shudder for the possibility of even more genocides of minorities who have temerity to advance, while majorities sluggishly lag, and incite more hate.

The Eugenic Message

We must admit to the probability, the evidence, that even in their enforced isolation, the Ashkenazim absorbed much Christian genetics within their various communities throughout Europe.[3] This is certainly true of the Sephardim, living under a variety of super-ordinate ruling dynasties, Visigothic, Berber, and Christian. Especially in the latter two ruling entities, the pathways toward integration and partial assimilation were open, the Jews then rising up to become part of the elite social classes. Such openings into the mainstream of national life inevitably drew many licit and illicit draughts of new blood. Within a highly enclosed ethnic or religious group, as were the Jews at their advent into Europe, new blood is healthful to the group. The key to the future of any ethnicity is what the ethnicity does with even a minimal measure of bio-genetic refreshing.

In the case of the Jews of Europe, from the end of the pagan Roman Empire, the theme was, *defense*, protect the community of belief and worship. Without knowing the scientific content of the concept of intelligence, smartness, 'sechel,' behavioral distinctions became the key to ethnic survival. From the earliest days, Rabbis, from Shammai and Hillel, died c.25 CE, through Ben Zakkai, the two Gamaliels, Akiba, later 1st century and 2nd century CE, the Tannaim—teachers, all had advocated universal literacy in the Hebrew scriptures, for males. The coming of the Amoraim, from c.200-250 CE, and Judah ha Nasi's codification of the various *Mishnahs*, this followed by the writing of the fully-evolved Talmud, a high critical literacy became a key element in Jewish cultural and religious life.

Leadership in the Jewish communities derived from intellectual as well as moral standing. Attaining to the rabbinate would normally represent the highest intellectual fulfillment of community life, not only by attained knowledge of the Holy Writings, but also in achieving high wisdom of societal affairs, and always, moral probity. The rabbi, especially in Europe, earned his livelihood outside his religious calling, as butcher, baker, cabinet maker. Beyond that, he himself was called upon to marry, the wife, with good fortune, usually from an economically successful family. He was thus, when so mated, allowed to concentrate on his studies as well as community obligations. Above all, he and his wife were to be fecund, to bring many intelligent, healthy children into this precarious Jewish world.

"He who learns receives but one fifth of the reward of that which goes to him who teaches." "I call heaven and earth to witness that every scholar who eats of his own and enjoys the fruits of his own labor, and who is not supported by the community, belong to the class who are called happy—'If , thou eat of the fruit of thy hands, happy art thou.'" "If a scholar engages in business and is not too successful, it is a good omen for him. God loves his learning but does not want to enrich him." "He who occupies himself with the study of the Torah only is as if he had no God" {Midrash}.[4]

How does a people survive, (not even to think), flourish, in an environment of unending hostility, social discrimination, often outright pogroms? Answer: no weak links of stupidity and social indiscipline to undermine the safety of the majority. That was the unspoken theme for over a thousand years of Jewish life. But discipline had to have more than a negative imperative, more than the 'thou shalt not' commandments against impetuous and risky behaviors, drunkenness, sexual wantonness, lazy impecuniousness, plain old stupidity, inability to learn to read, think, and work.

Here is the clue. The Jews carried with them this heritage of inner knowledge, the key to their unique relationship with God, the sign of being chosen, chosen to undergo much privation with the hope of individual and community redemption, perhaps with the coming of the *Messiah*. Jewish fulfillment, an eternal life of blessedness to atone for the millennia of sacrifice and privation. The Holy Writings, the Hebrew Bible, the Talmud, gave them a never-ending source of moral and intellectual fortification with regard to the day-to-day decisions of life.

The writings of guidance required ever modern interpretations, analyses. Except in Spain, where the Jews enjoyed the privileges of entrance into an environment of universal intellectuality, where they produced a Maimonides, the northern Ashkenazim were blocked by northern ignorance. This, until the late Gothic university system began to open the doors to secular debate. Throughout this millennia of isolation, the Ashkenazim were thrown back upon the internal resources of a self-generated intellectualism.

They had their own stars, 'Greek Olympiads,' as in the ancient 5th century CE Kallahs of Nehardea, Pumbeditha, and Sura in Mesopotamia. These were evolving Talmudic disputations, perhaps scholastic hairsplitting, but it created a high bar standard as to what it meant to be intelligent, and thus successful in climbing the Jewish social ladder. In the background, the foreboding clouds, death and expulsion at the hand of Islamic and Christian violators. Thus, the famous slaughters along the Rhine, at the beginning of the First Crusade, c.1096 CE, again and again, to the pogroms in late nineteenth-century Czarist Russia, next, in Kishenev (now in Moldova), and in the Ukraine, after W.W. I.

We must remember that even if women were not primed for a Yeshivah education, most of them were taught to read by their parents. They were also the managers of the worldly wealth of the family, ran the 'home front'; critically judged by their peers in their endeavors in creating an efficient home life for husband and children. Here, too, there was a social hierarchy that judged a women's intelligence by her work ethic, her home of cleanliness, orderliness, financial efficiency, child rearing skills, in general her practical intelligence in handling the affairs of the family.

Arthur Ruppin, a German-Jewish sociologist first raised these issues in writings completed between 1906-1910.[5] More recently, Ernest van den Haag, a non-Jew, has developed the theme of Jewish eugenic practices, which also led to a much higher infant survival rate in spite of the Jews' millennial poverty.[6] Van den Haag worked the other side of the equation also, dealing with comparative eugenic practices within the Christian communities. Here, he like many others has contrasted the celibacy of the most intellectual of Christian sons as they entered the priesthood, populated the university faculties, and in general, removed their genes from European history. Consider also the constant feudal wars in which the aristocratic cream of Christian European communities were killed off.

There are other elements in this Jewish/Christian eugenic comparison. Whereas the Jews did suffer from periodic pogroms in which they had severe losses, these killings of Jews were random, not focused in particular on men, women, children, or the aged. They were intermittent, sporadic, the evidence being that they did not permanently decimate Jewish demographic trends. More likely the Jews were expelled, wandered to new climes, sometimes readmitted to their old residencies. Thus, even where there was not much intermixing, genetically, with gentile communities, there incessant 'wanderings' afforded them the possibilities for new genetic rearrangements, and thus avoidance of the worst consequences of intense inbreeding.

Still, the high incidence in Jews of genetically-transmitted diseases and disabilities, Tay-Sachs, Cystic Fibrosis, Canavan, and Goucher, testifies to the fact that genetic inbreeding in Eastern European *shtetl* life was a reality. Today through eugenic testing and medical 'filtration,' this heritage of physical disabilities is being gradually eliminated.[7]

There is another factor not usually discussed in these matters. European society was always hierarchical. Though it is truer than any Marxist would concede, the social flow from the lower recesses of the economic/cultural hierarchy was constant and impactful, especially in Britain, where the universities themselves were often repositories for the most talented yeoman, working, agricultural class youngsters, here sponsored by the clerisy as well as the aristocratic classes. Nevertheless, there was always a market for unskilled/uneducated labor within feudalism.

From c.1750, with a world population of about 650 million humans, through the middle of the 19th century, a world population of one billion, the demographic explosion in Europe and the rest of our planet has been propelled by the great technological inventions of the West, food production, medical death prevention. These innovations were produced by elite intellectuals of the West. This demographic expansion came mainly from the lower ends of the social scale. As the socialists complained, the peasantry went directly from one form of exploitation, agricultural feudalism, to modern industrial forms. The need for the labor masses in the factory and mine grew. The poor of Europe and the world went into the industrial revolution in great human waves.

The intellectual profile of this expansion, as between Christian Europe and Jewish Europe, showed a sharp deviation. It must be granted that in spite of whatever debilitations the gentile genetic/intellectual profile suffered from, i.e., priestly celibacy, the vast destruction of young men in the wars, as per example the conflicts between the Italian Renaissance cities, the sixteenth and seventeenth century religious wars, Christian Europe still produced a bountiful harvest of genius. Modern Western Civilization is indeed a product of European Christian society. However, the Jews on their release from ghetto isolation in the towns and villages of Europe by the middle of the eighteenth century still seem to have been on average, better advantaged, intellectually, than their emerging Christian neighbors.

The Jews had never suffered from a hierarchical social structure in which Jew enslaved or oppressed fellow Jews. Such was considered abhorrent, and against Holy Writ. The few rich and advantaged had a philanthropic obligation to assist all Jews in need; never, to take advantage of the poor. Jews who for one reason or another were not able to participate in the defense of the community were quietly shunted to the biological sidelines. No self-supporting Jew would consider marrying his/her children, male or female, to the children of incompetents. There was no place in Jewish life, the rabbis insisted, for the muscular, without a brain and the will to use it.

Thus, when the Jewish demographic expansion began in the 18th century, that now-noted 15-18 point I.Q. advantage that ultimately produced a relatively homogeneous Jewish intellectual elite, was revealed. This is the fact that so threatened the anti-Semites, and then the German Nazis.

There was, if only we had understood its nature and cause, an explanation communicable to the world outside as to why so many Jews moved to the top, economically, in the universities and in the sciences and the arts. Just as had happened in the Hellenistic, in high Gothic intellectualism, the Jews had joined, as part of a massive majoritarian move, the path that led to the highest levels of creativity blazed by their gentile predecessors.

In summary, it must be emphasized that this Jewish intellectuality, even in its aggressive thrust toward the top, was totally European, in that the participation of the Jews took place in all of the ongoing institutions of Western progress. Here was the paradigm of minority integration into the social/cultural framework of the majority.

The advantage of the Jews, in terms of their self-created cultural ambience, the drive to know and succeed, was rooted in their ability to maintain a heritage of perpetual ethnic defense, of which learning was at the core. Social survival within the Jewish community demanded of each individual both equality of responsibility, and equality of reward. There did not exist nor could there be tolerated any self-created subjugated Jewish minorities within the Jewish Biblical and Talmudic codes of ethics, as these had first evolved under the teachings of Rabbis Gershom ben Yehuda, d.1028 in Mainz-on-the-Rhine, and Rabbi Shelomoh ben Yitshaq (Rashi), d.1105, Troyes-sur-Seine.

Israel and the West

Let us consider the situation of the Jews today, in their re-created national independence. The Zionist vision for a Jewish homeland in Palestine was assisted by the events of World War I. The Ottoman Empire was broken. Palestine became a British Mandate. The Austrian and German defeats, the overthrow of the Romanov Czar in Russia, and the establishment of a communist state in that nation, allowed for an entirely new sense of opportunity for the Jews. Then the United States would pass a series of immigration laws which would essentially halt the massive immigration of Jews out of Eastern Europe.

The Balfour Declaration, and the British Mandate, 1917-1920, which promoted Palestine as a homeland for the Jews, tipped the weight of Jewish idealism and opportunity to this new and ancient homeland. Here it was hoped that the Jews could remake themselves as a people, independent, cultivating land that they owned and nurtured, a socialistic cooperative environment where the capitalist evils of the West could be sloughed off. The dream was to create a wholly new kind of Jew, bereft of the historic chains of Europe, a modern Jew here to be reconstituted in the ancient homeland, so long foreign controlled these 2000 years.

Here was also a vision of socialism with a human, democratic, egalitarian, communal face. The Kibbutz movement became a herald for this magnetic ideal, to create this new Jewish person, without the caricature of personality self-abnegation and self hatred, that product of a millennial anti-Semitic incubus. Palestine was then an empty desertified land inhabited by a few Bedouins, several Arab towns, including Jaffa. Tel Aviv adjoined, a Jewish city now created by the draining of its mosquito laden swamps.

For the first time, however, Jews found it necessary to carry and use weapons in the defense of their farms and towns, an unusual deviation from two thousand years of vulnerability without the right or opportunity to resist criminal violence directed against them.

The ending of World War II and the cessation of the *Holocaust* brought many more immigrants to what would become the land of Israel, 1948, first, to be fought for as an independent nation. Since the founding of the state of Israel many more wars have been fought resisting the aggressions of their Arab neighbors. These nations were intent of eliminating the Jewish nation. In addition, violent terrorism has been promoted by the indigenous Arab populations.

The enormous subsequent demographic expansion in numbers by the Palestinians, 6.5 children per female, this mandated policy imposed by their leadership, Yasser Arafat, had as its eventual goal the driving of the Jews into the Mediterranean. It has added great stress to the attempt to forge a permanent peace. Today the Palestinians live off the largess of anti-Semitic Europeans, international agencies and some begrudging giving, including surreptitious arms, from Arab nations. In a real sense Arab Palestine, without resources or internal economic productive capacity is today and will likely always be a ward of the international community.

Of course, this condition is true of much of the Arab and Islamic world, which without the largesse of Mother Nature's oil and natural gas, would quickly descend into poverty, return to desert and the camel instead of the Mercedes. The Arab world today lives under the thumb of medieval-like tyrannies. It is a deep and questionable dilemma as to whether these people can rise up to meet the intellectual and educational standard that could allow them to shed the chains of their theocratic subjugation; then to join the modern, egalitarian, democratic, scientific and technological world which the West, now including the Northeastern Asiatic nations, has created.

Israel, on the other hand, without such natural resources is a thriving modern democratic scientific/technological society which has more companies (technological) on the Nasdaq Wall Street listings than any nation besides the United States, over 70. The Jewish people in Israel, perhaps except for a small group of ultra-orthodox Jews who choose to live as their ancient Ashkenazi ancestors did and refuse obedience to Israel's modern educational and military obligations, enjoy a Western European standard of living and life style. They have achieved this despite the constant internationally supported violence against them. Not even ancient Athens was able to maintain its democratic institutions in such a context.

Israel also has absorbed a 20 percent profile of indigenous Arab Muslims into their democracy, giving them full rights. But Jewish Israel must still face up to this future, a much higher internal Arab birthrate. There are approximately four million Arabs living in the Gaza Strip, West Bank, and in Israel. Israel's present population, in a land smaller than the size of the state of New Jersey, is approximately five million, including other religious and ethnic persuasions.

Is there a future for the Jewish heritage, in Israel? And if so, how will it survive the above endemic pressures, a heritage of this ancient geography. The Jews in the present Diaspora, now comprising some nine million scattered individuals, most now in the United States, are themselves undergoing great stress. Intermarriage rates with non-Jews are now at least fifty percent, most of these children lost to the Jewish community.[8]

In the United States there is yet within the citizenry a realization of the importance of Israel and its liberal secular conception of Judaism. Also, the non-Jewish leadership in the United States is aware of this nation's crucial geographical and symbolic position for the international furtherance of liberal, secular Western ideals of the democratic life.

Arab societies of the mid-East, North Africa, Iran, Pakistan, Bangladesh, Indonesia, are extremely backward. There is little evidence of a general awareness of the need to create modern institutions compatible with Western achievements. Demography is here, out of control. They are thus ripe for social dissolution, their fleeing migrants creating the conditions for international *jihad*. Is it possible for both Israel and the West to live with these nations in peace and equality?

For the Jews of Israel, indeed for Israel now, as a beacon of Western Civilization in a desert of despotism, the above questions are of life and death importance. The Israelis themselves realize that periodic and opportunistic peace making by these implacable enemies, is usually prelude to renewed attempts, with ever changing means, to obliterate Israel from its presence in the heart of the Islamic, Arab world.

For the West, now including Europe, face to face with its own volatile Muslim minorities and the terrorist component within them, the fundamental question the Israelis must constantly face, has now risen to self-conscious awareness. Can these people, here Israel's neighbors ever join with the West in its three hundred year old commitment to the Enlightenment? Can they internalize tenets of life lived according to scientific rationality, democratic processes of debate and choice that flow from educated secular thinking into political and social policy making?

The Jews quickly caught onto the scientific world view, even as their Ashkenazi Talmudic tradition had eschewed such scientific study of the world of nature and man. And while a small minority of the Islamic educated elite are secular in outlook and modernistic in their aims for the social re-organization of their nations, the masses follow the fundamentalist injunctions of the Mullahs, the terrorist gangs, obedient and obeisant to the vision of a medieval Caliphate.

The truth of the matter, if one delves deeply into bio-social and historical issues, is that the Arab and Islamic world as it has evolved over a millennium of time, is today far different from the civilizations that the Sumerians, Pharaonic Egyptians, Assyrians, Persians created. The Muslim world in engaging in massive sub-Saharan slavery, concubinage, polygyny over the centuries, now suffer from the same social and educational weaknesses that afflict those tragic peoples in the African homelands derivative of the Arab slave trade.

We may eventually have to concede that the attempt to bring these peoples into the mainstream of the West is beyond our means. These nations and peoples have failed to move, as did the Jews of the 18th century and the Israelis of the twentieth century into the mainstream of modern life. Note how the Koreans, Japanese, and Chinese, each ethnic group itself weighed down by a history of feudal oppression, but now with self-created and modern educational and intellectual profiles, have quickly thrown off the incubus of their respective recidivistic histories. They are now intent on surpassing the old West at its own game.

The now embalmed Muslim world may be afflicted by deeper disabilities than mere immersion in a reactionary faith.

Why the hatred by the Muslim world toward the United States, still the most powerful nation on earth. Why the proclamations of never ending hatred and genocide against Israel and its Jews. Partially, it lies in the fact that the Israelis, have beaten them in war and modernity, despite Arab oil and human masses. Failure is never lightly internalized. If the failed, an individual or a group cannot win by orthodox means, (here meaning against the United States, the West, and Israel), then the end, vengeance, justifies the means: terrorism against any of their vulnerable innocent.

When the German masses were unable to compete, one on one, with their minority Jewish neighbors, they turned to Nazism as an emotional palliative, gaining comfort in irrational togetherness, hatred the lure for unlimited revenge at the least to assuage their incapacity. But also, they had the numbers, thus the subversive power to lure the industrial/military infrastructure of Germany into their nightmarish plans. Their seeming success in subjugating the few pacific Jews, led to their hallucinogenic vision that they could conquer the world.

The Muslim terrorists are little different. They were foiled in their attempts to co-opt Afghanistan and Iraq. They failed to destroy Israel by conventional military means, and then failed with their successive terrorist *intifadas*. They have been unable to bring their people into positions of modern economic, technological, scientific and political competitive strength in spite of the wealth of oil. Failure brings on envy and hatred, the attempt by any means to invoke a measure of tangible material revenge, bombing of subways (London), train plat-forms (Madrid) burning of cars in Paris, crashing airplanes into great symbolic structures (World Trade Center, Pentagon), anything to give themselves a sense of empowerment, to be able to inflict anguish on their betters.

Can there then be a future for the Jewish people in their homeland sur-rounded by an exploding demography of hundreds of millions of people who will look upon Jewish modernism and middle class scientific/secular achieve-ments as a testament to their own permanent sense of self-humiliation? Can a fence around the West Bank be more than a temporary and symbolic separation of two very different ways of life, ethnic capacities to deal with modern knowl-edge? Will not the Arabs follow on their plan to exact revenge in any way pos-sible, and into an infinite future? Given the oil wealth, the numbers, and the ca-pacity to purchase whatever weapons of mass destruction that can be leveled at innocent populations; will not the Islamic destruction of Israel get done, some day?

It will not be easy for the West, Europe, North America, and now the mod-ernizing nations of Northeast Asia, to allow Israel to be written off once the dream of turning Iraq or Syria into a Netherlands/Sweden turns sour. For Europe with its own subversive Islamic underclass, the dangers are close at hand. They face an implosion from within, not too dissimilar from the possible long term fate of Israel.

Israel, within two generations will face an internally restive Arab under-class comprising some 30-40 percent of its population. The Western Europeans, with a declining birth rate could see their own Muslim underclass at some 20 percent of their respective national populations within the same time-frame. The present ideology of environmental amelioration, the transferring of the wealth of the West to the dependant peoples of the world, essentially wards of the interna-tional system, will, as the world demography increases from 6.5 billion people today to some 9-10 billion by 2050, render redistribution moot. Triage, the effort of all nations and their peoples to survive, will by then become the great preoc-cupation of the political/economic decision makers.

At that time, Israel may not have to stand alone, in a crisis created by the sprouting seed sown by a failing West.

The Jews: Conservators of Western Civilization
The high on average intelligence of the Ashkenazim, and their significant contributions to Western civilization in spite of their small numbers, argues they carry with them the most paradigmatic representation of this original human evolutionary potentiality for creative civilizational endeavor Of course, the Europeans and the creators of the great civilizations of South and Northeast Asia today share in this repository of human possibility. But the Jews have shown

how this intelligence can be distilled and enhanced, protected within a real social and ethnic community. Finally, they have paid the supreme price for preserving for the West the essential kernel of hope for a truly international human civilization, richly diverse, yet united in pursuit of a rational future.

The Jews have learned how to realign their ancient repository of wisdom, in meeting the ever-dynamic challenges of civilizational progress. Such shifts in Judaic outlook will continue to be refined. There is no need to abandon totally, the ancient heritage, the synagogue, the Yeshivah, the medical philanthropy, the aspiration toward higher education, above all the commitment to search out the most modern functional interpretations and understandings of Torah, the larger Hebrew Bible, and the Talmud, as a source of perennial moral wisdom.

To balance heritage and modern ethnic/religious survival requires a new modernism within Judaism, and indeed for all ethnicities and religions on our planet. The alterations induced by the Enlightenment for a more progressive Christendom, exemplified in the American Constitution, testifies to the political intellectual sensitivity of high intelligent citizens when led by visionary peers.

As for the Jews, the desire, as with the Hellenistic Jews of Judea and Alexandria, to go out and welcome new participants in a modern belief system, as with those ancient "God fearers," would bring new life to Judaism, a hungry constituency of those who today would want to go beyond the cults and superstitions of the times. In so attracting much new blood to this ancient intellectual and moral heritage there could be created a Judaism that would not fade into a tiny ritual committed synagogue minority.

It is the poison that is national and ethnic failure that has created the modern world's anti-Semitism. The Jews are a tiny minority in the world. Why the continuing virulence? The hint is given by the former Malaysian Prime Minister, Mathathir Mohammed, Muslim, *quasi*-dictator, suppressor of minority (Malaysian) Chinese/Indians rights. As he left office several years ago, he expounded on the weakness of his own Muslim confreres, but mostly about the great power of and threat by international Jewry to the fate of the world. It was a speech that would have made Adolph Hitler proud. His was not an isolated example of an attempt to rationalize and bewail in self-hatred the modern failure of his co-religionists around the world, and, naturally, to blame one's own catastrophic failure on the Jews.

The President of Iran, Mahmoud Ahmadinejad has several times questioned the reality of the *Holocaust,* threatened to "wipe Israel off the map," *i.e.,* annihilate the Jews of Israel. Another kind of anti-Semitism, hatred of Israel's desire to survive, cloaked in supposed pity for the condition of the terrorist laden Arab Palestinians, is heard more and more often around the world, especially resonant in today's Europe. And early in 2006 we have heard implicit anti-Semitic mutterings by a new would be dictator, Hugo Chavez of Venezuela.

The reason is clear: too many Jews in public life, governmental and other, too many Jews of prominence and wealth, too many Jews seemingly "running things." Let us ask what in reality happens in a world that is dependent on high intelligence in order to function. Humans of high intellectual ability in a vast variety of fields of endeavor, public, scientific, cultural, become the bricks and mortar of civilizational life. And the Jews have responded both with ambition and responsibility. Soon, we will hear the same envious chant about the Chinese. They, not few in number, are destined, given their evidenced high intelligence and educational achievements, to make their truly powerful mark. But they will not be outnumbered.

The Chinese are yet on the runway. The three Northeast Asiatic ethnicities, Korean, Japanese, Chinese, are homogeneous within their territories. They will not even whisper their well perceived understandings about the relationship of intelligence to national social and economic advance. The ideologically moribund West certainly would not listen. These latter, including the United States are still hallucinating in their quasi-Marxist superstitions, that forcible wealth redistribution constitutes the utopian pathway to an egalitarian future.

The irony is that with the passing of every decade, high human intelligence in science and technology makes a larger and larger proportion of the working masses, today and yet to come, redundant. High intelligence is creating a world of social potential where bare muscle and brawn, human bodies without high brain-power will be redundant.

What is coming to be is a social economy of high intelligence and education, the same social structure that has existed amongst the classless Ashkenazim for over a thousand years. The high 115 I.Q. (at a minimum), their major role in the civilization building of Eur-Asia throughout its thousand fold history, is reflective of what modern knowledge is now creating in potential for all of humankind. This modern technological economy of literacy and education mimics what the Jews have worked for during these thousand years of subjugation by Christendom and Islam.

The Jews, under their moral and religious codes could not enslave their fellows or exploit them as serfs or feudal colons. The first and primary principle of Maimonides' ethical code was the injunction for all Jews to help the needy to be independent by finding them work. {Shabbat 63a, bot}

"Give justice to the weak and the orphan; maintain the right of the lowly and the destitute. Rescue the weak and the needy from the hand of the wicked." {Psalm 82}

"So I will send a fire on Judah, and it shall devour the strongholds of Jerusalem....because they sell the righteous for silver, and the needy for a pair of sandals—they who trample the head of the poor into the dust of the earth, and push the afflicted out of the way…" {Amos 2, 5-6}

"Ah, you who join house to house, who add field to field, until there is room for no one but you, and you are left to live alone in the midst of the land! The LORD of hosts has sworn in my hearing: Surely many houses shall be desolate, large and beautiful houses without inhabitant." {Isaiah (I, of Jerusalem, c. 700 BCE) 5, 8-9}

"You shall not withhold the wages of poor and needy laborers, whether other Israelites or aliens who reside in your land, in one of your towns. You shall pay them their wages daily before sunset, because they are poor and their livelihood depends on them; otherwise they might cry to the LORD against you, and you would incur guilt". {Deuteronomy 24, 14-15}

"You shall not deprive a resident alien or an orphan of justice; you shall not take a widow's garment in pledge. Remember you were a slave in Egypt and the LORD your God redeemed you from there; therefore I command you to do this". {Deuteronomy 24, 17-18}

The Ashkenazim created a classless society of mutual egalitarian impoverishment, except for a very few, and then never allowing such fixed class structure to extend over the generations.

The Jews are the contemporary exemplars of the high intellectual civilizational creators in history. They have also made the millennial sacrifice, almost six million destroyed, and by those who hated the high intelligence of the "other" within their midst. The Jews today have the primal responsibility for shouting out this knowledge to the world. Today, the world is deaf. Not too long into our future, our species will be forced to listen:

The above is not a plea for the moment. With the Jews, this pathway became a rule of social life, for the millennia. Were the Jews to take their heritage seriously, and practically, Judaism could become a rallying center for ethical, scientific and transcendental understanding, an earthly pathway and beyond, into a future where the hatred of intelligence and rationality would shrivel. All humans could potentially share in this universal and ancient, bounty.

Endnotes, Chapter 11

[1] Renan, E. 1853. "L'histoire du peuple d'Israel," in *Etudes d'histoire religieuse*, Paris: Calman-Levy, pp. 44, 75-76.

[2] Leroy-Beaulieu, A. 1893. *Israel among the Nations,* tr. F. Hellman, N.Y.: Putnam, p. 261.

[3] Patai, R., and Patai, J. 1989. *The Myth of the Jewish Race* Detroit: Wayne State; Comas, J.1951 *Racial Myths* Paris: UNESCO.

---

[4] Quoted in Konvitz, M. R. 1955. "Judaism and the Democratic Ideal," in *The Jews*, ed. by L. Finkelstein, N.Y.: Harper, pp. 1102-1105.

[5] Ruppin, A. 1911. *Die Juden der Gegenwart*, Cologne: Judischer Verlag.

[6] van den Haag, E. 1969. *The Jewish Mystique*, N.Y.: Stein and Day.

[7] Kolata, G. 2003. "Using Genetic Tests, Ashkenazi Jews Vanquish a Disease," *The New York Times*, July 4.

Index